AF291059

OXFORDSHIRE FROM THE AIR

Published titles in this series:

Berkshire from the Air
Dorset Coast from the Air
Essex Coast from the Air
Essex from the Air
Hertfordshire form the Air
Isle of Wight from the Air
Isle of Wight & Hampshire Coast from the Air
Kent Coast from the Air
Kent from the Air
North Cornwall Coast from the Air
North Devon Coast from the Air
Somerset Coast from the Air
South Cornwall Coast from the Air
South Devon Coast from the Air
Sussex Coast from the Air

Forthcoming titles in this series:

Dorset from the Air
Gloucestershire from the Air
Somerset from the Air
Surrey from the Air
Wiltshire from the Air

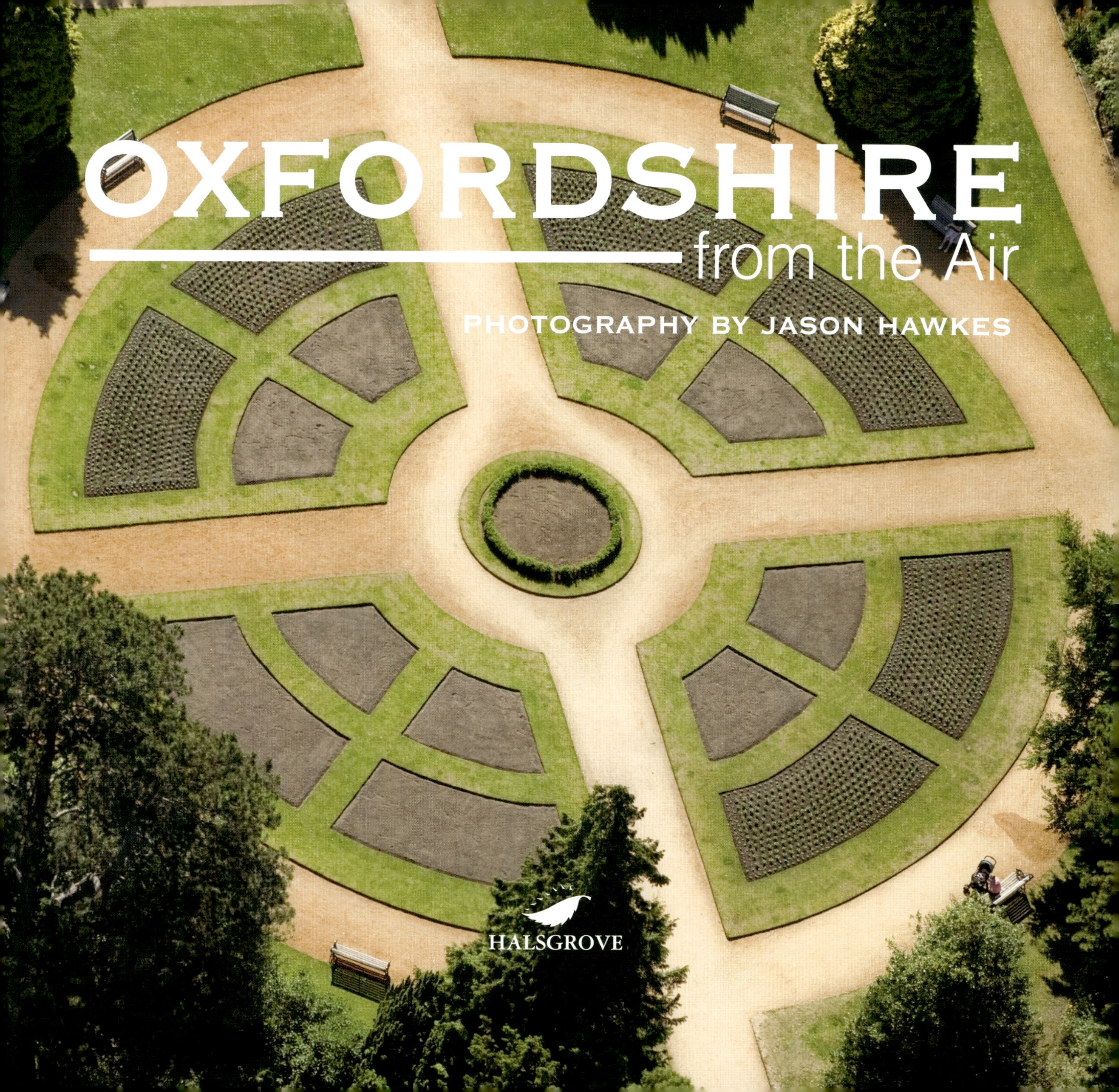

OXFORDSHIRE
from the Air
PHOTOGRAPHY BY JASON HAWKES
HALSGROVE

First published in Great Britain in 2010

British Library Cataloguing-in-Publication Data
A CIP record for this title is available from the British Library

ISBN 978 1 84114 939 4

HALSGROVE
Halsgrove House,
Ryelands Industrial Estate,
Bagley Road, Wellington, Somerset TA21 9PZ
Tel: 01823 653777   Fax: 01823 216796
email: sales@halsgrove.com

Part of the Halsgrove group of companies
Information on all Halsgrove titles is available at: www.halsgrove.com

Printed and bound in India on behalf of JFDi Print Services Ltd

INTRODUCTION

While in many people's minds it will be the City of Oxford that dominates this county, not least through its association with its ancient University, Oxfordshire itself contains many landscape and historic gems that are often missed from the usual guidebooks. In this book of aerial photographs the concentration has been as much on the lesser known places as on the major tourist sites.

Although not a large county (it is ranked 22nd in size with an area of around 1000 square miles [c.2600km], and with a population of 635 000), because of its historic connections, it remains one of the most visited of all English counties. Through the landscape winds the River Thames, bordered by ancient towns and quintessentially English villages. The vast stately home of Blenheim Palace (birthplace of Sir Winston Churchill) contrasts with the simple beauty of the prehistoric White Horse carved into the chalk hillside at Uffington.

Oxford was founded in the 9th century when Alfred the Great established it as one of a network of fortified towns, called burghs, across his kingdom. Today Oxford has a population of just under 165,000. The rivers Cherwell and Thames flow through Oxford and meet south of the city centre. For a distance of some 10 miles (16 km) along the river, in the vicinity of Oxford, the Thames is known as The Isis. As the oldest university in the English-speaking world, Oxford is a unique and historic institution. There is no clear date of foundation, but teaching existed at Oxford in some form in 1096 and developed rapidly from 1167, when Henry II banned English students from attending the University of Paris.

The 'dreaming spires' of Oxford continue to exert their romantic appeal despite a significant amount of modern building development within the city and much urban sprawl beyond. Even so it is possible to find many quiet corners within the college precincts which immediately take the visitor back over the centuries.

The fascinating aerial photographs in this book are selected to provide the reader with an overview of a variety of landscapes and settlements, with many historic sites included. Where the county boundary follows a particularly scenic course, such as the River Thames, aspects of neighbouring counties are also included.

The principal attraction of aerial photographs is that they are literally a bird's-eye view, allowing us to look down on the landscape from a perspective that we never normally see. Such pictures reveal to us things that are normally hidden from view, and often surprise us when we find that what we had imagined the layout of the land to be is in reality quite different. The best practitioners of this genre of photography also strive to capture an aesthetic in the images they take, and these pictures, sometimes quite abstract in appearance, are often strikingly beautiful in their own right.

Jason Hawkes is one of the country's best-known photographers specialising in aerial photography. From his base near London he travels worldwide to produce images for books, advertising and design. Since 1991 he has provided photographs for major international companies including Nike, HSBC, Ford, Rolex, Toyota and BP. The images in this book and the sister publications in the series were specially commissioned by Halsgrove.

For more information regarding Jason Hawkes' work visit www.jasonhawkes.com. For a complete list of titles in this series and other Halsgrove titles visit www.halsgrove.com.

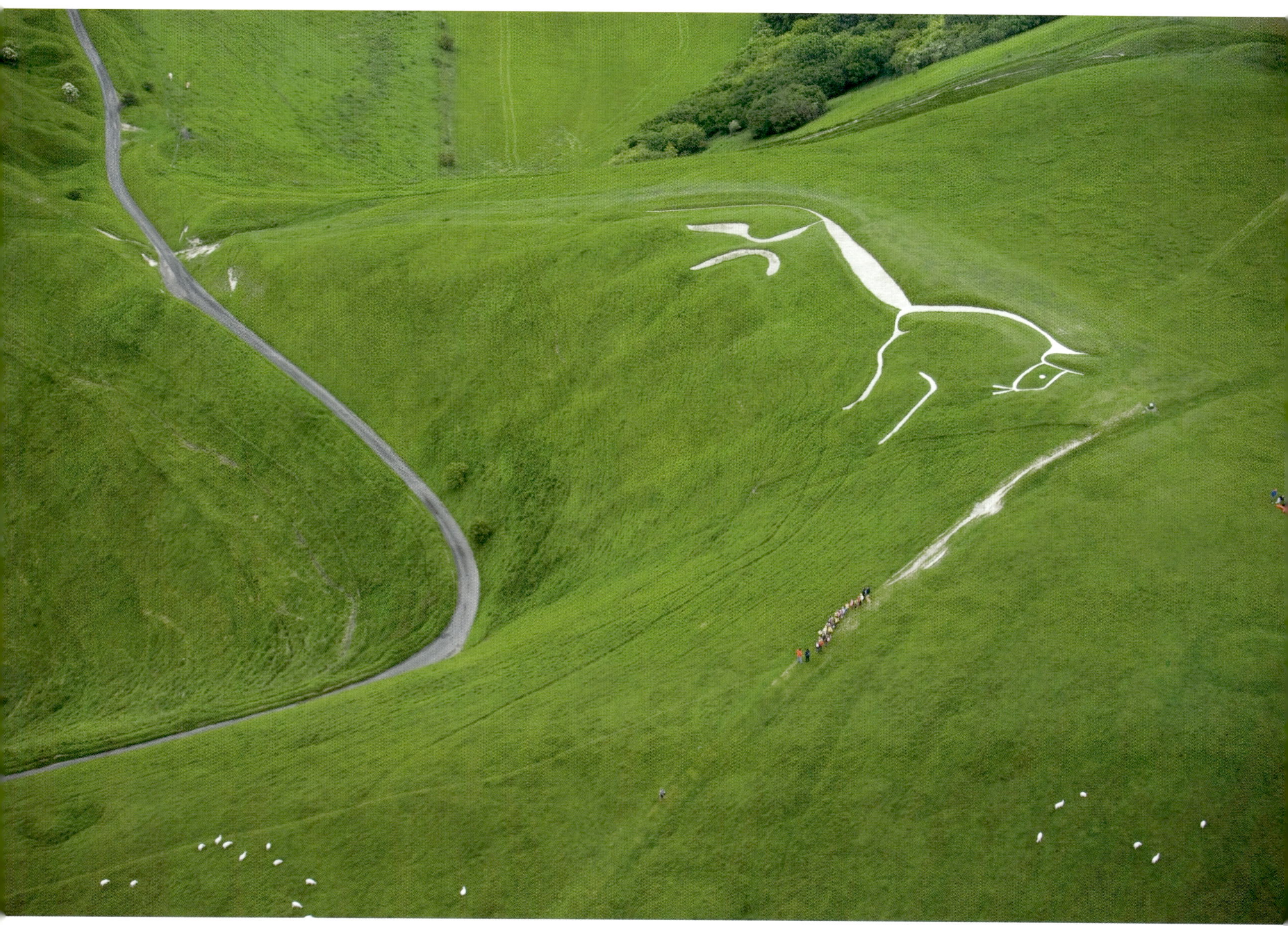

The Uffington White Horse is a highly stylised prehistoric hill figure, 374 feet (110 m) long, formed from deep trenches filled with crushed white chalk. It lies on the upper slopes of White Horse Hill in the parish of Uffington some five miles south of the town of Faringdon. Best views of the horse are obtained from the air, or from directly across the Vale, particularly around the villages of Great Coxwell, Longcot and Fernham. The site is owned and managed by the National Trust.

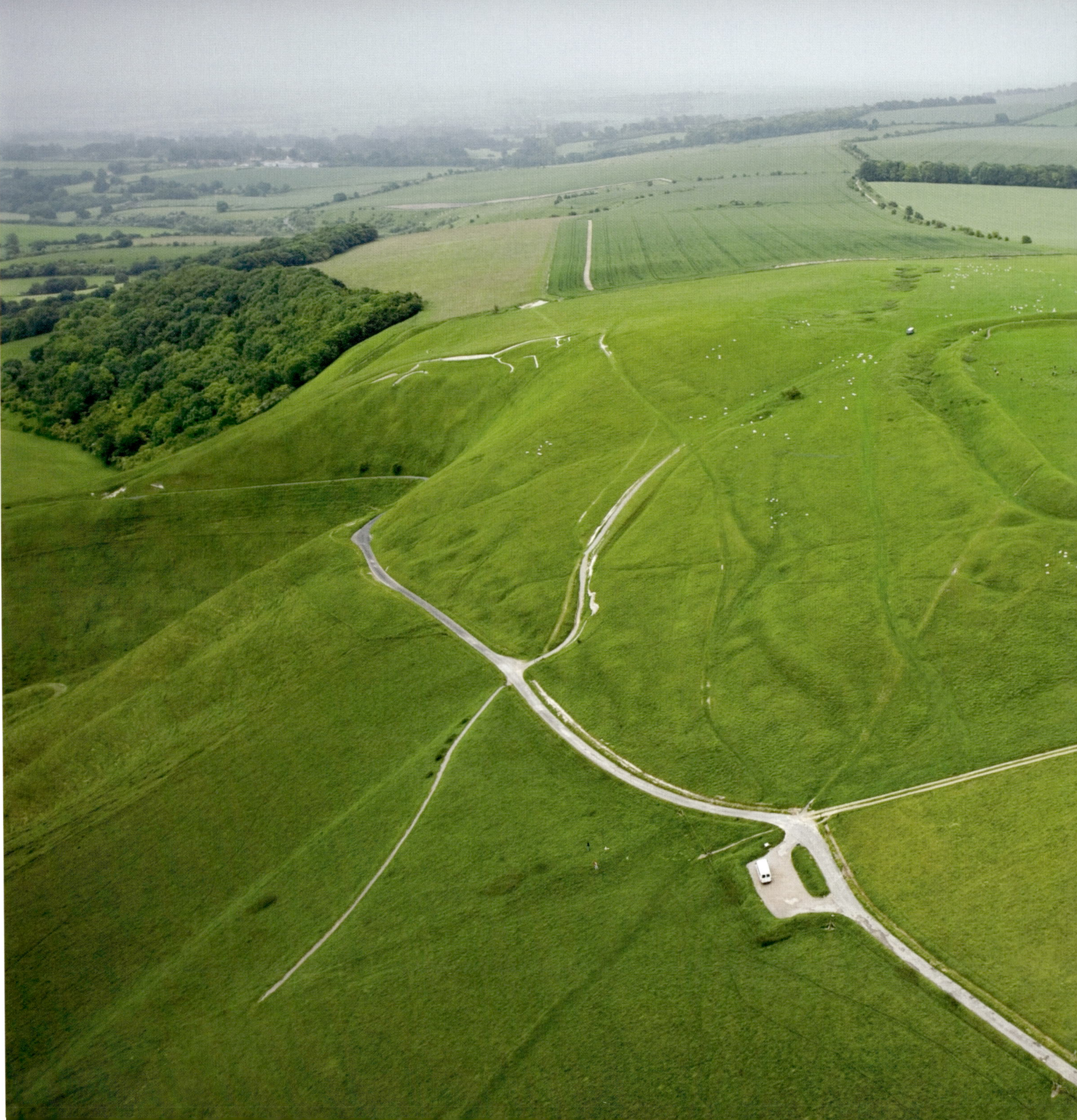

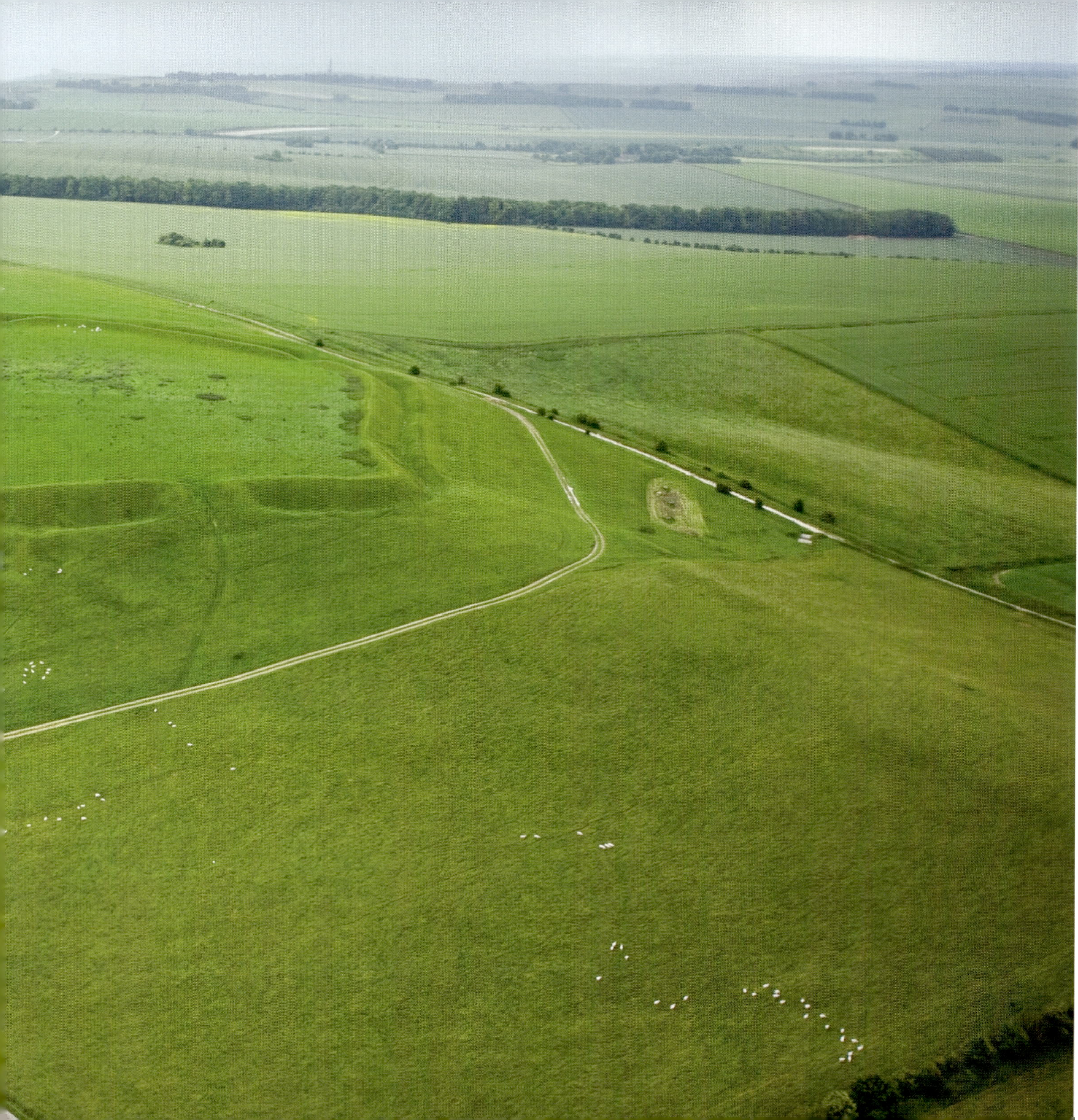

Previous page: Uffington Castle is an early Iron Age hill fort. It covers about 32,000 square metres and is surrounded by two earth banks separated by a ditch, with an entrance at the eastern end.

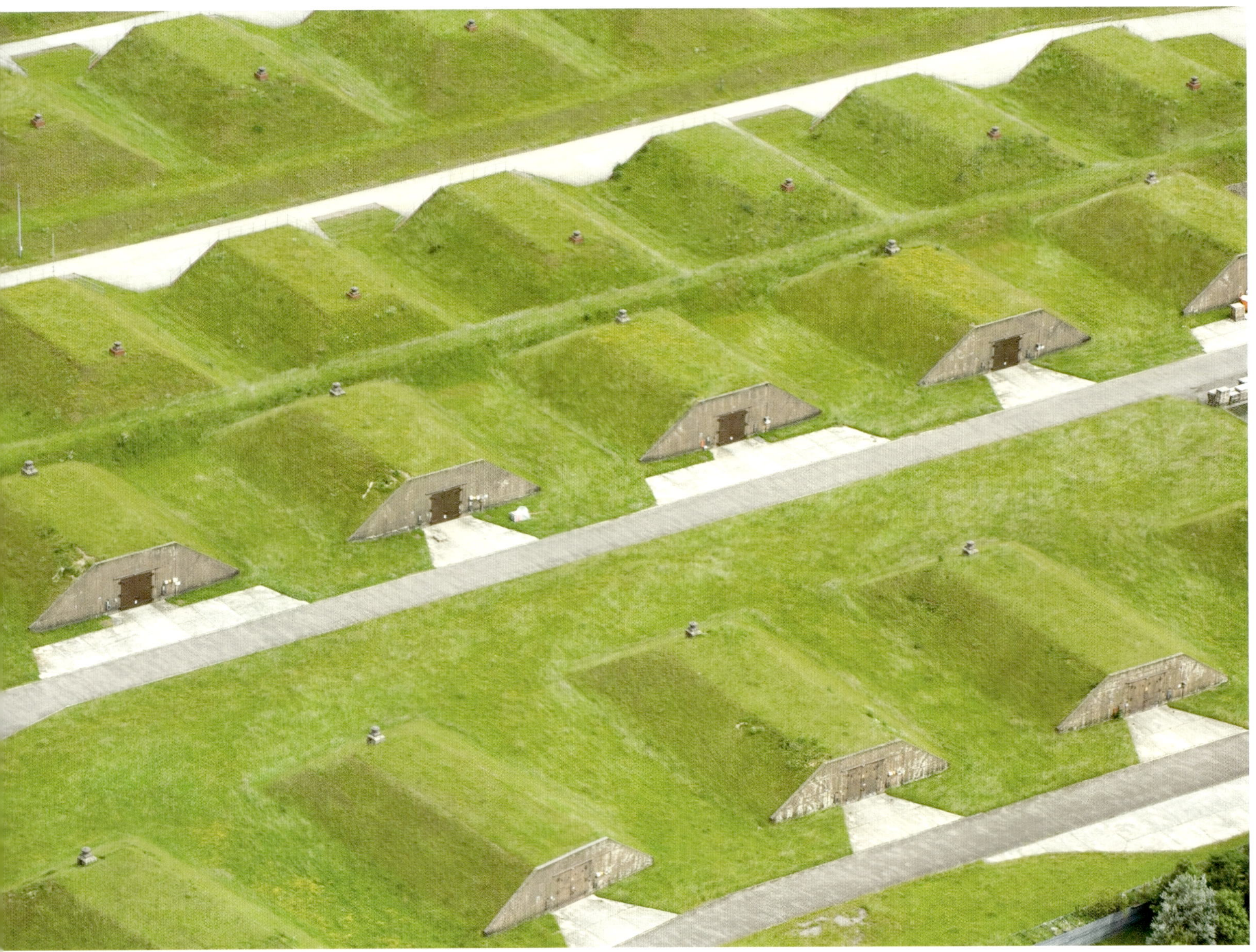

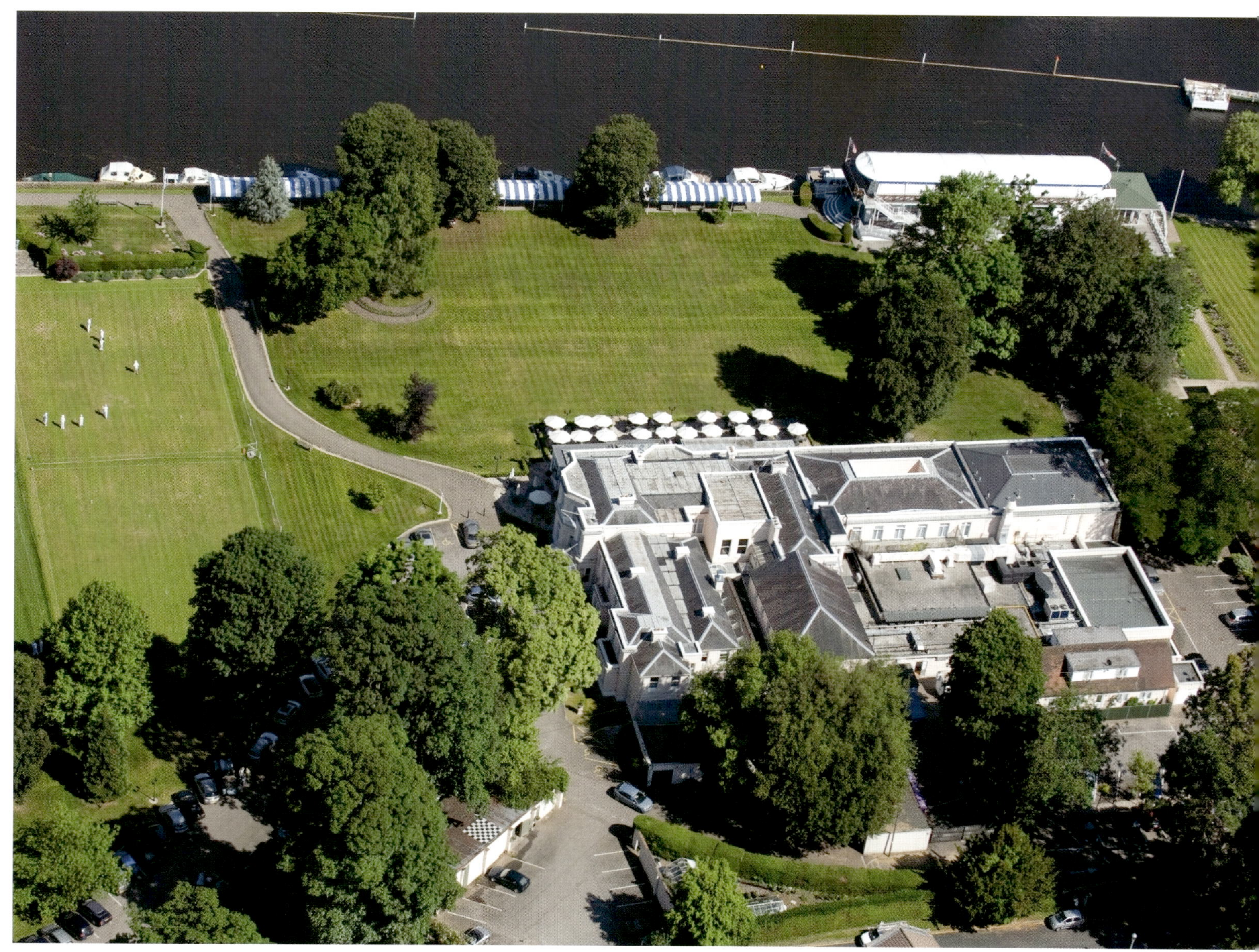

Left: The almost abstract shapes of concrete shelters as seen from the air at RAF Upper Heyford.

Above: Phyllis Court, was established as a private members club in 1906. It commands a superb position alongside the River Thames, Henley-on-Thames.

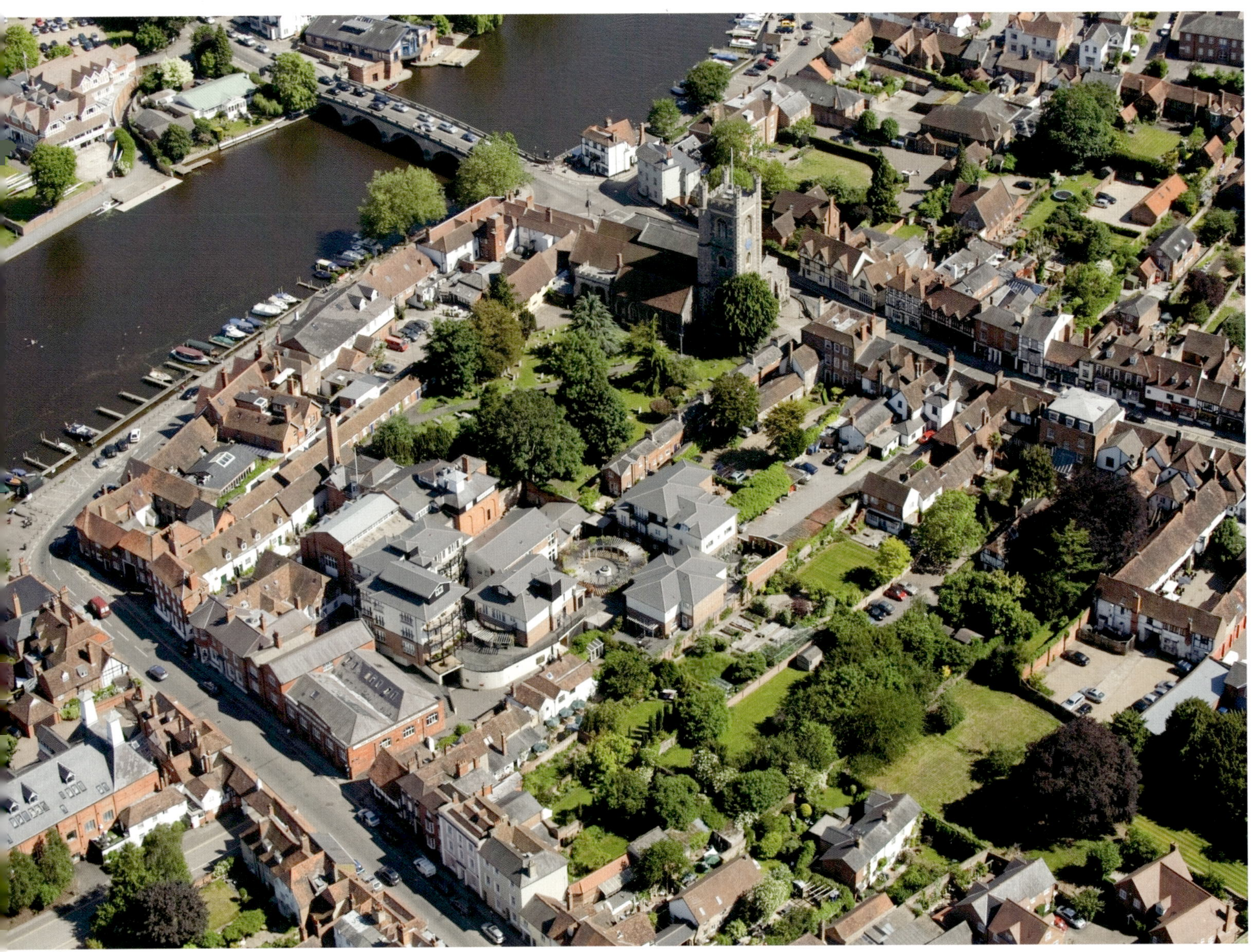

Above: Henley-on-Thames town centre.

Right: Looking down on to the church of St Mary the Virgin, Hart Street, and bridge over the River Thames, Henley-on-Thames.

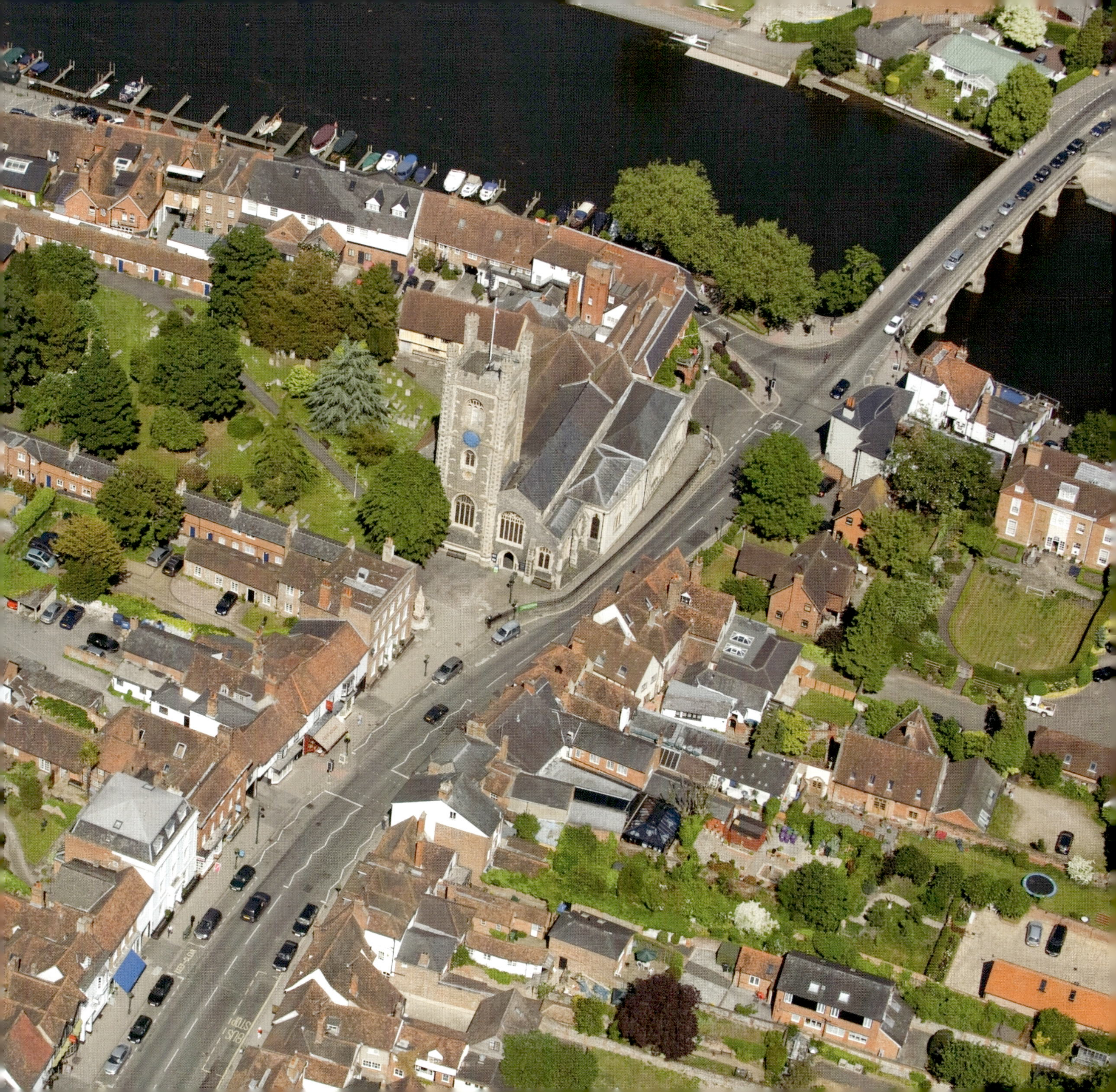

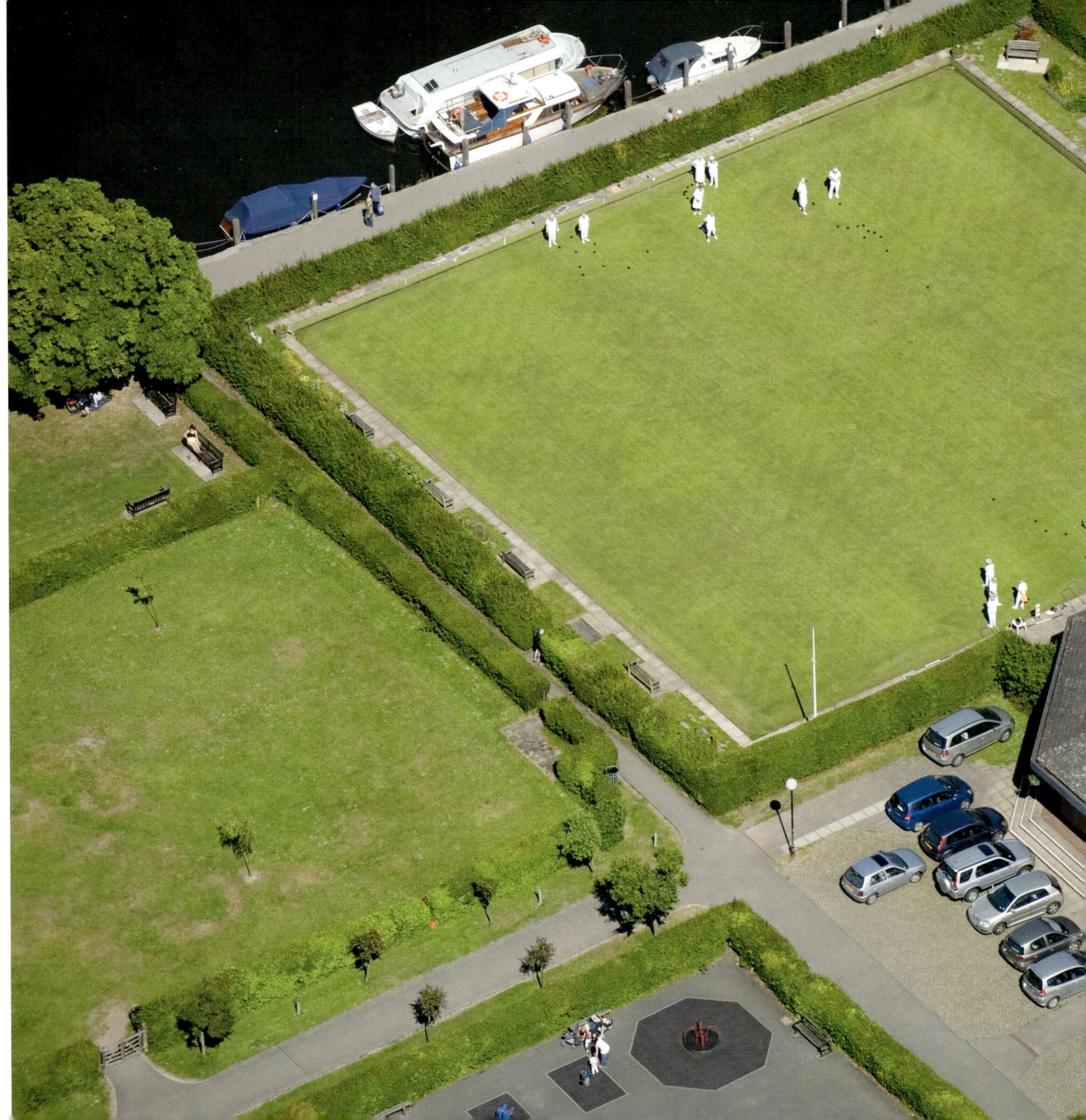

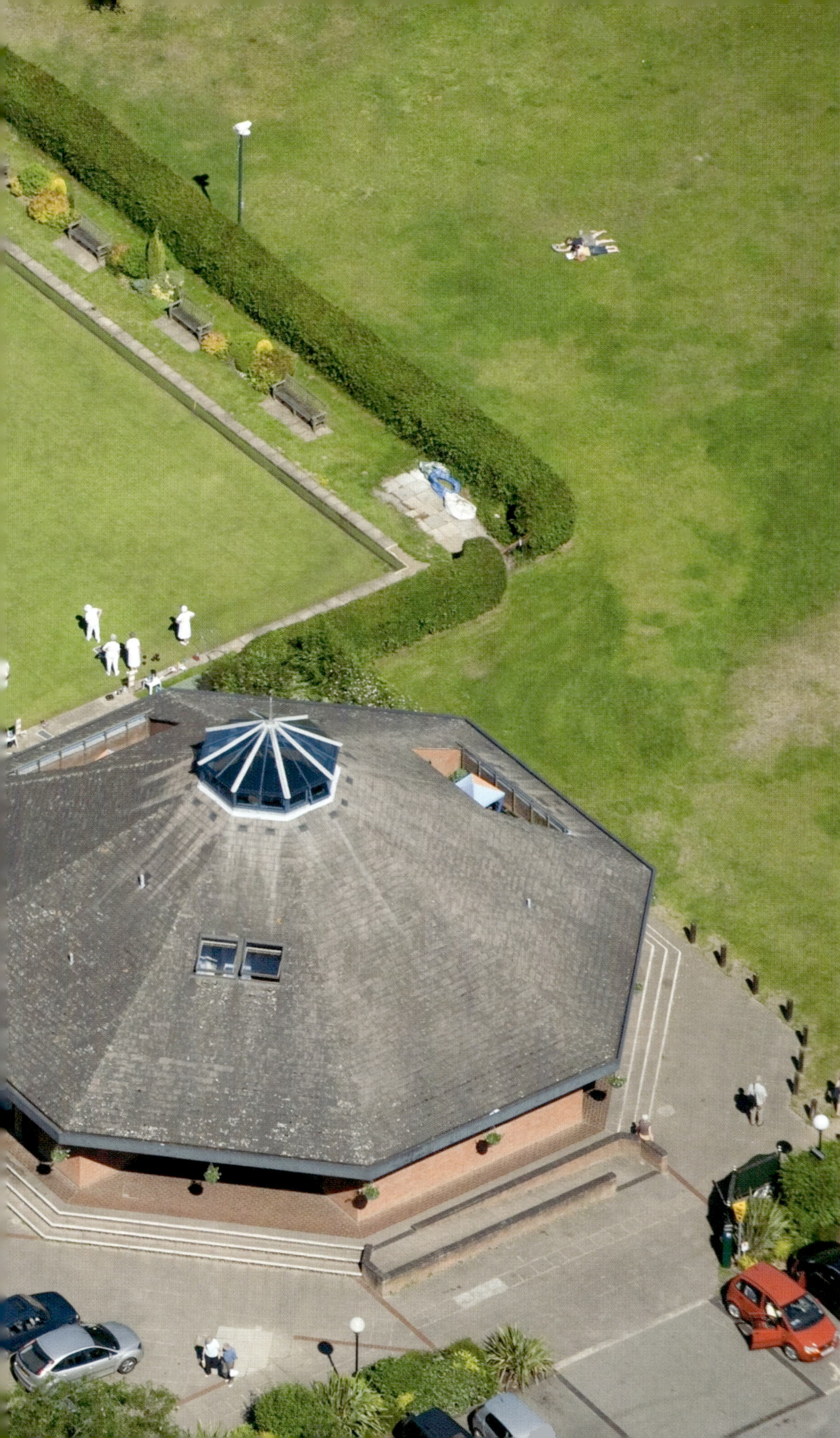

Henley-on-Thames Bowling Club, Mill Meadows.

Marsh Lock is a lock and weir on the River Thames, near Henley-on-Thames. The first pound lock was built here by the Thames Navigation Commission in 1773.

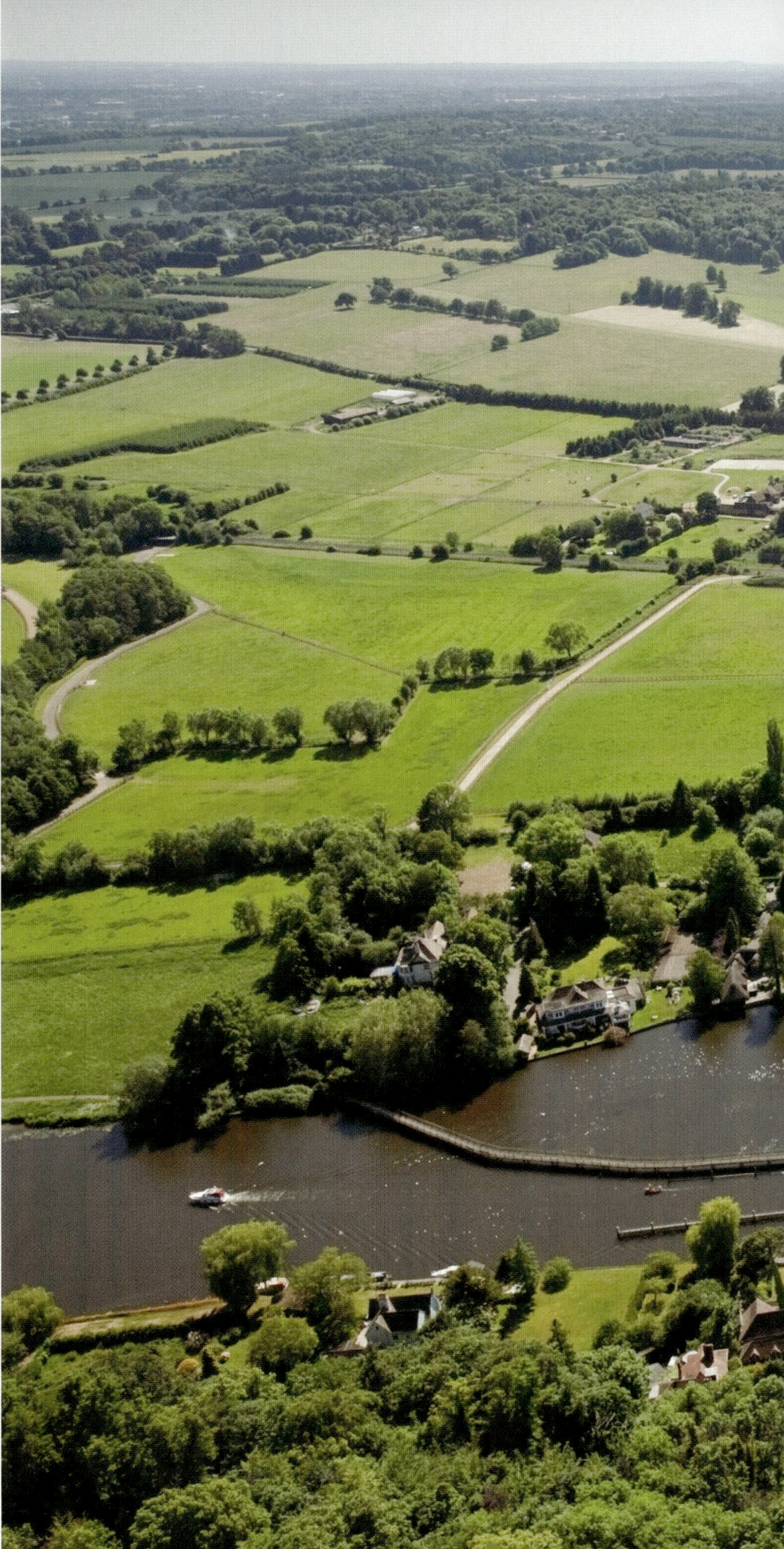

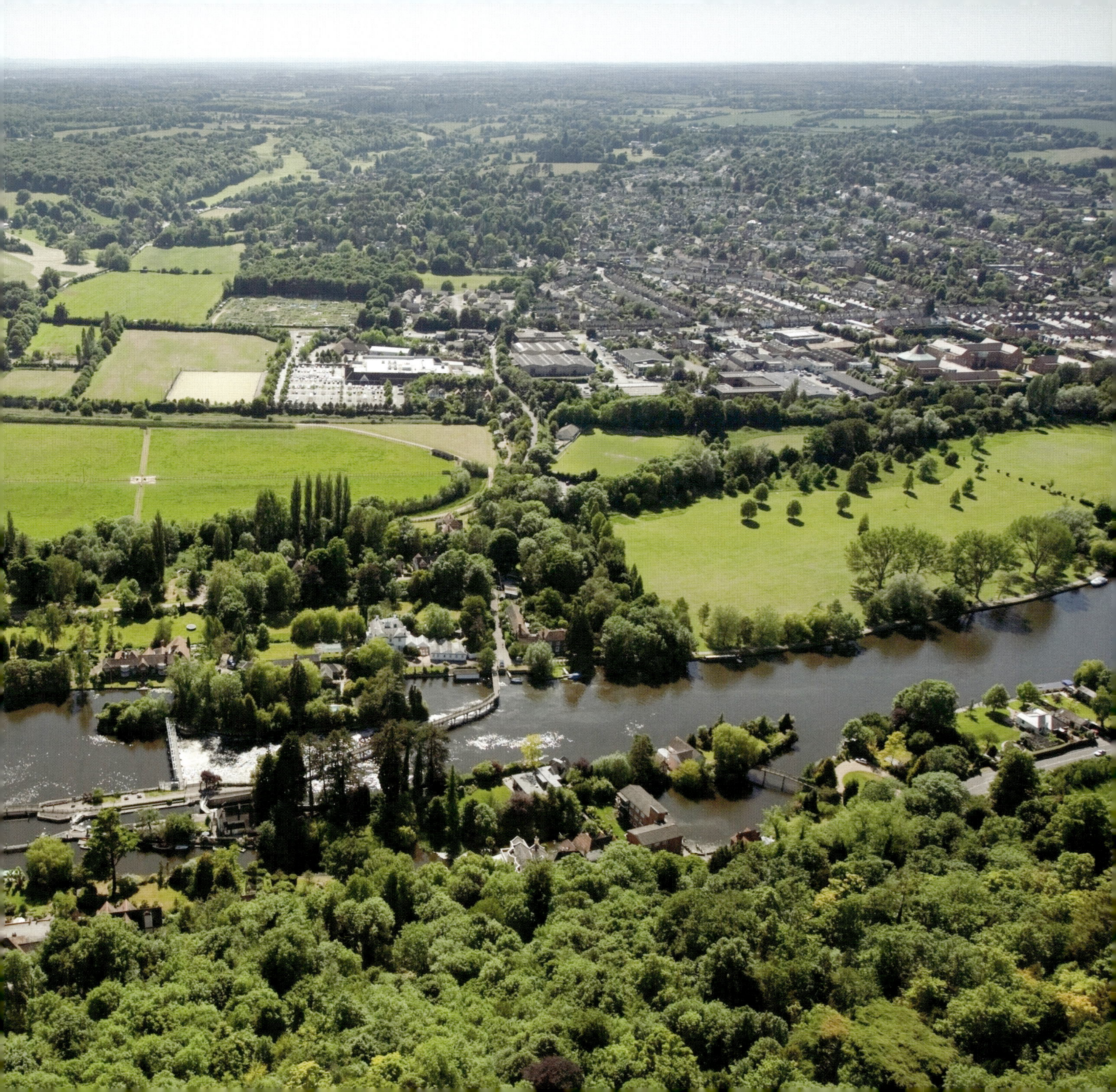

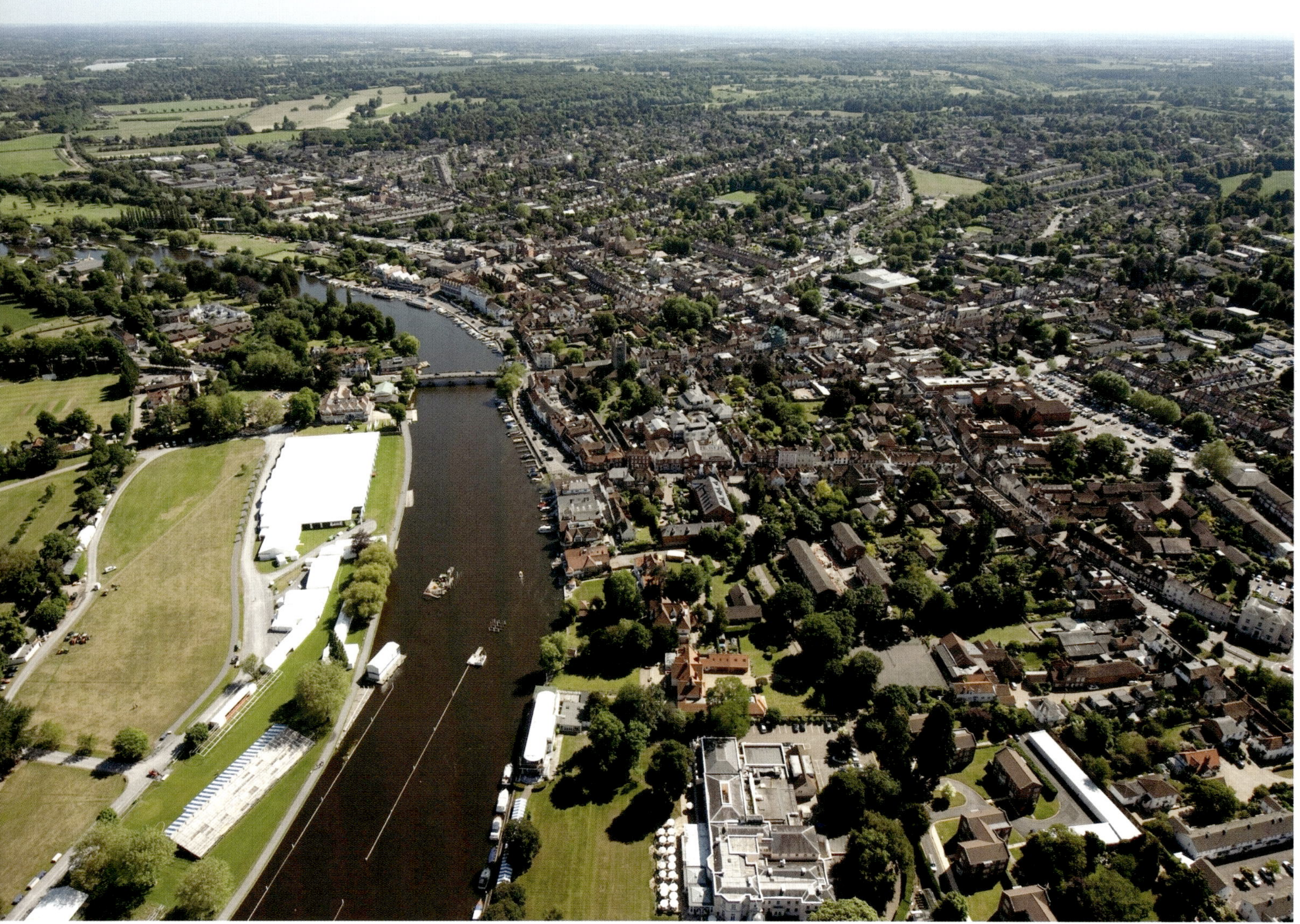

Above: Henley-on-Thames during the construction of the marquees for Henley Regatta, held annually in early July. It was first held in 1839 and since has become the world's premier event of its kind.

Right: The village of Shiplake lies about 3 miles (4.8 km) south of Henley-on-Thames. This view looks south-west towards Wargrave on the opposite bank of the River Thames.

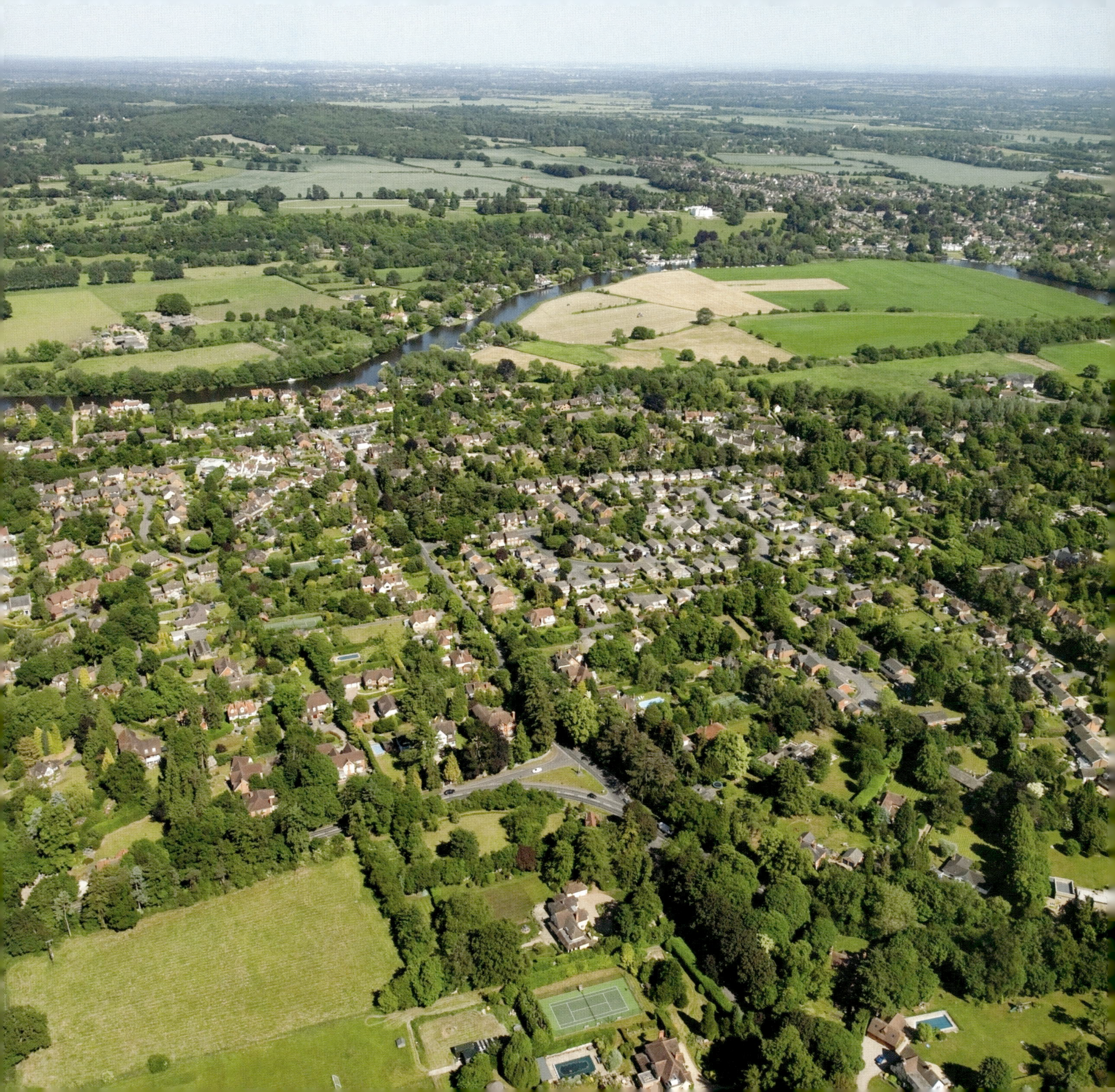

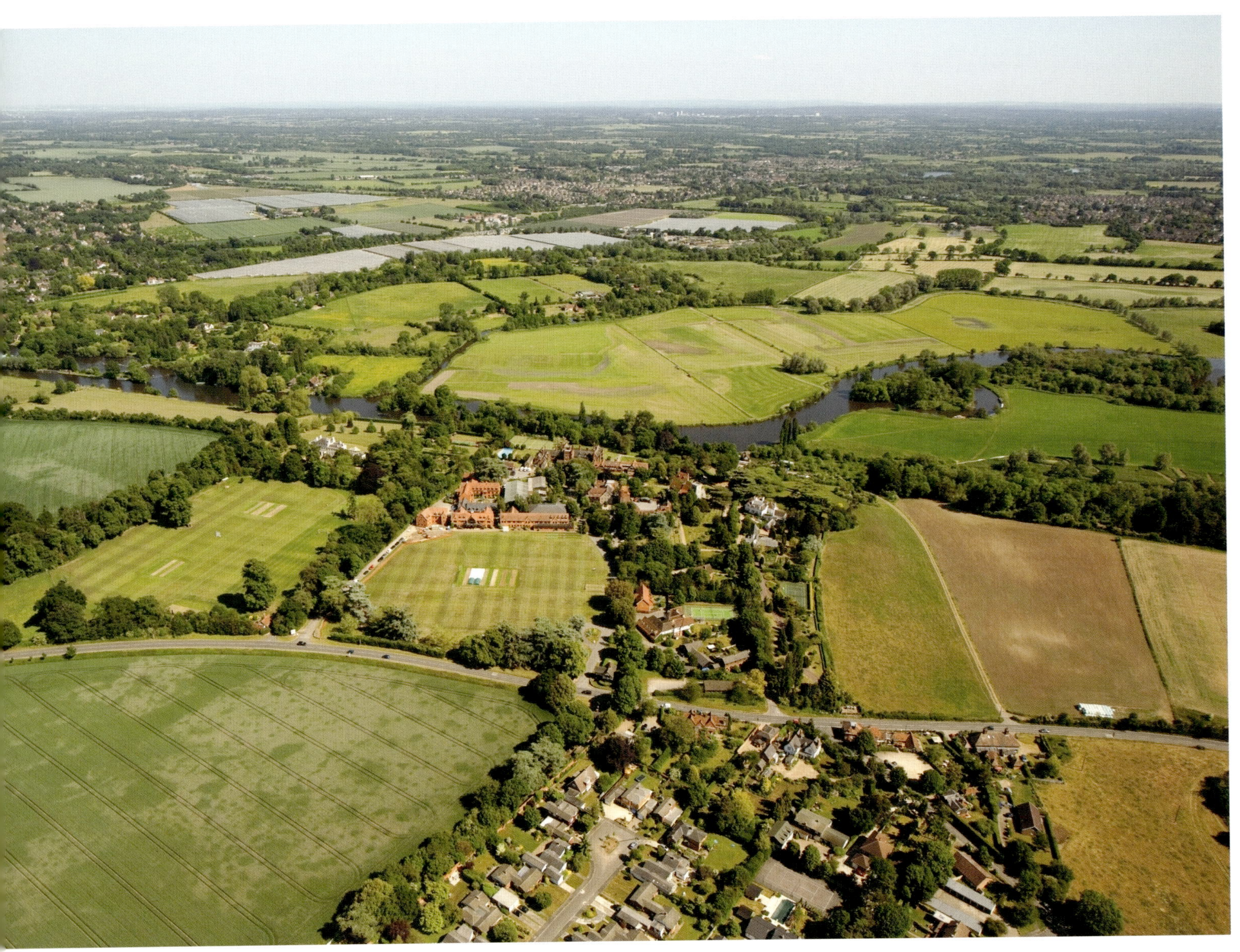

Above: Shiplake College lies in the foreground with the Berkshire towns of Wargrave glimpsed far left, Twyford in the centre distance and Charvil distant right.

Right: Mapledurham House is situated on an ancient estate lying to the west of Caversham. Among other attractions, it now plays host to golfers, holidaymakers and wedding parties.

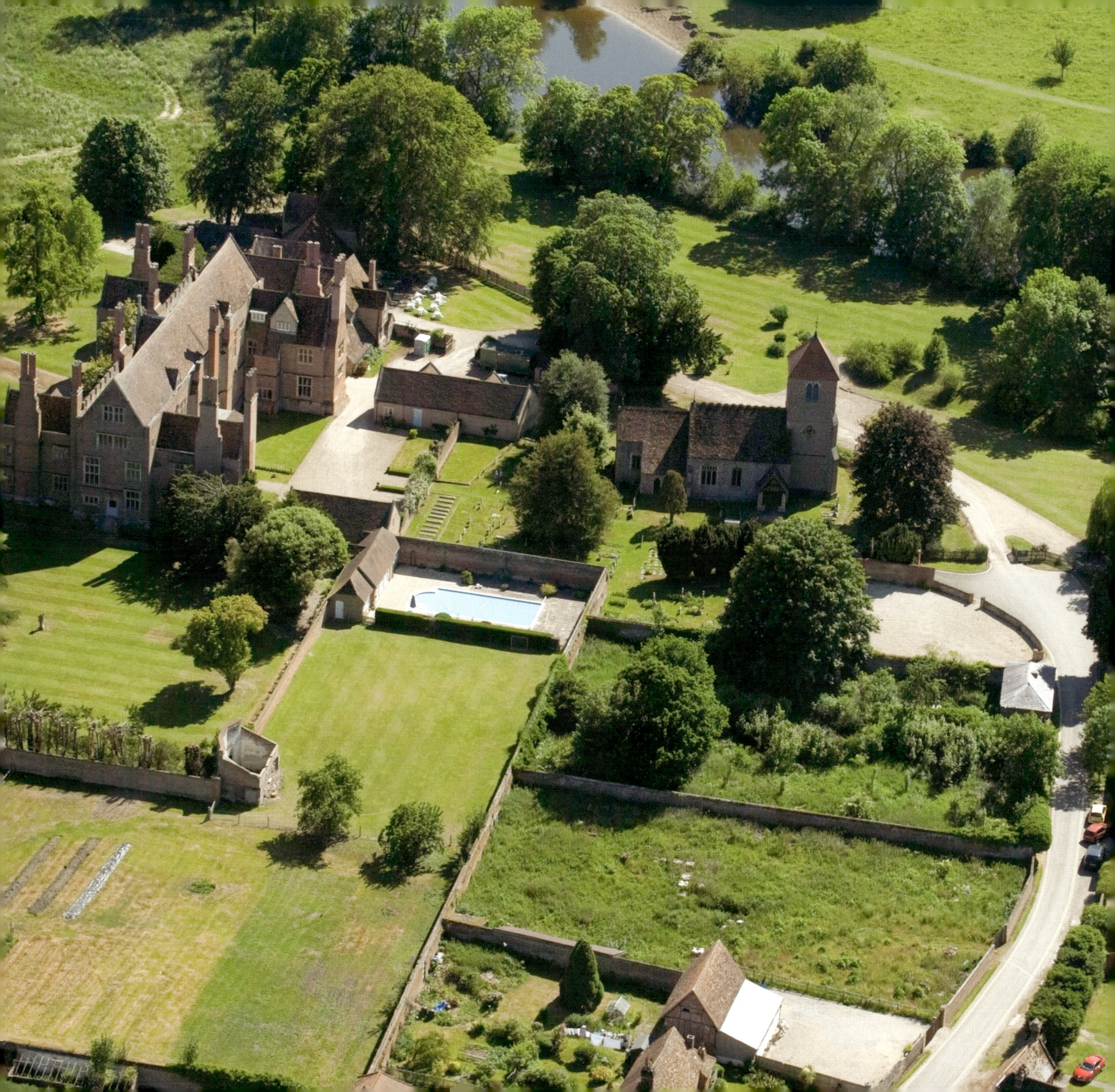

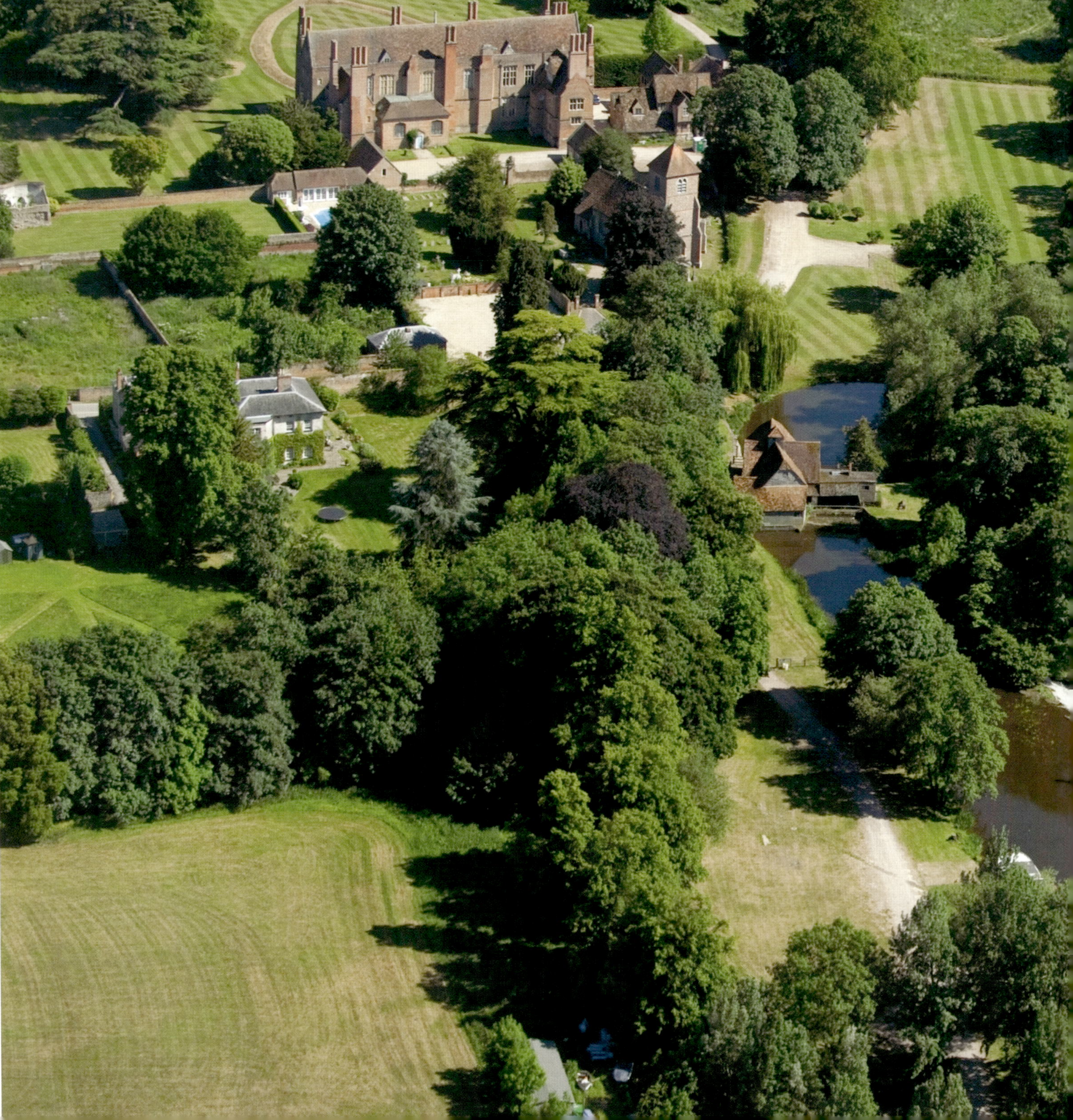

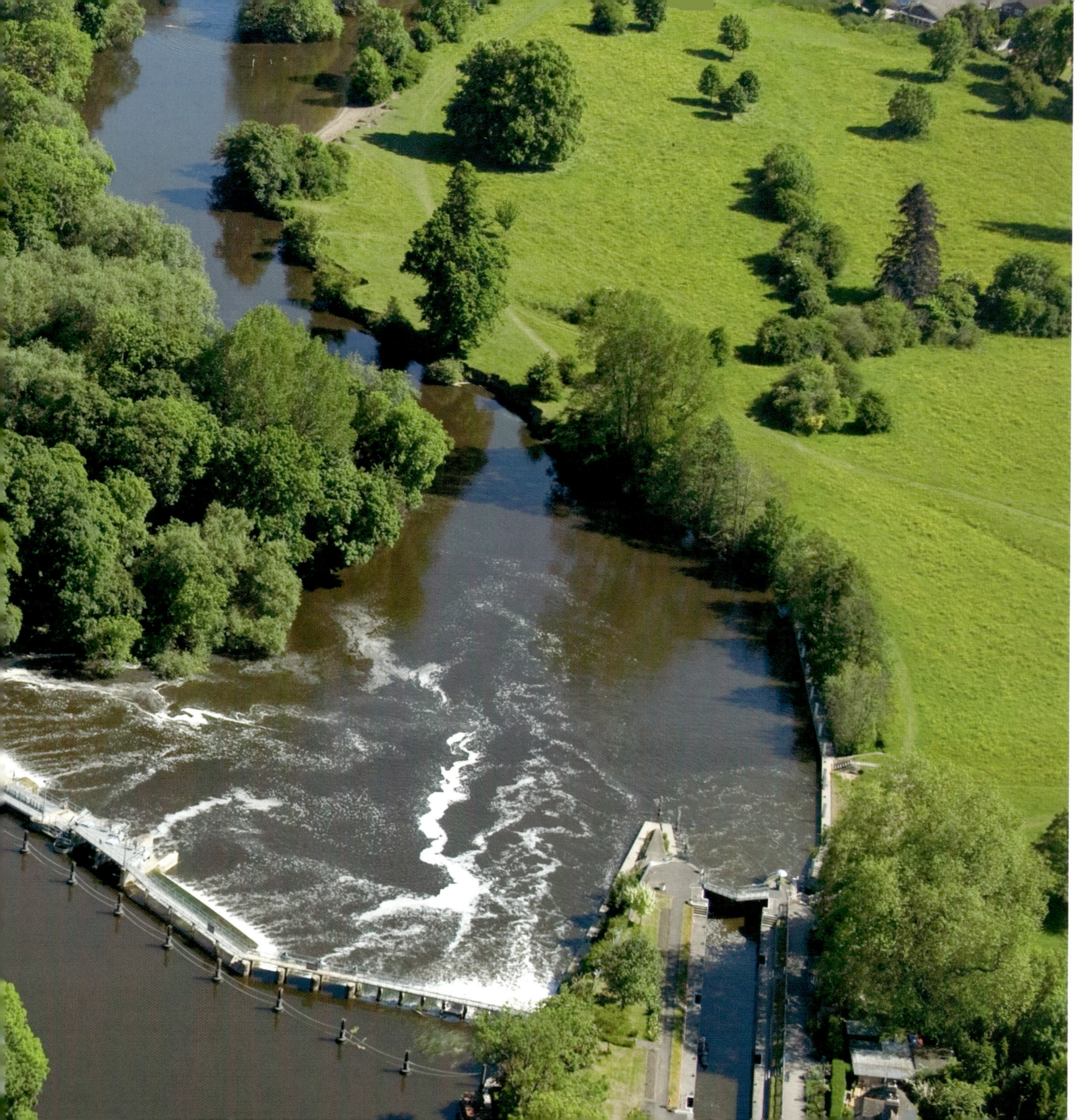

Previous page: A superb place to visit or stay, Mapledurham House. The ancient watermill, seen centre, is the only surviving working mill on the River Thames. Despite its name, Mapledurham Lock is located by the Berkshire village of Purley-on-Thames, rather than at the Oxfordshire village of Mapledurham which lies on the other side of the river.

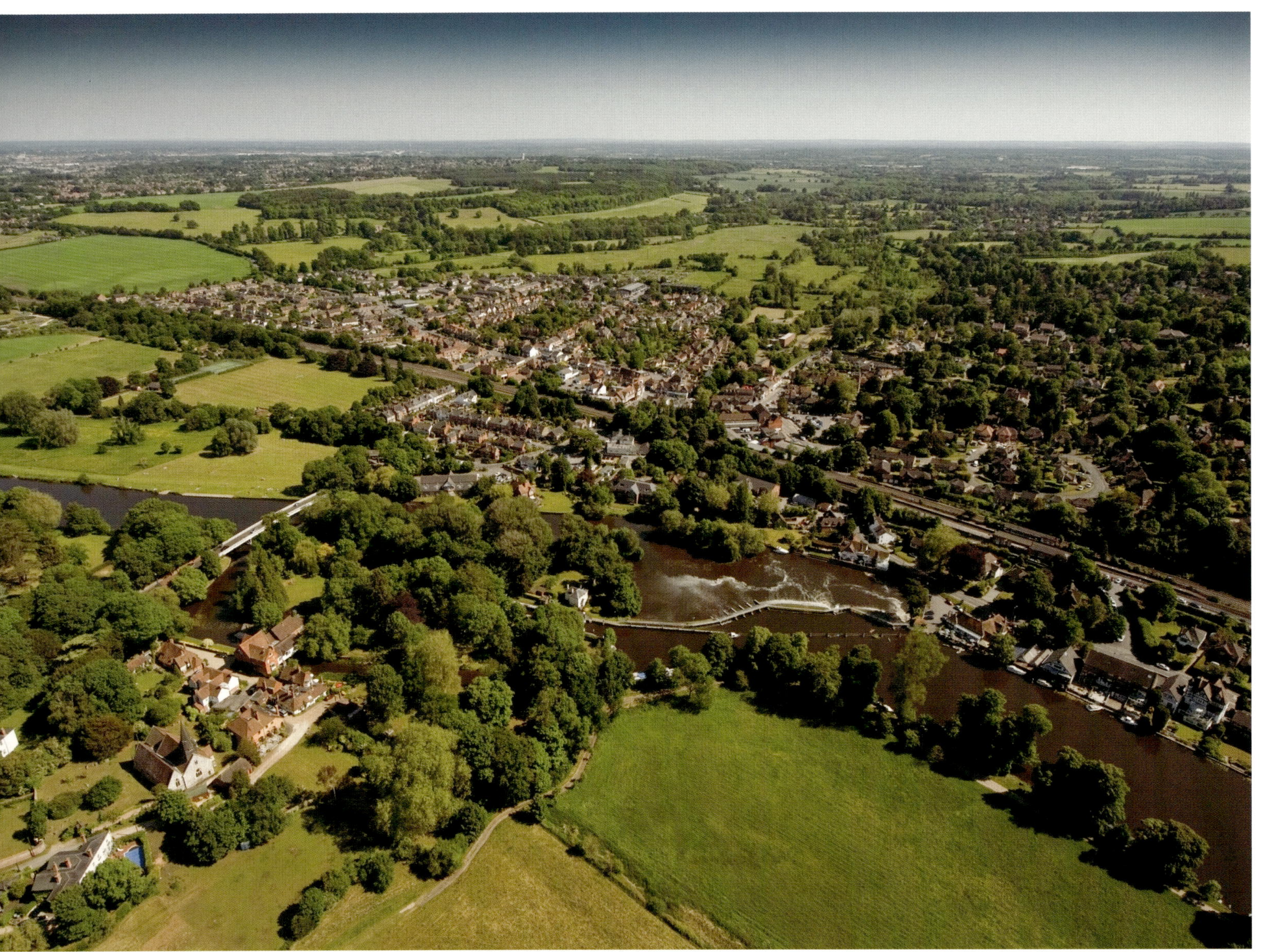

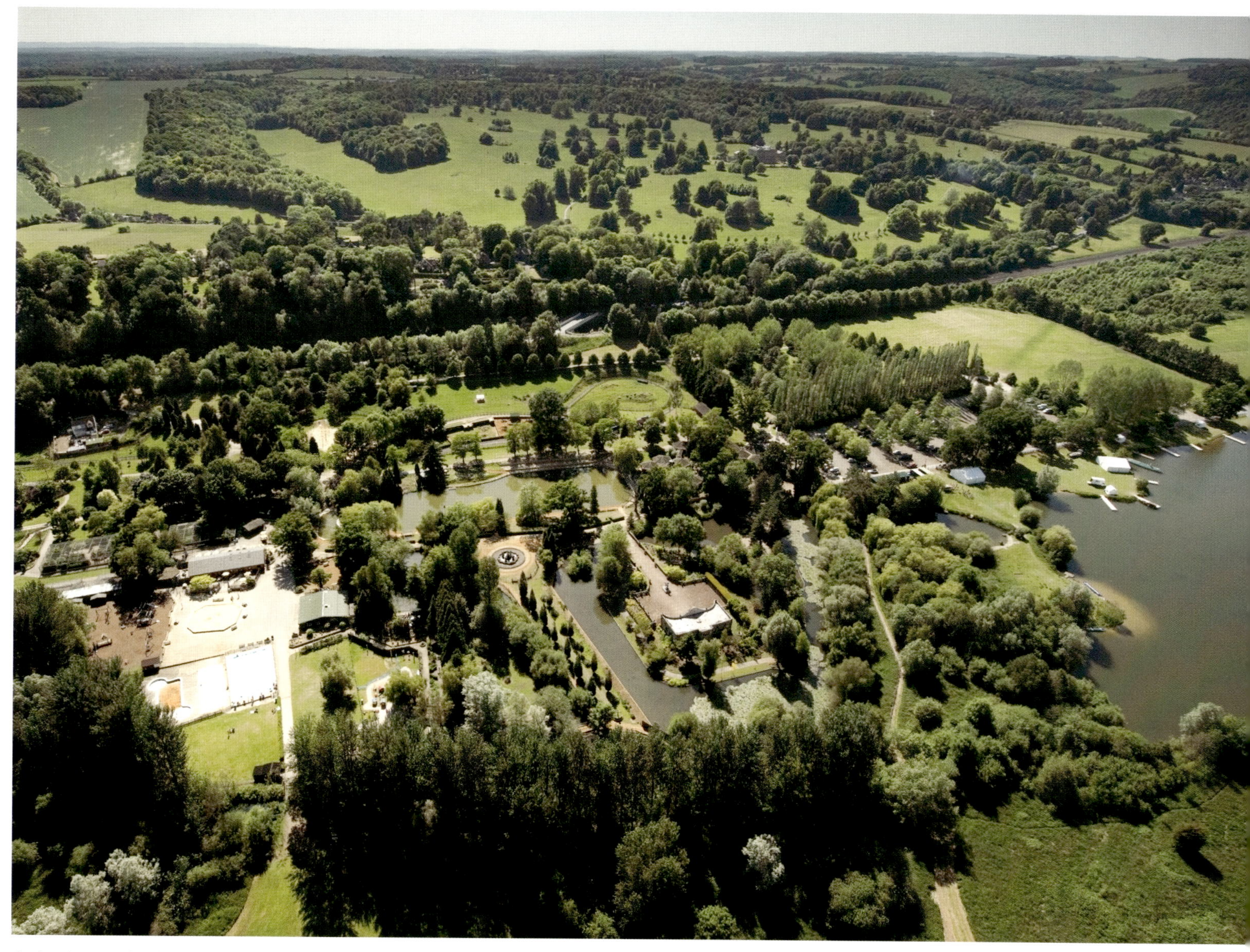

Left: A superb view looking from Whitchurch-on-Thames over the River Thames towards Pangbourne in Berkshire.

Above: Beale Wildlife Park in Berkshire lies between Pangbourne and Lower Basildon.

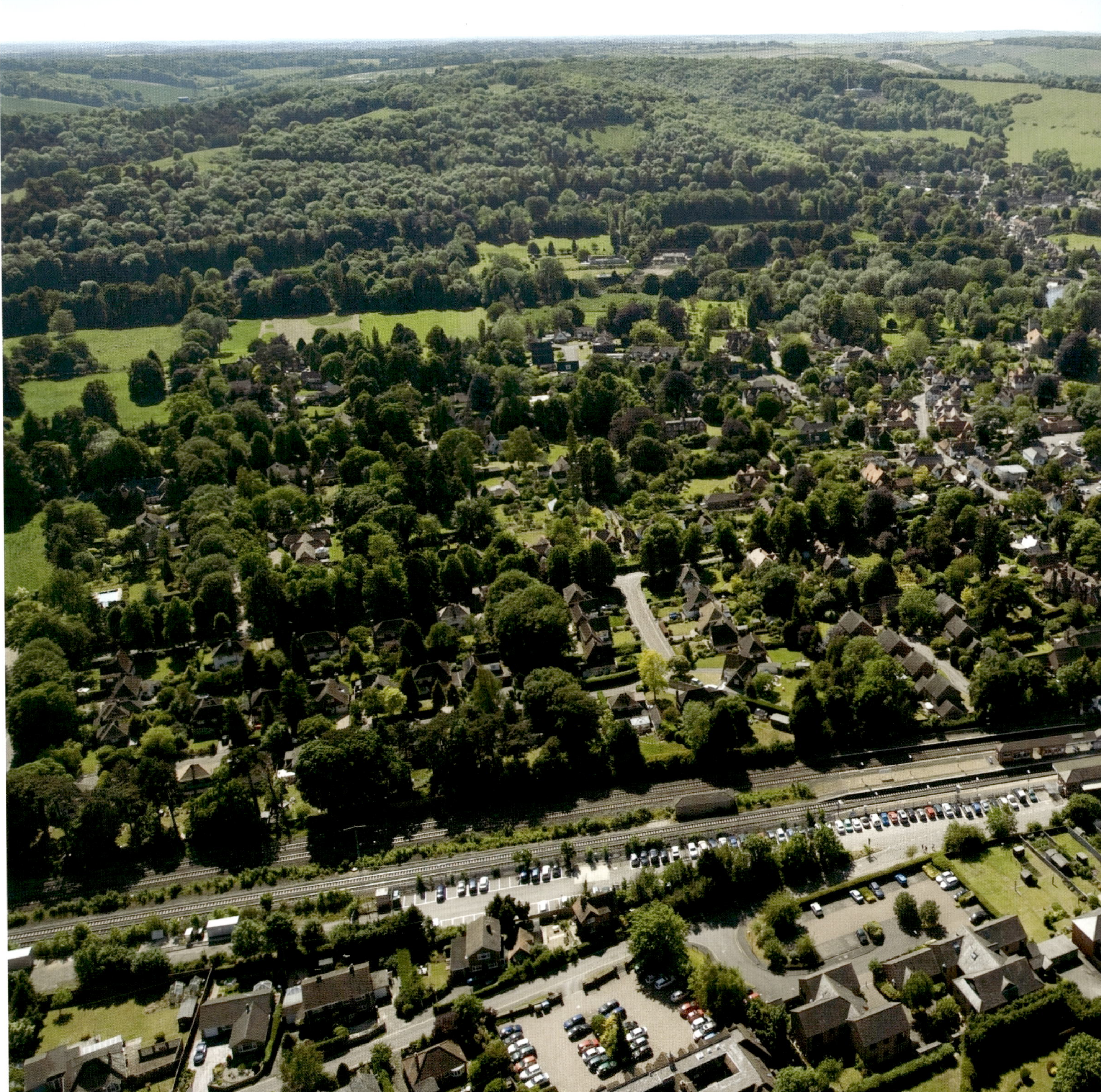

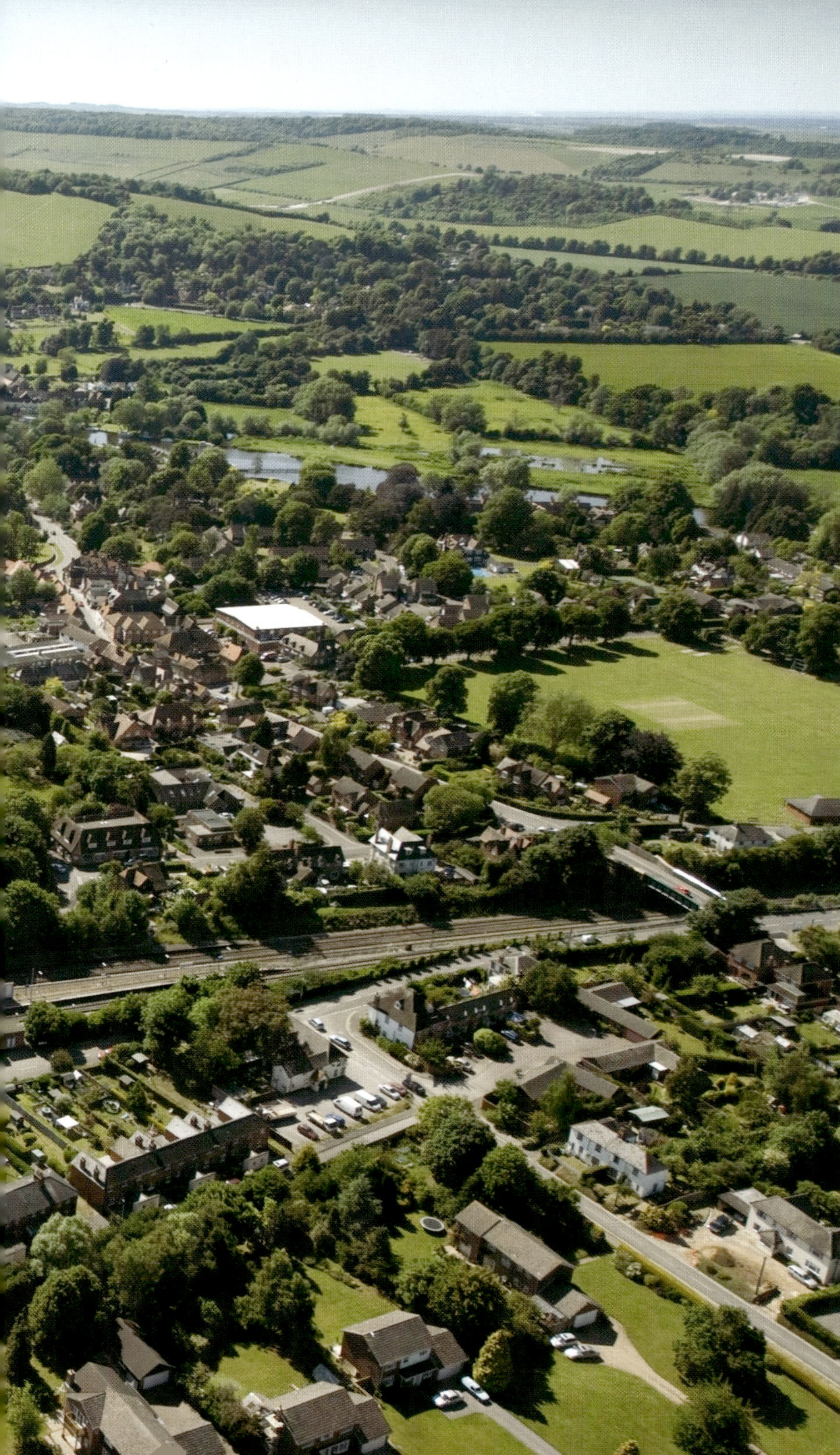

Looking east over Goring-on-Thames, with the River Thames glimpsed on the right.

The river and the railway line run alongside each other for a short distance at Goring-on-Thames. Here, in the still waters of the River Thames, river cruisers are tied up to wait their turn to enter a lock.

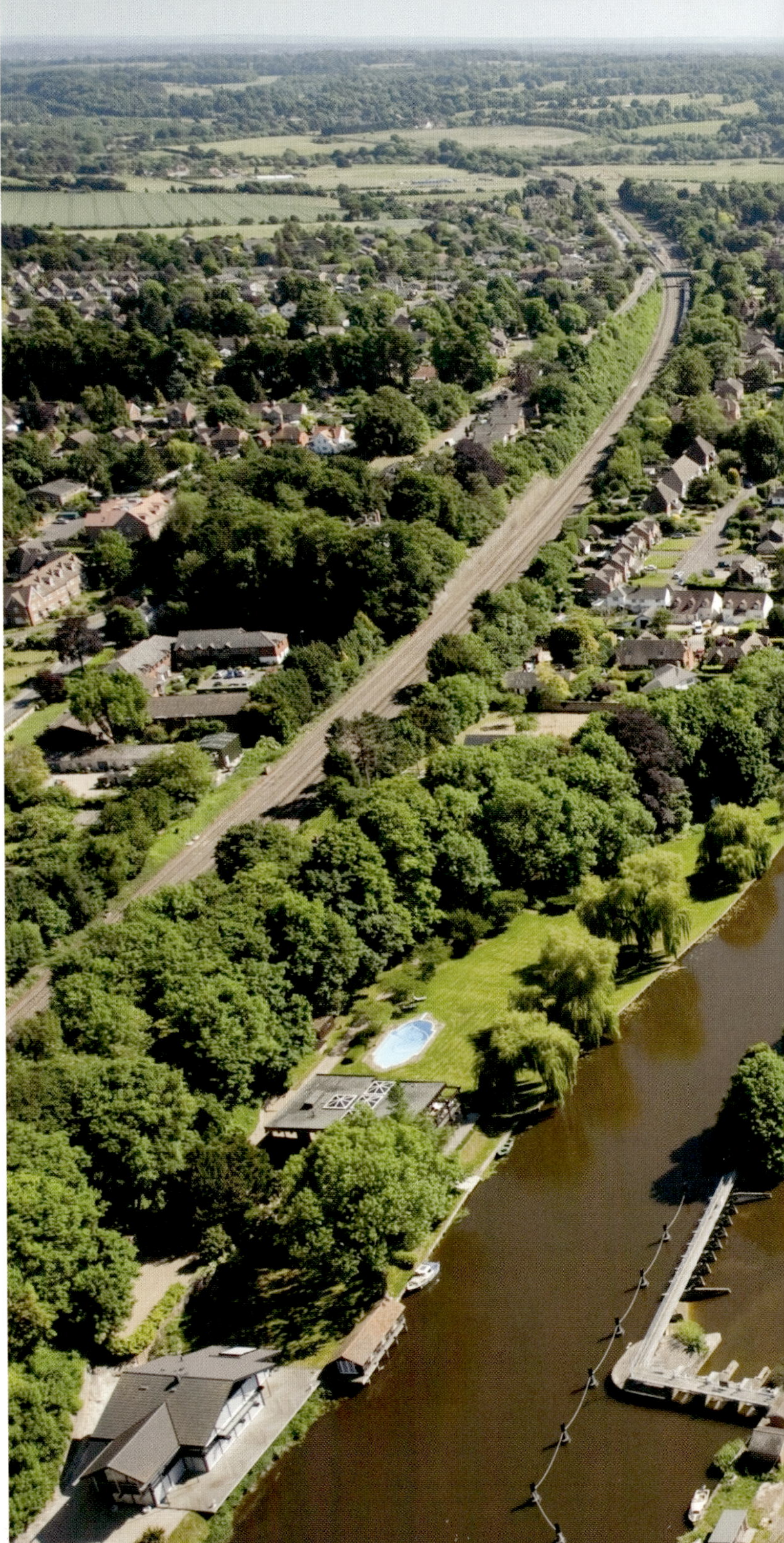

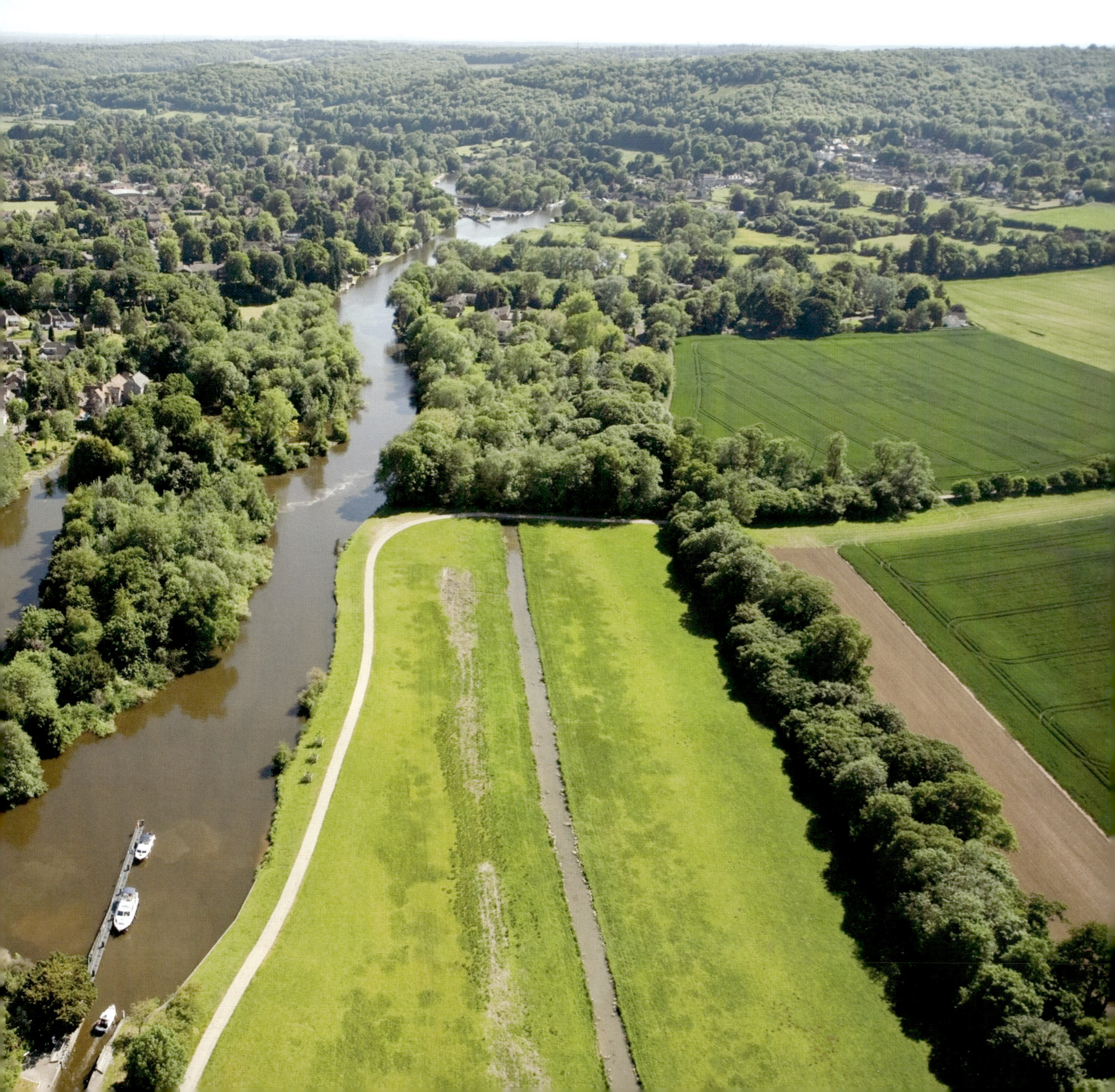

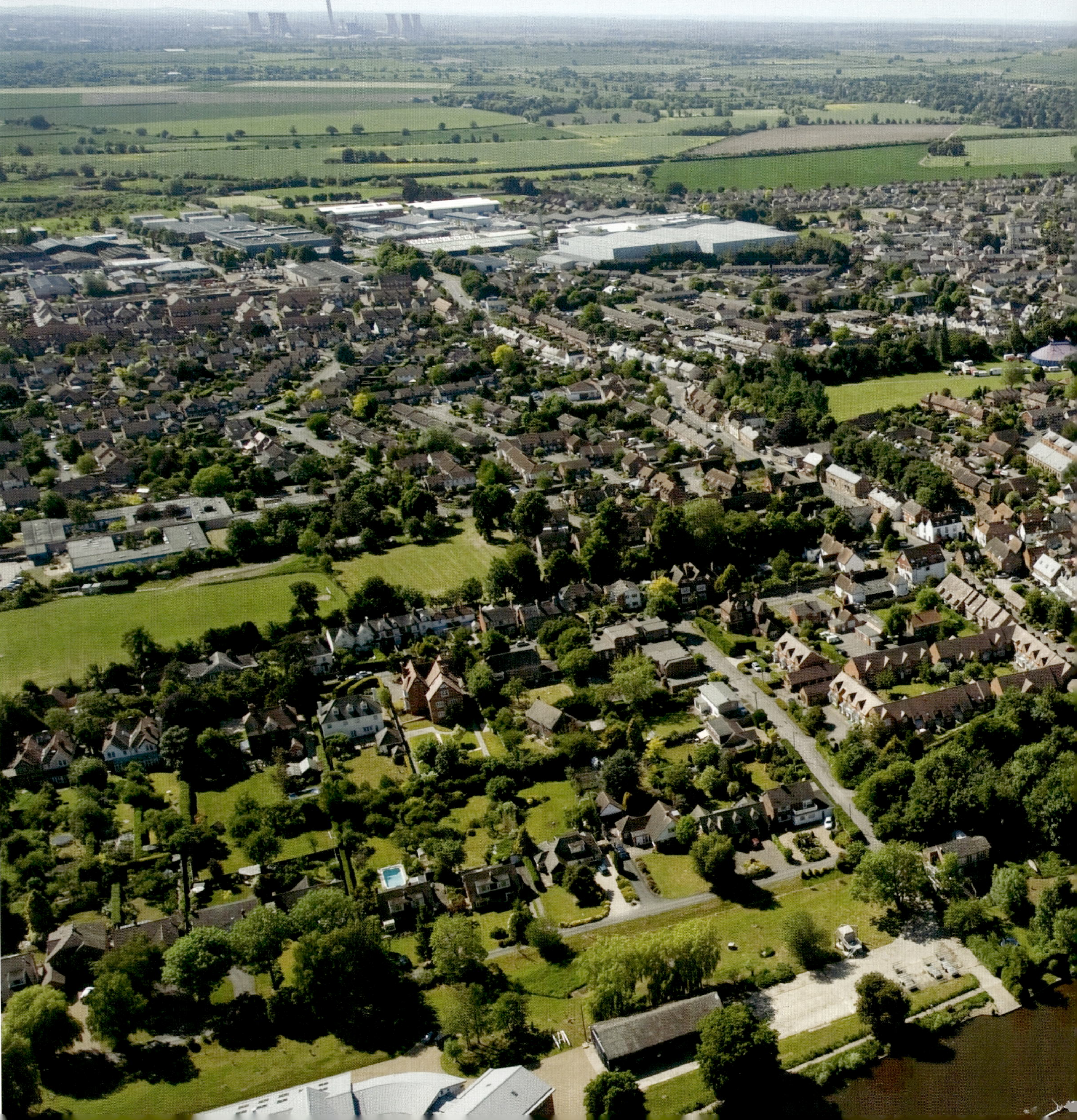

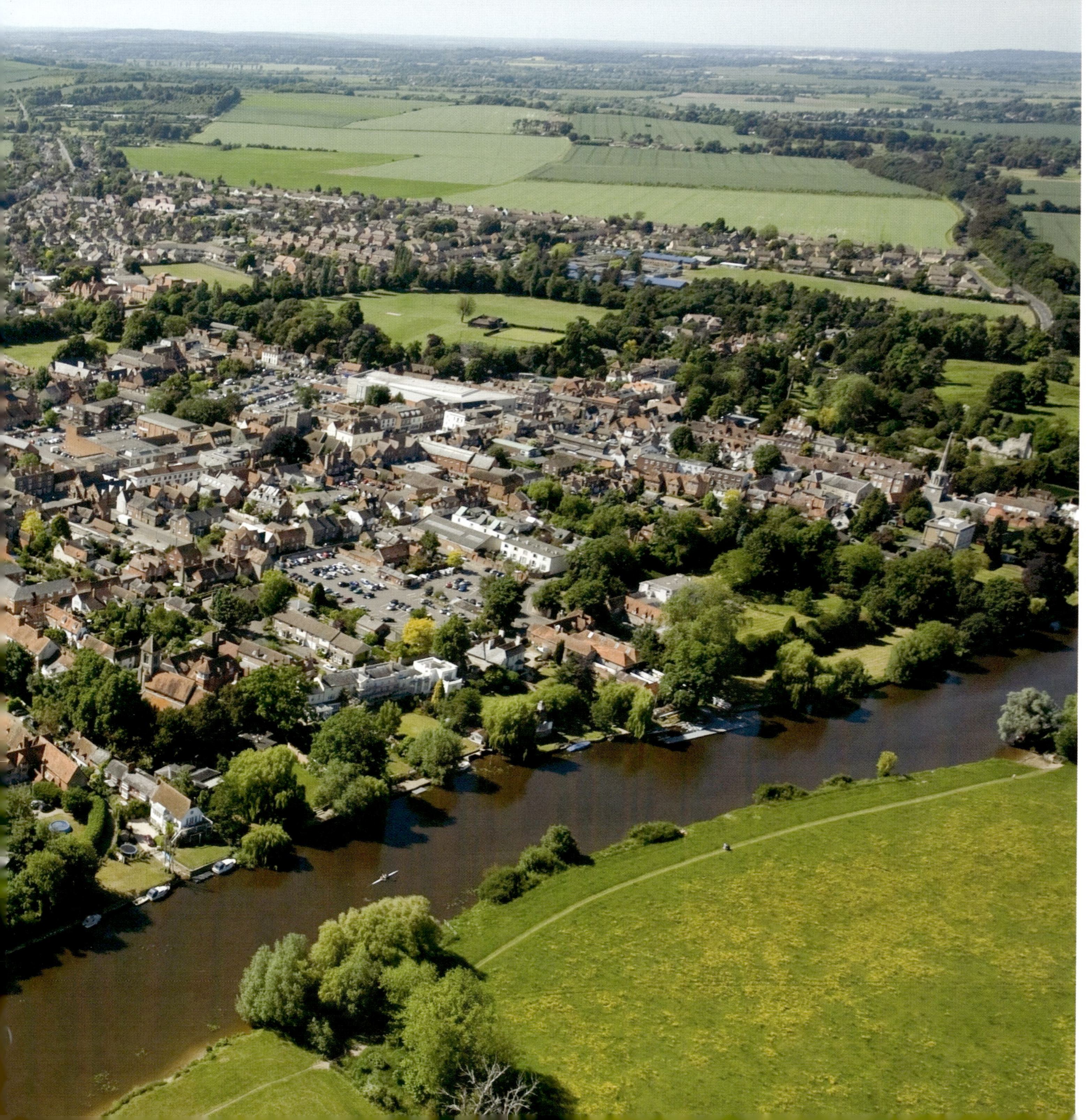

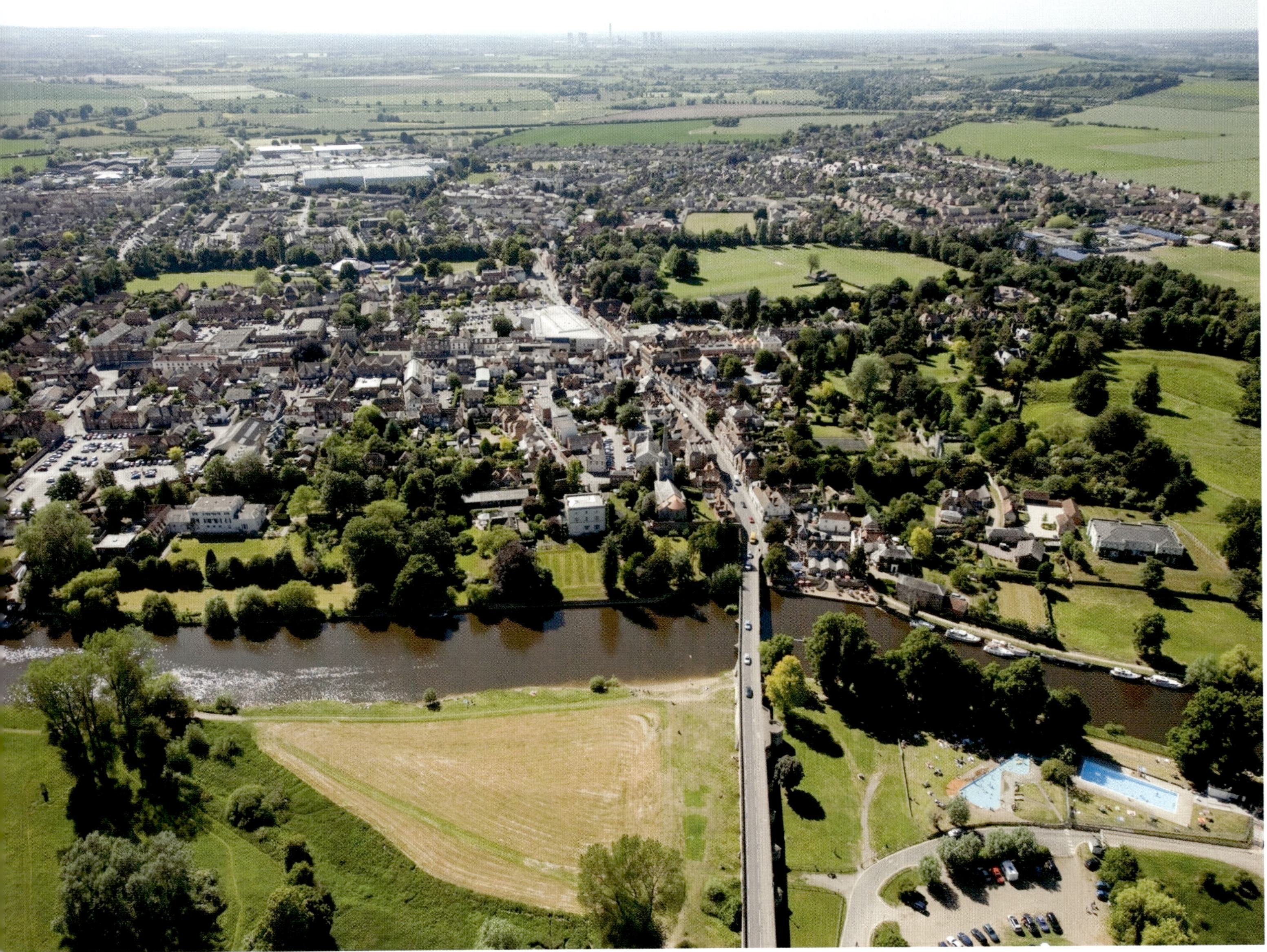

Previous page: The view north-eastwards over Wallingford, looking towards Didcot.

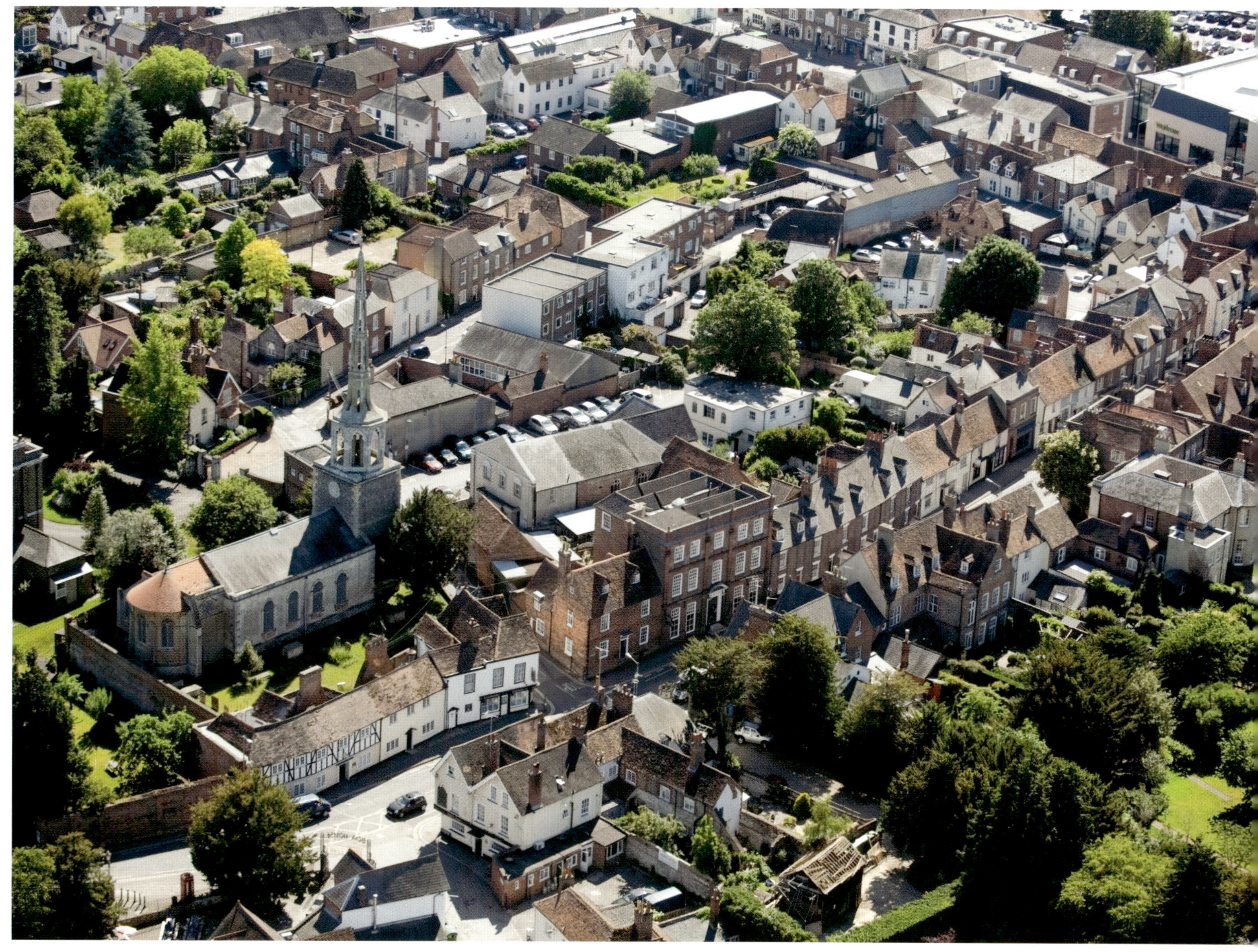

Left: Wallingford Bridge, looking east.

Above: Looking down into the High Street, Wallingford.

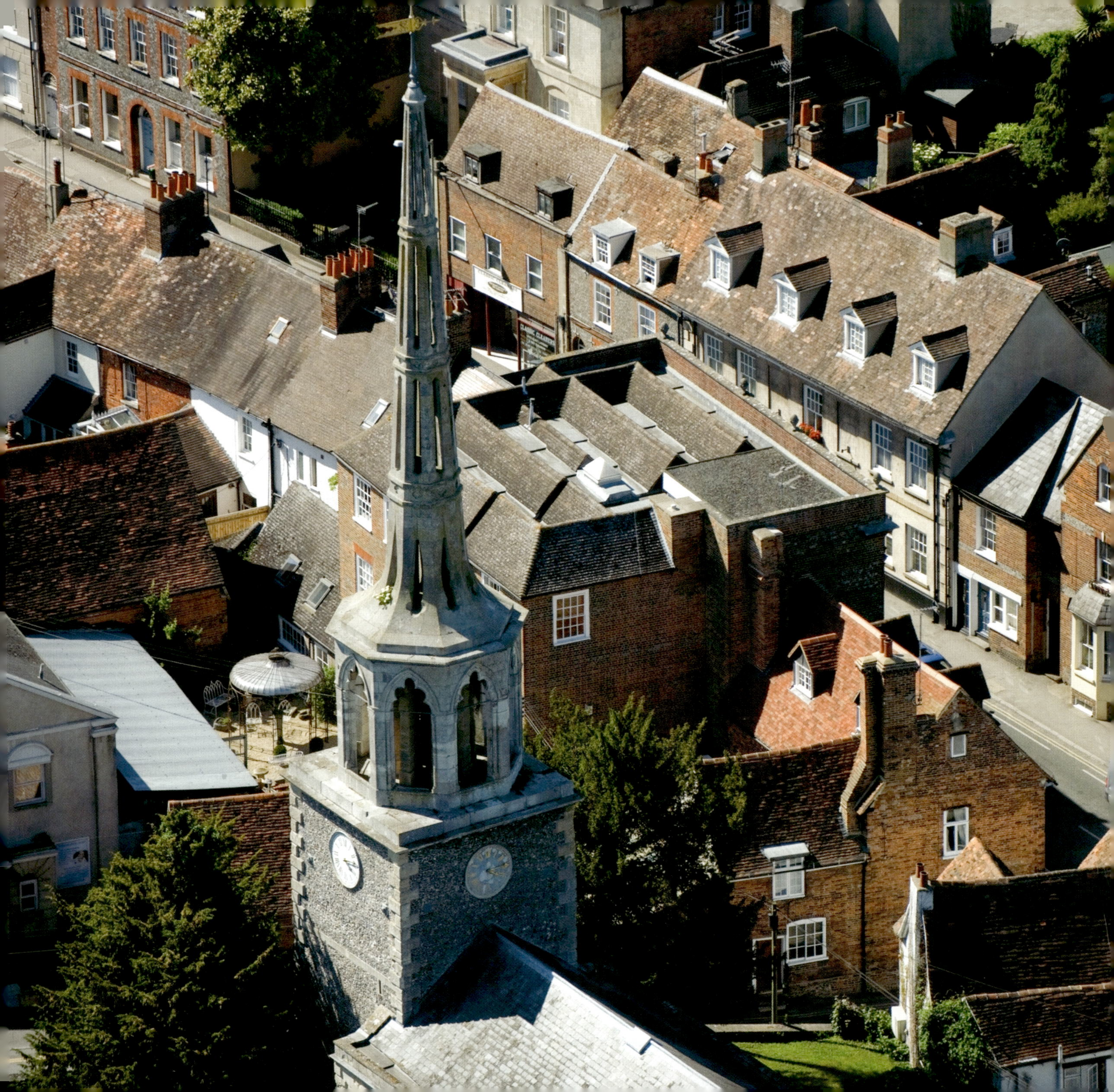

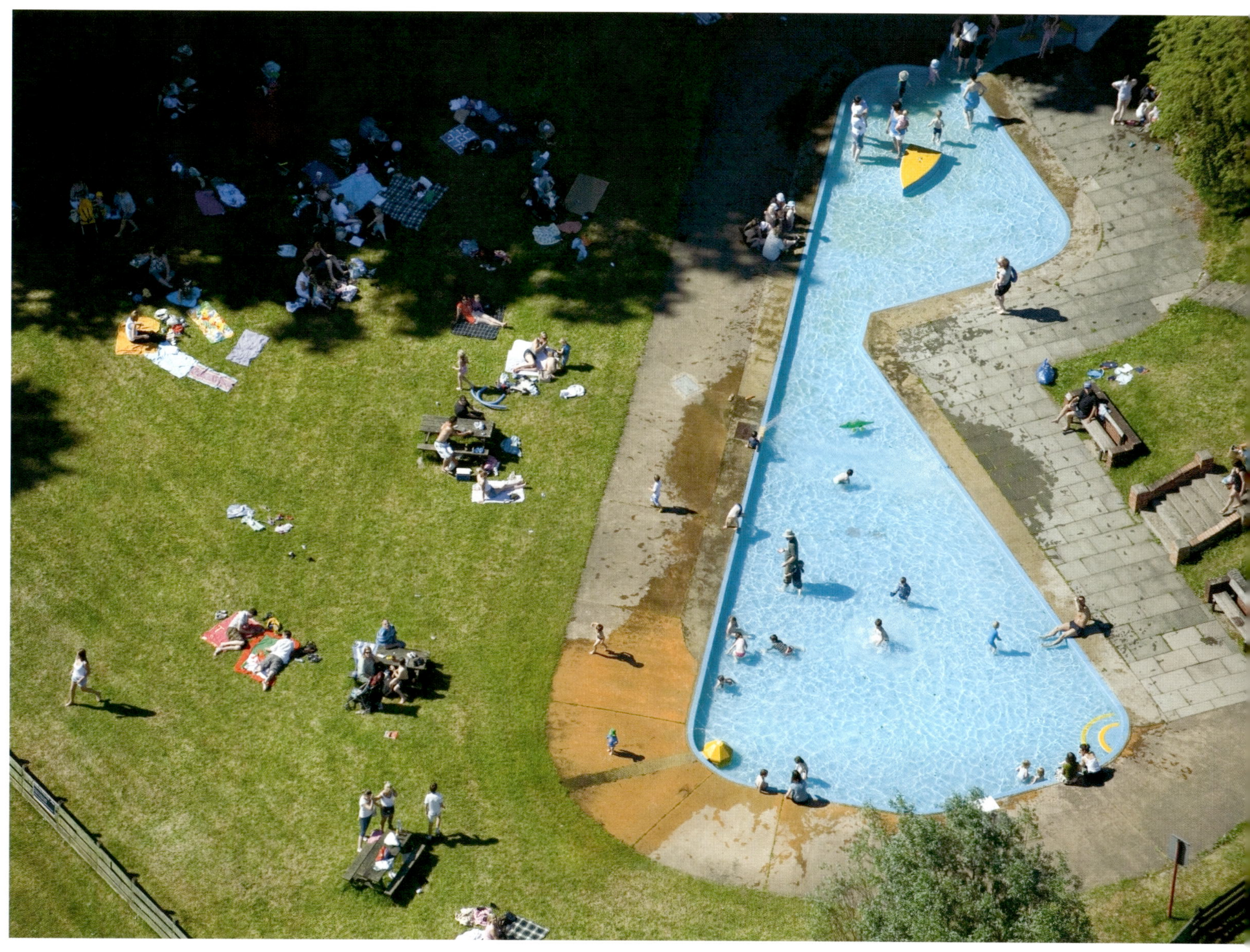

Left: St Peter's Church Wallingford. Its remarkable pierced spire dates from 1777.

Above: Fun in the sun at Crowmarsh Gifford which lies on the River Thames, on the opposite bank from Wallingford. These two communities are connected via Wallingford Bridge.

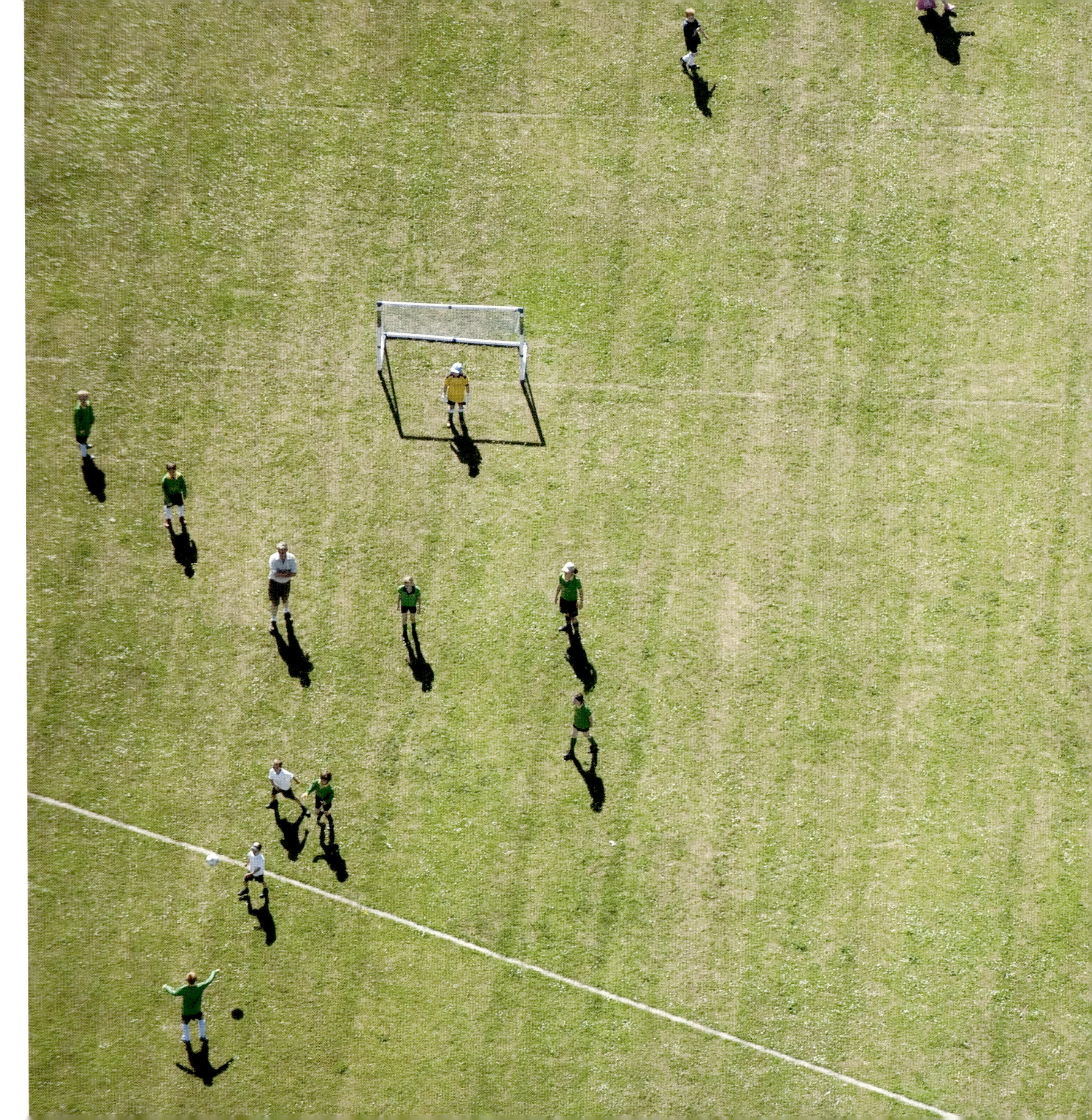

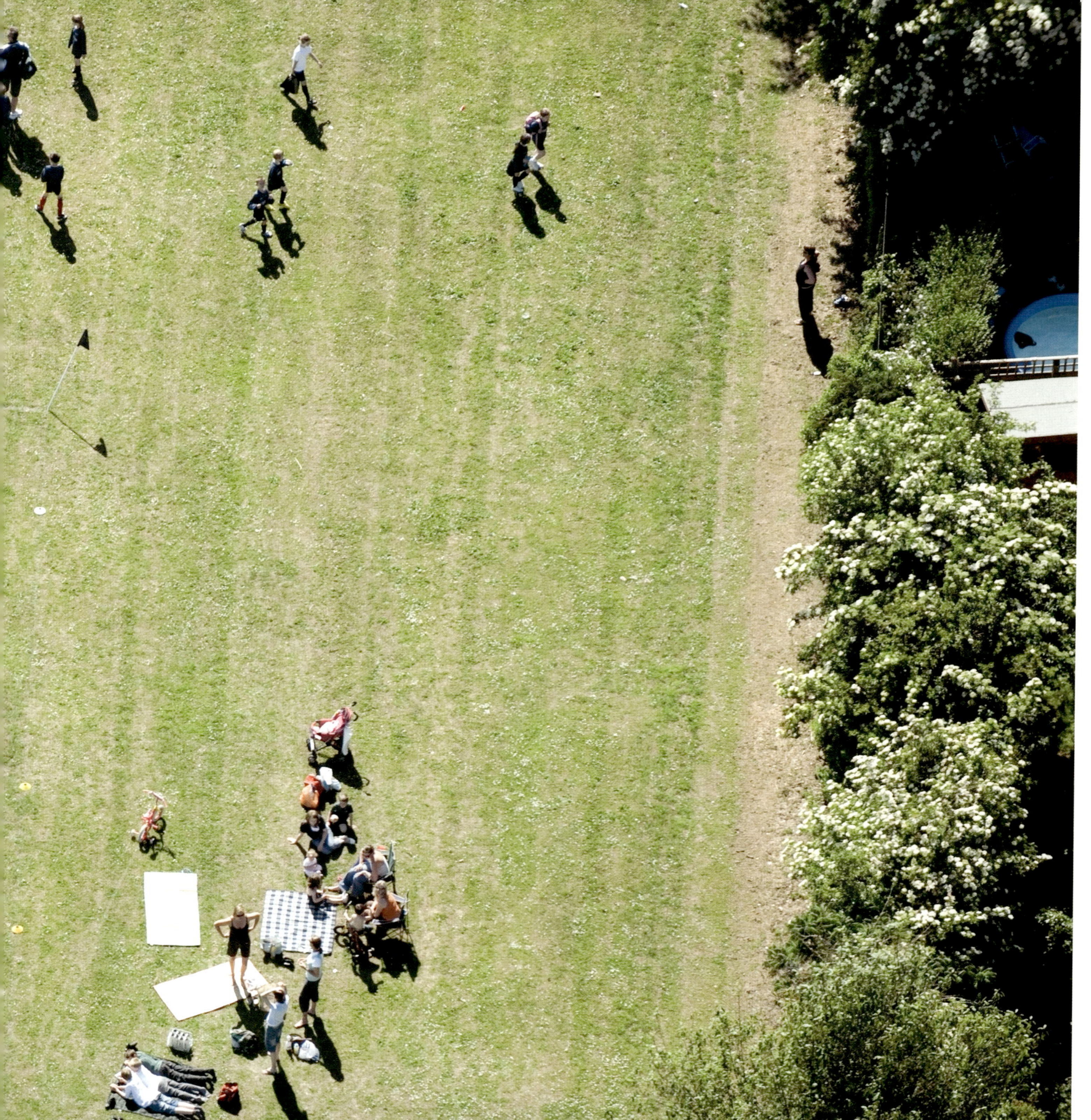

Previous page: Sports at Wallingford School, with families spectating.
This secondary school was founded by Walter Bigg in 1659 in association with the Worshipful Company of Merchant Taylors

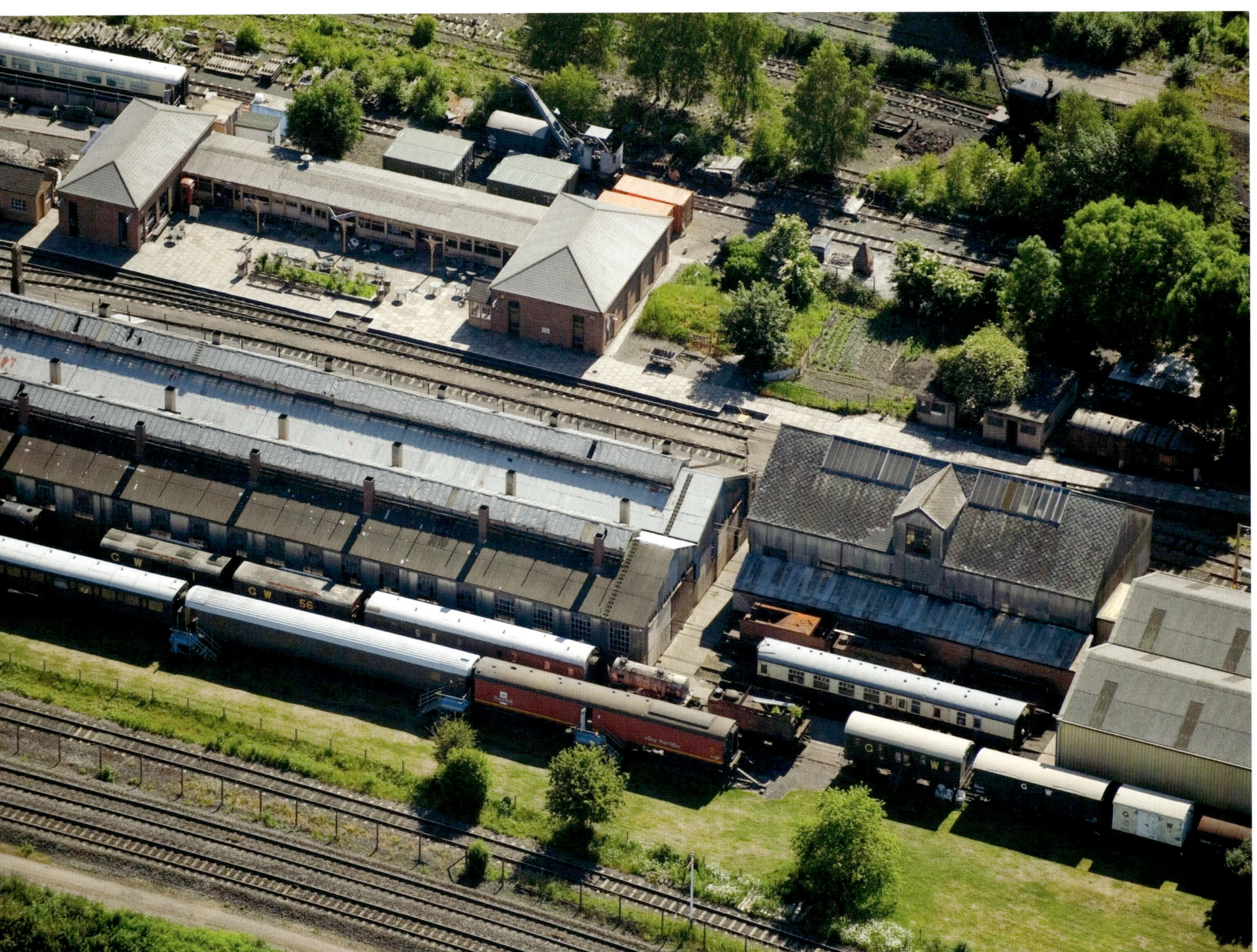

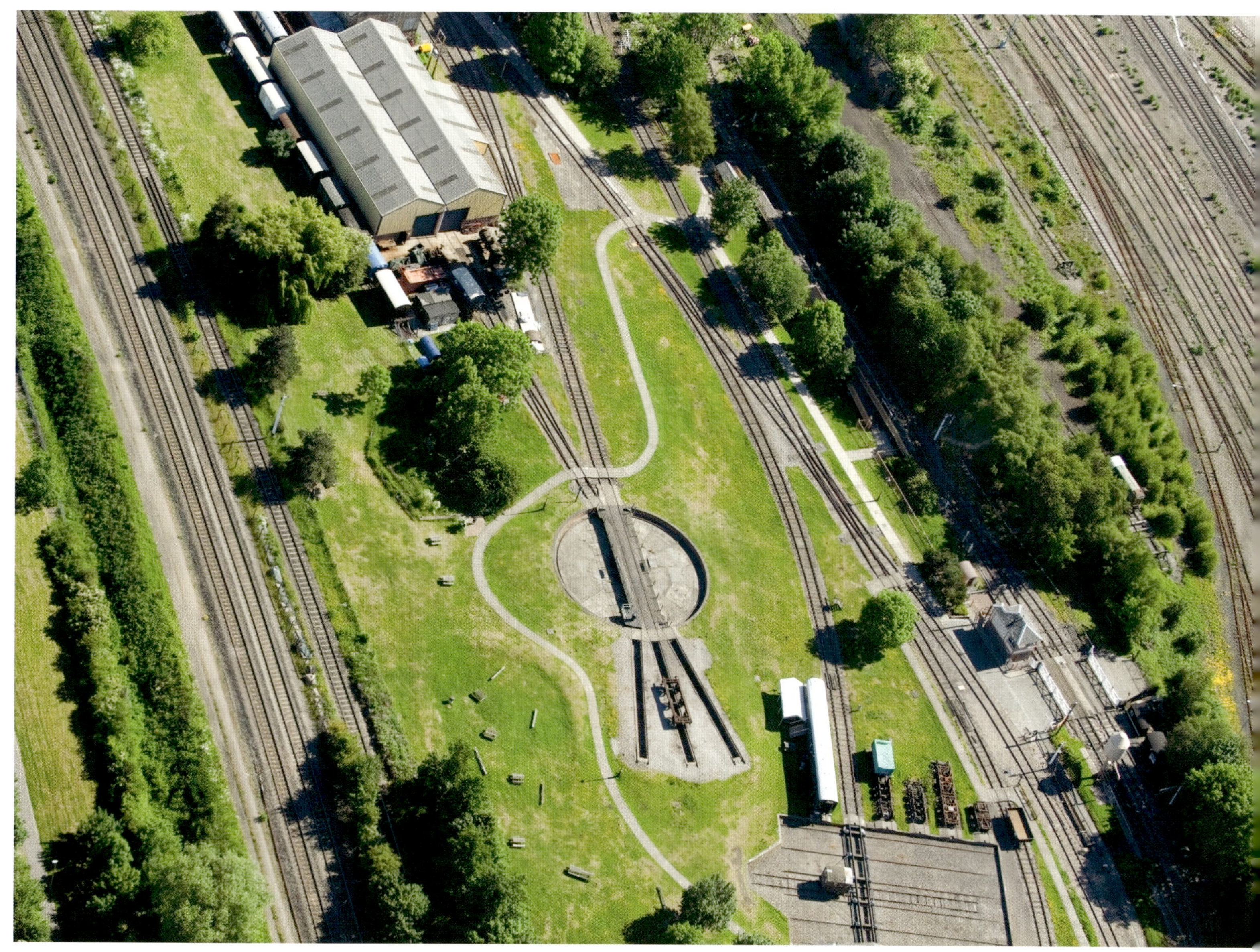

Left and above: Didcot's famous Railway Centre. Here visitors can see a unique collection of Great Western Railway steam engines, coaches, wagons, and buildings, along with a recreation of Brunel's broad gauge railway.

Didcot Rail Station - Didcot Parkway is served by local services operated by First Great Western from Reading to Didcot and Oxford, and by Inter-City services from London Paddington to Bristol and South Wales.

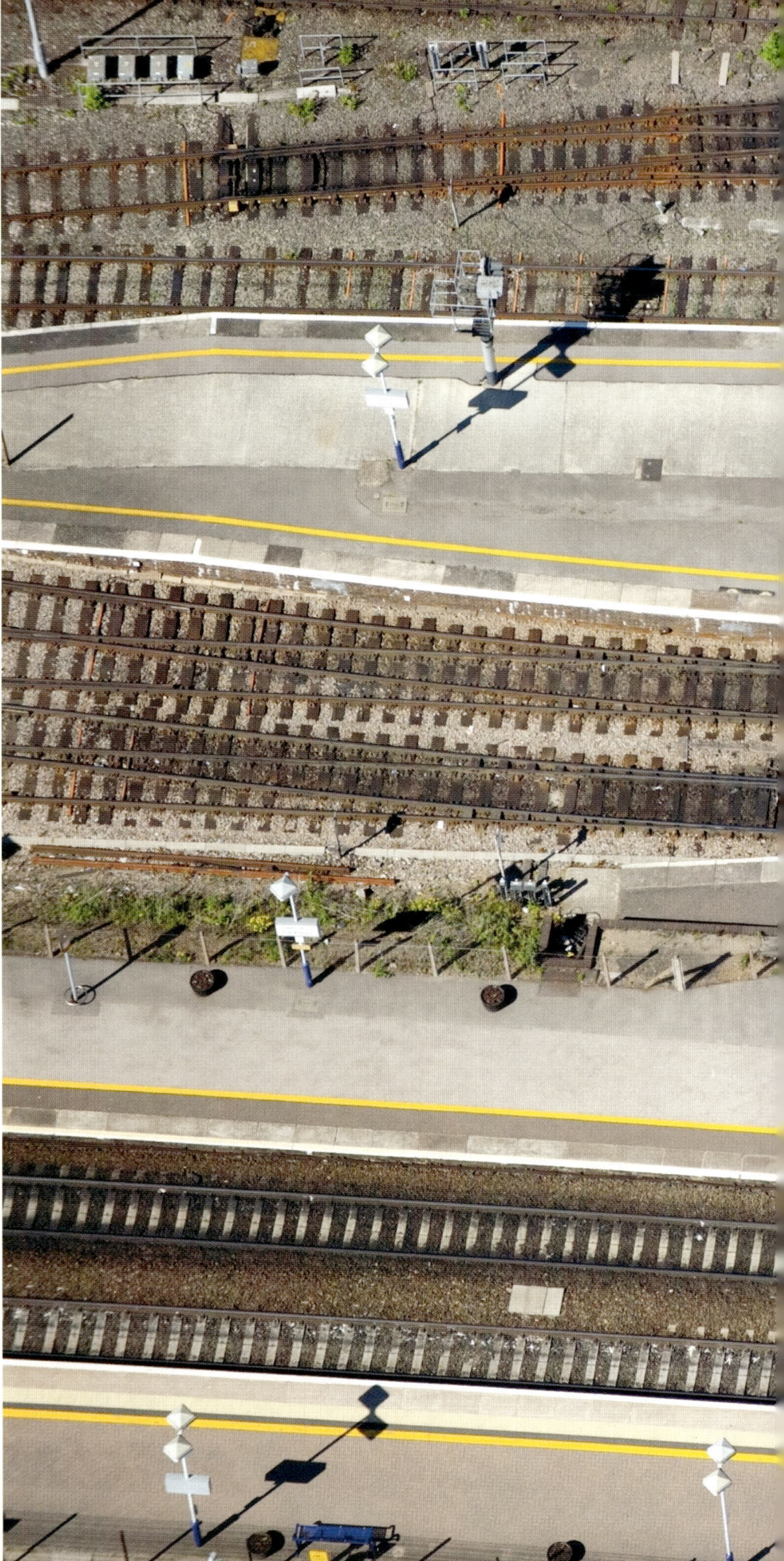

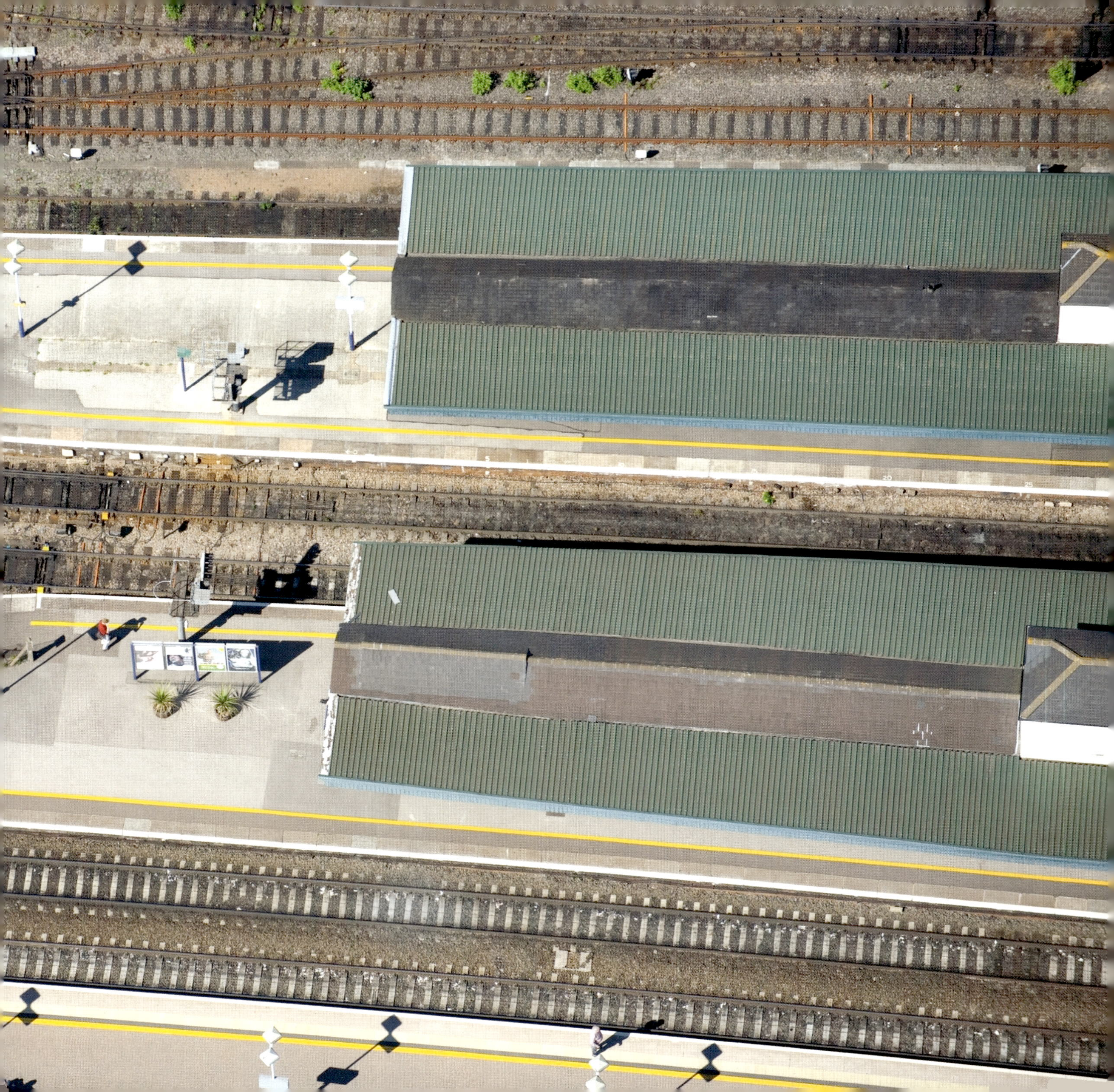

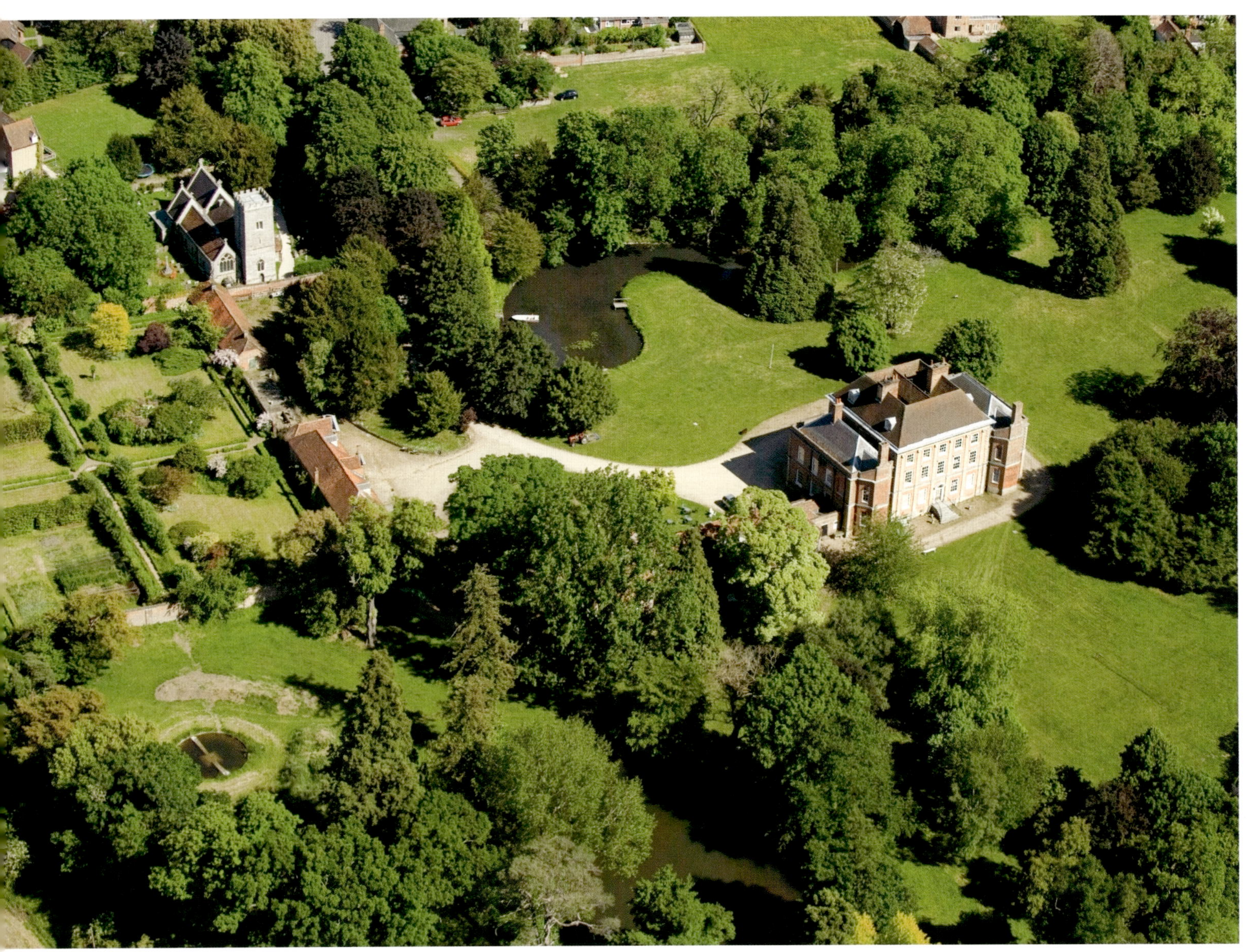

Above: Milton Manor House, near Abingdon, is an elegant eighteenth century house built by Inigo Jones. The house and gardens are occasionally open to the public.

Right: The Old Gaol, Abingdon, was completed in 1811 to house all prisoners for the county of Berkshire, From 1974 until 2002 it served as a leisure centre.

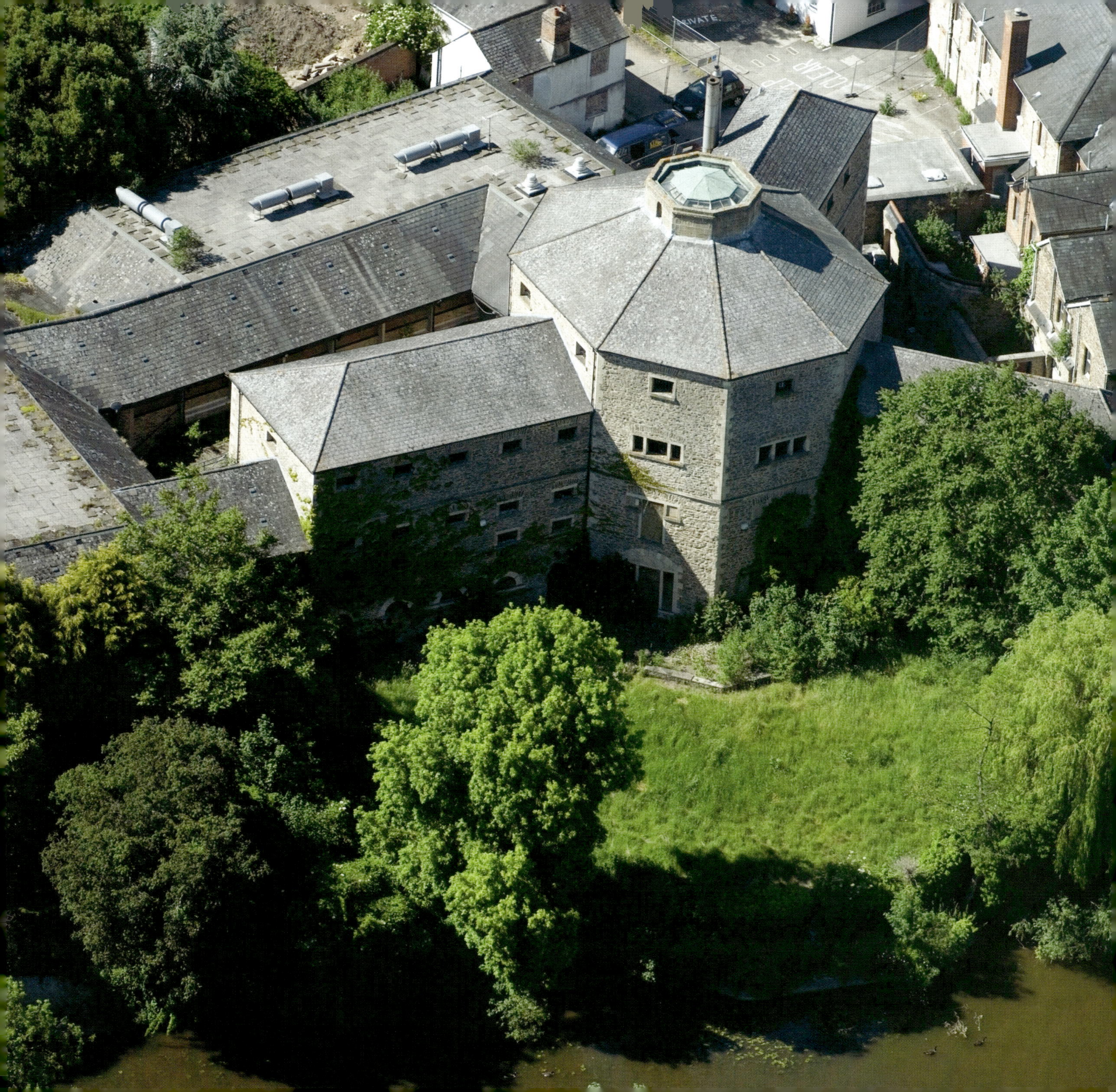

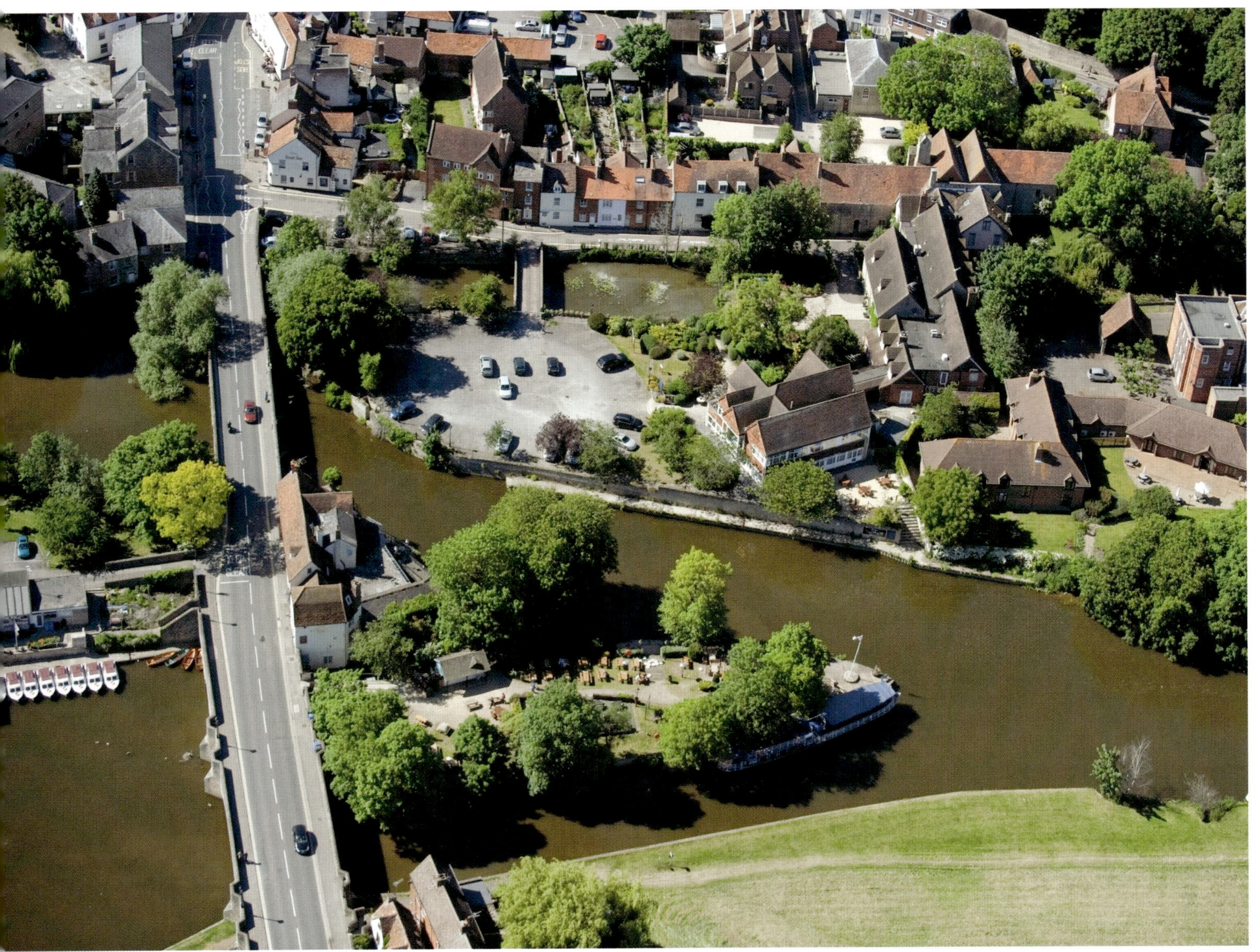

Above: Abingdon Bridge over the River Thames. It actually comprises a pair of bridges separated by Nag's Head Island.

Right: A bird's eye view of the centre of Abingdon. The old County Hall (seen left) now houses a museum.

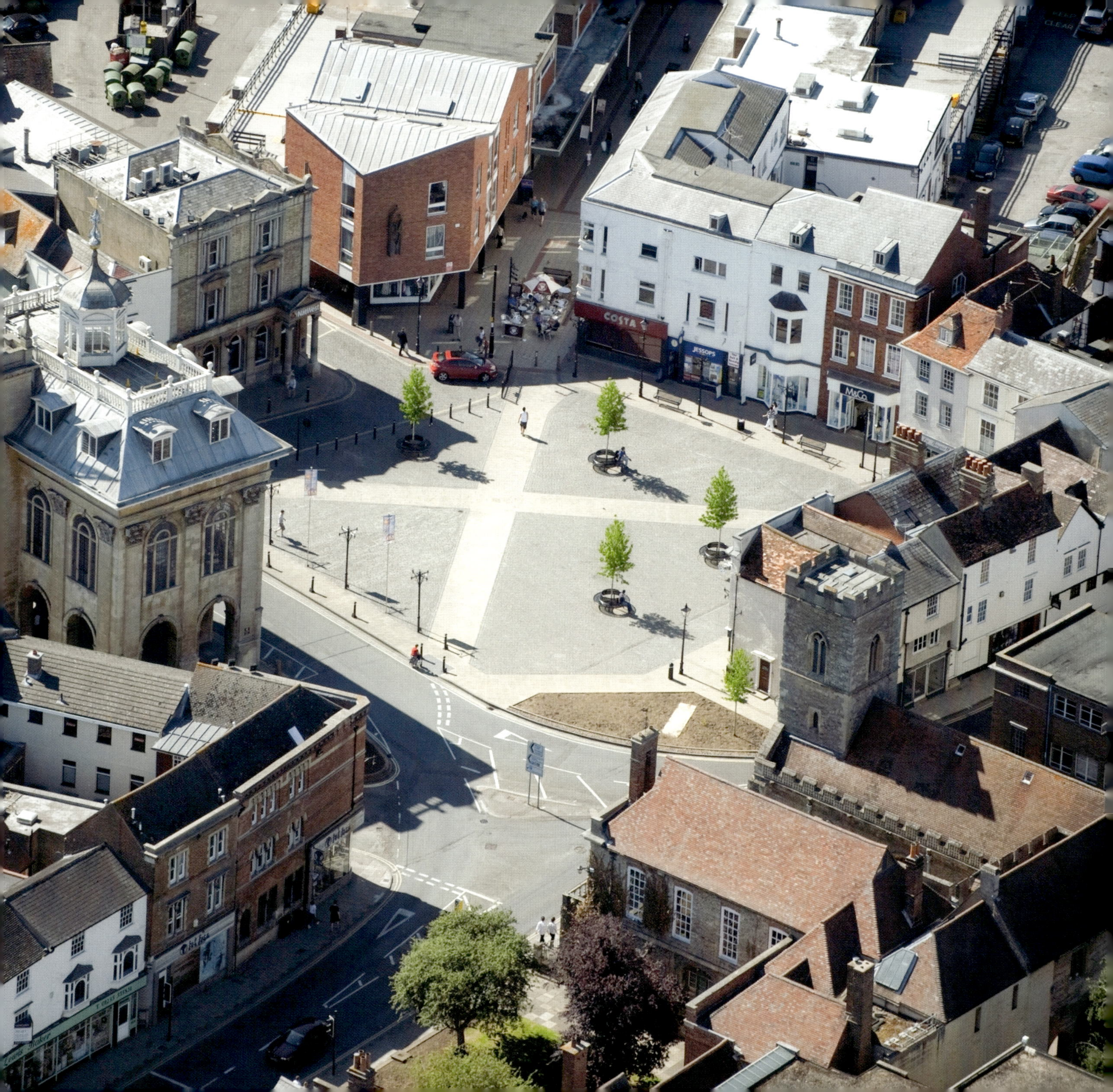

COSTA
JESSOPS
M&Co

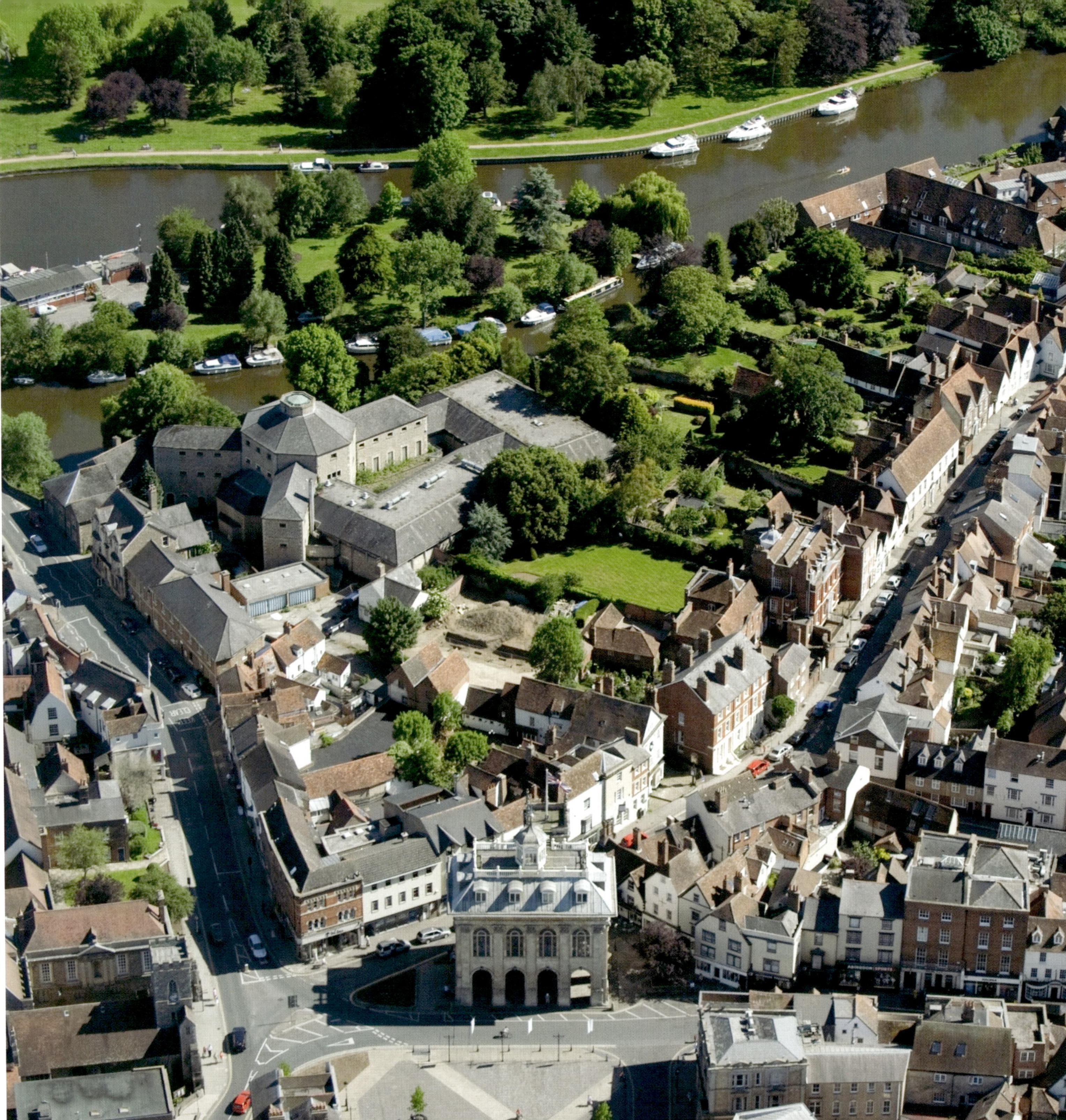

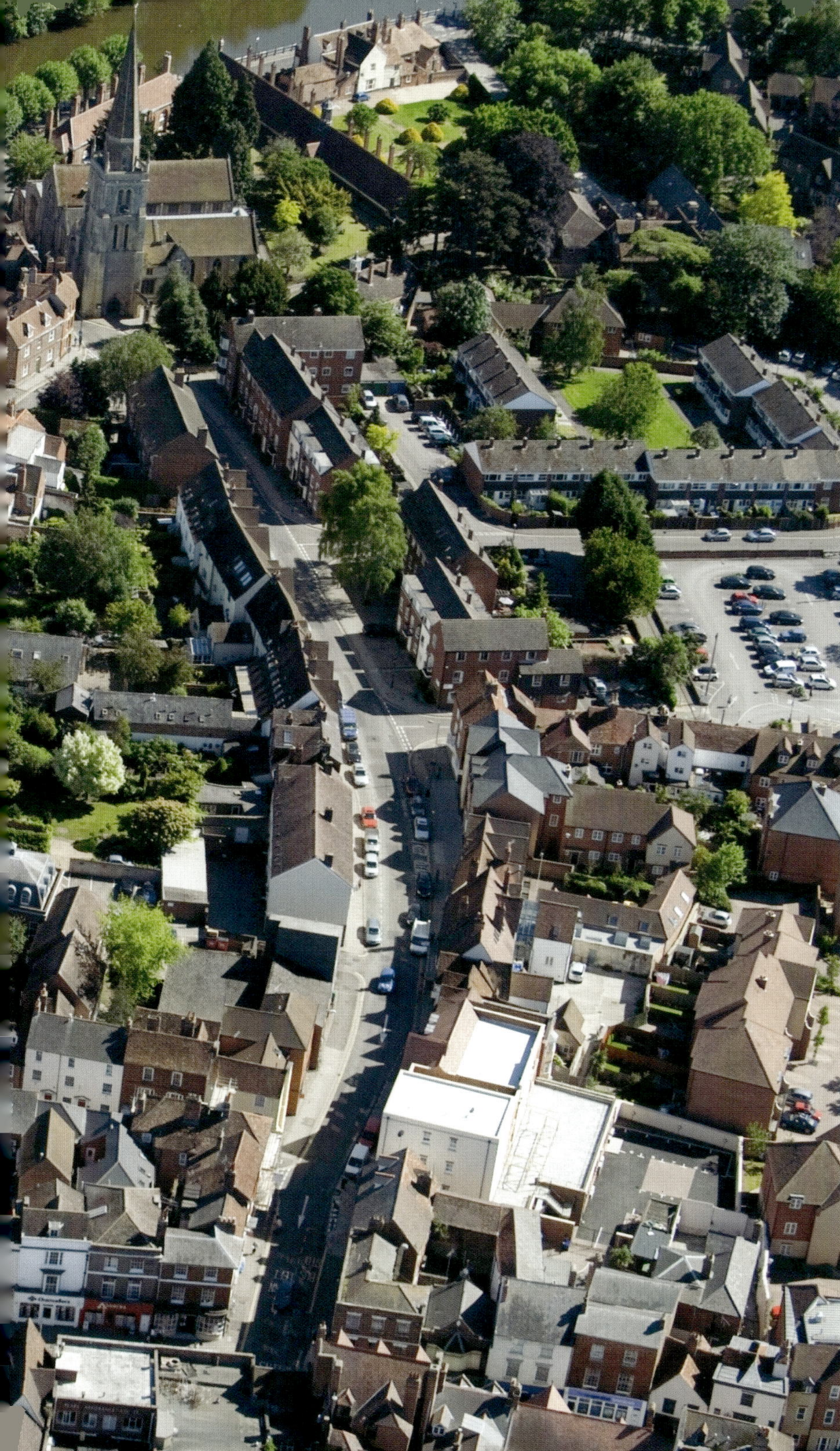

A superb view into the centre of old Abingdon empha-
sises its former important strategic position as a
crossing point on the River Thames.

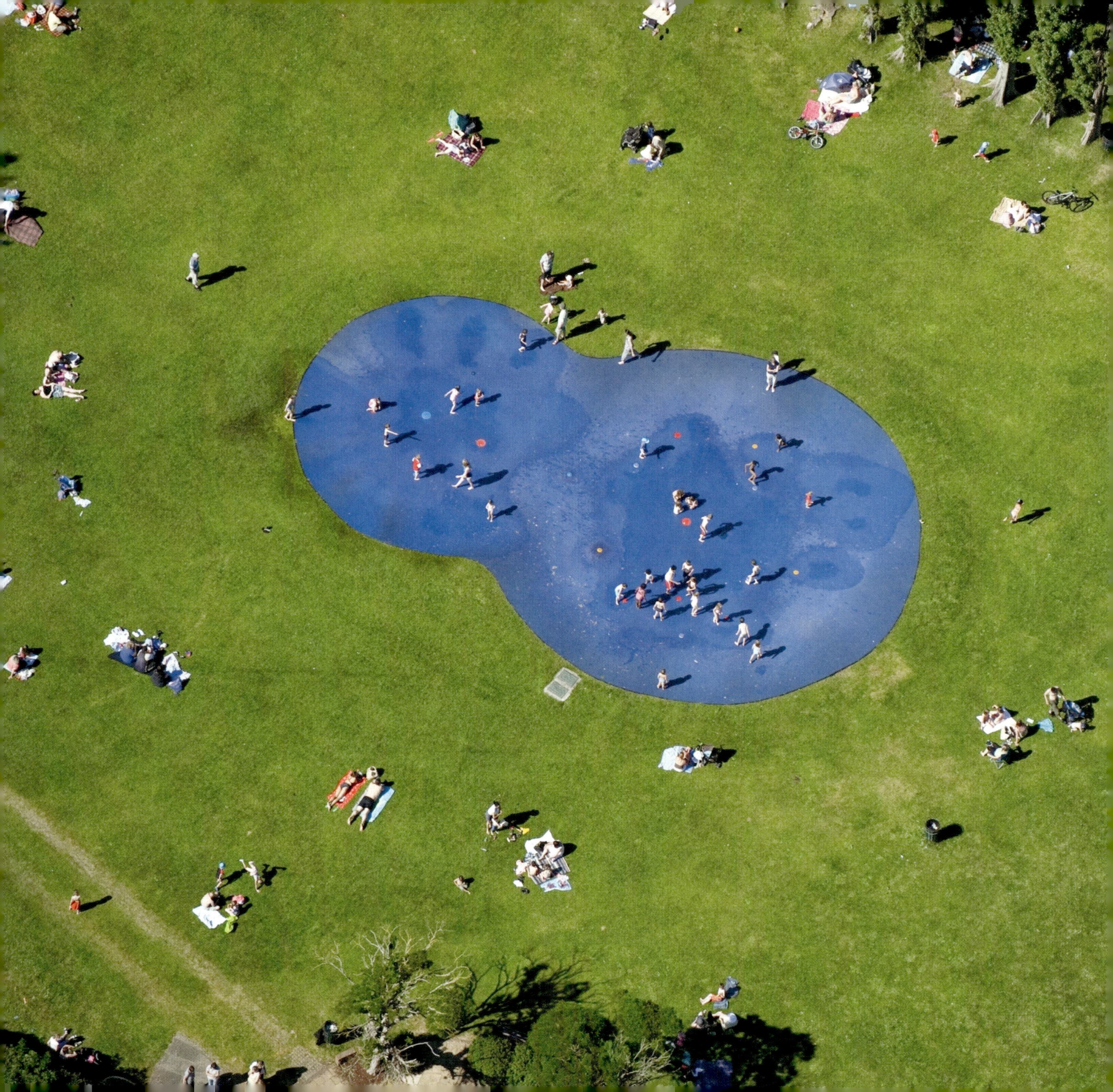

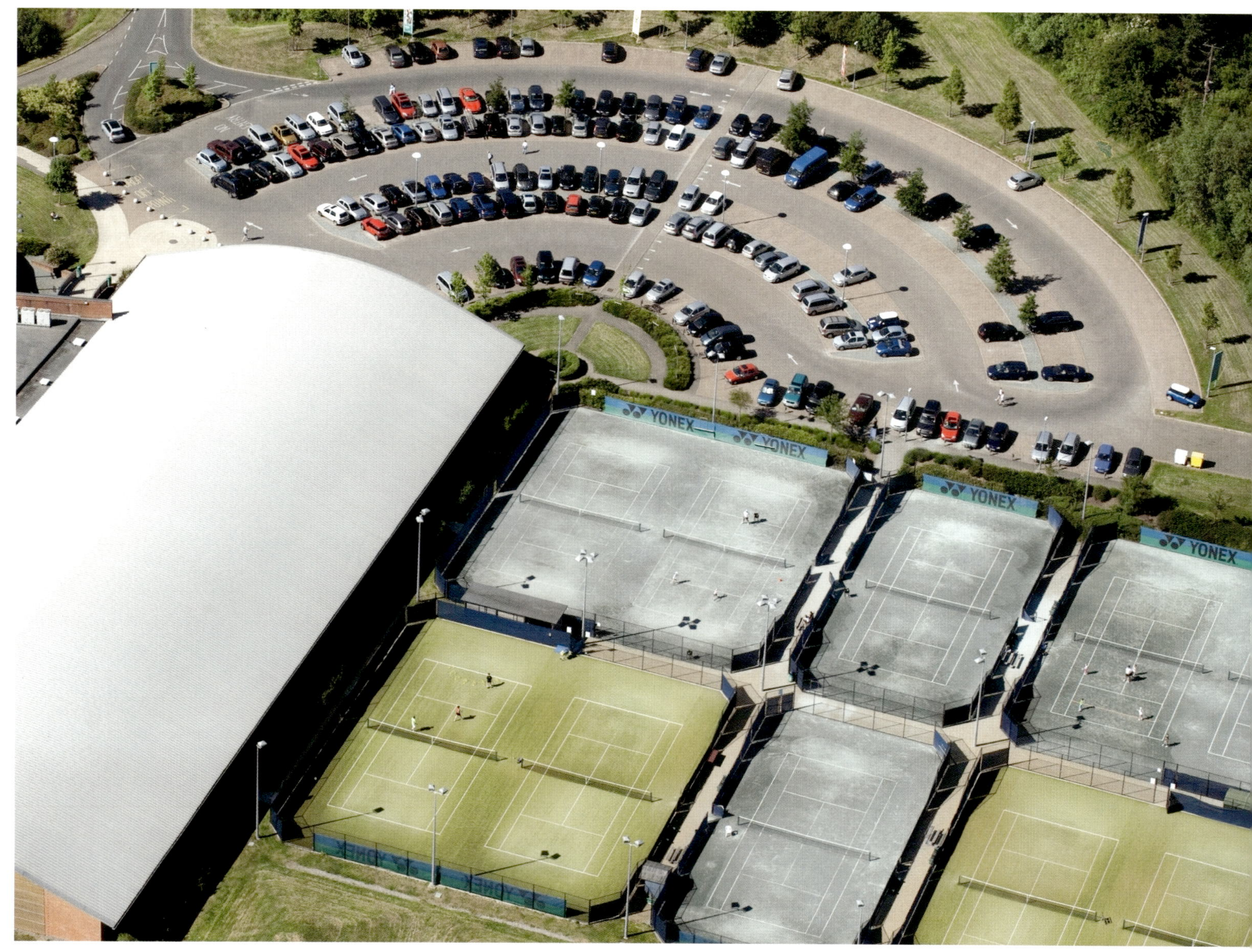

Left and above: Two views over Abingdon with people at play. The children's play pool at Abbey Meadows and the White Horse Leisure Centre. Abbey Meadows is a delightful park located at the end of Abbey Close in Abingdon, which has the River Thames forming the southern boundary.

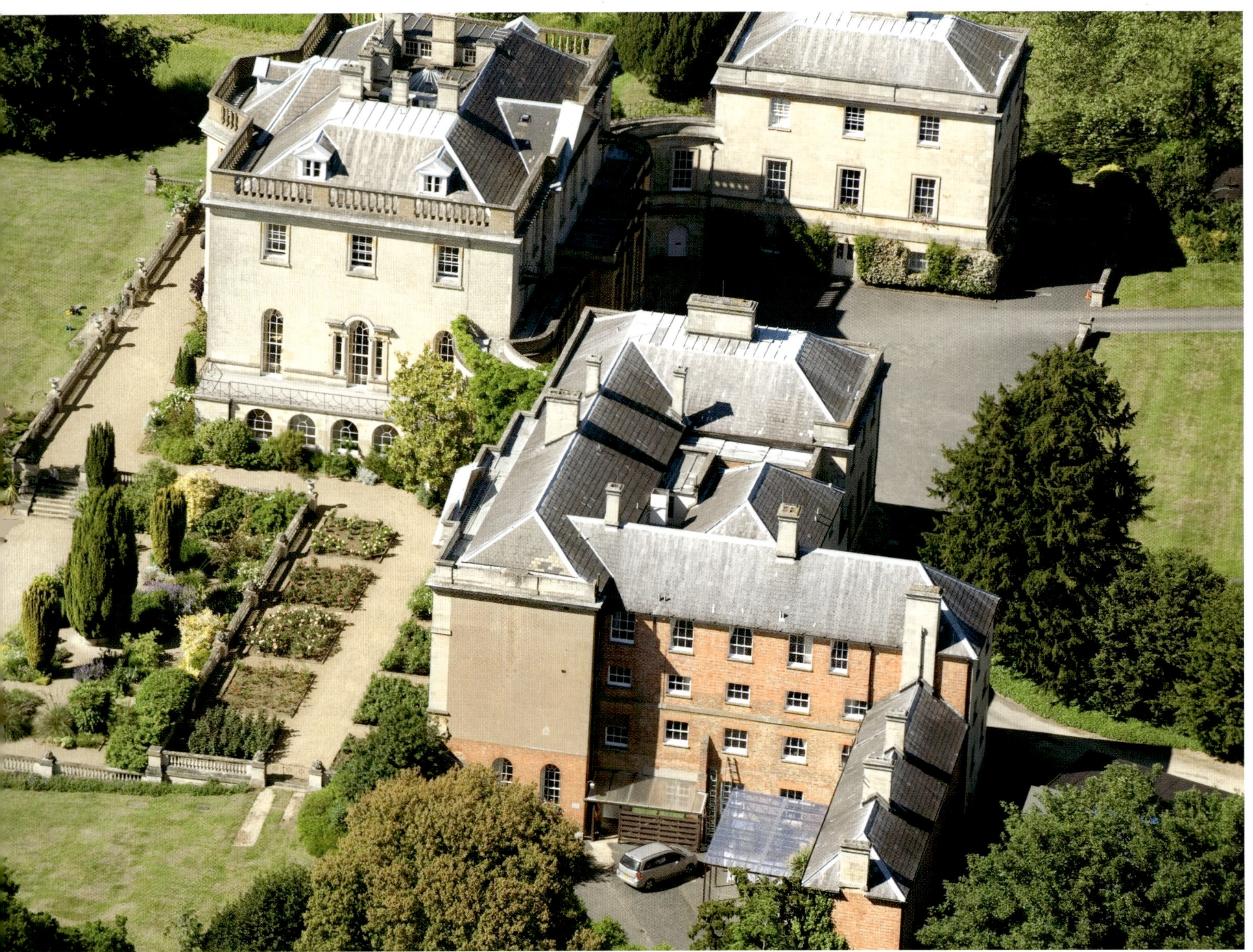

Above and right: Nuneham House, sited near the village of Nuneham Courtenay, is one of the finest examples of villa revival of the 1750s. It was built as a principal residence for Earl Harcourt, one of George III's leading courtiers. Lancelot 'Capability' Brown designed the landscaped grounds. The house and park is owned by Oxford University and is currently used as a retreat centre by the Brahma Kumaris World Spiritual University.

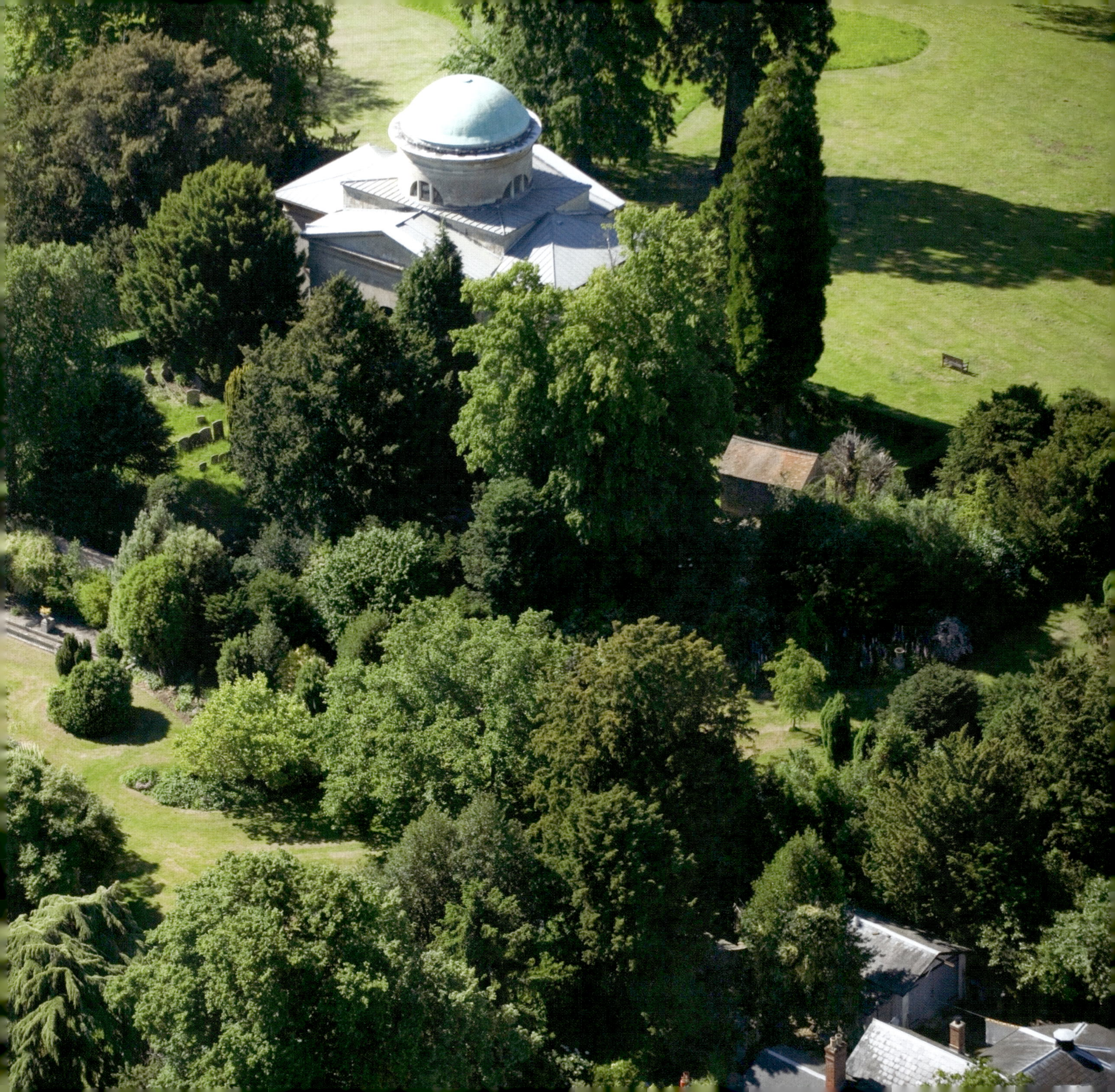

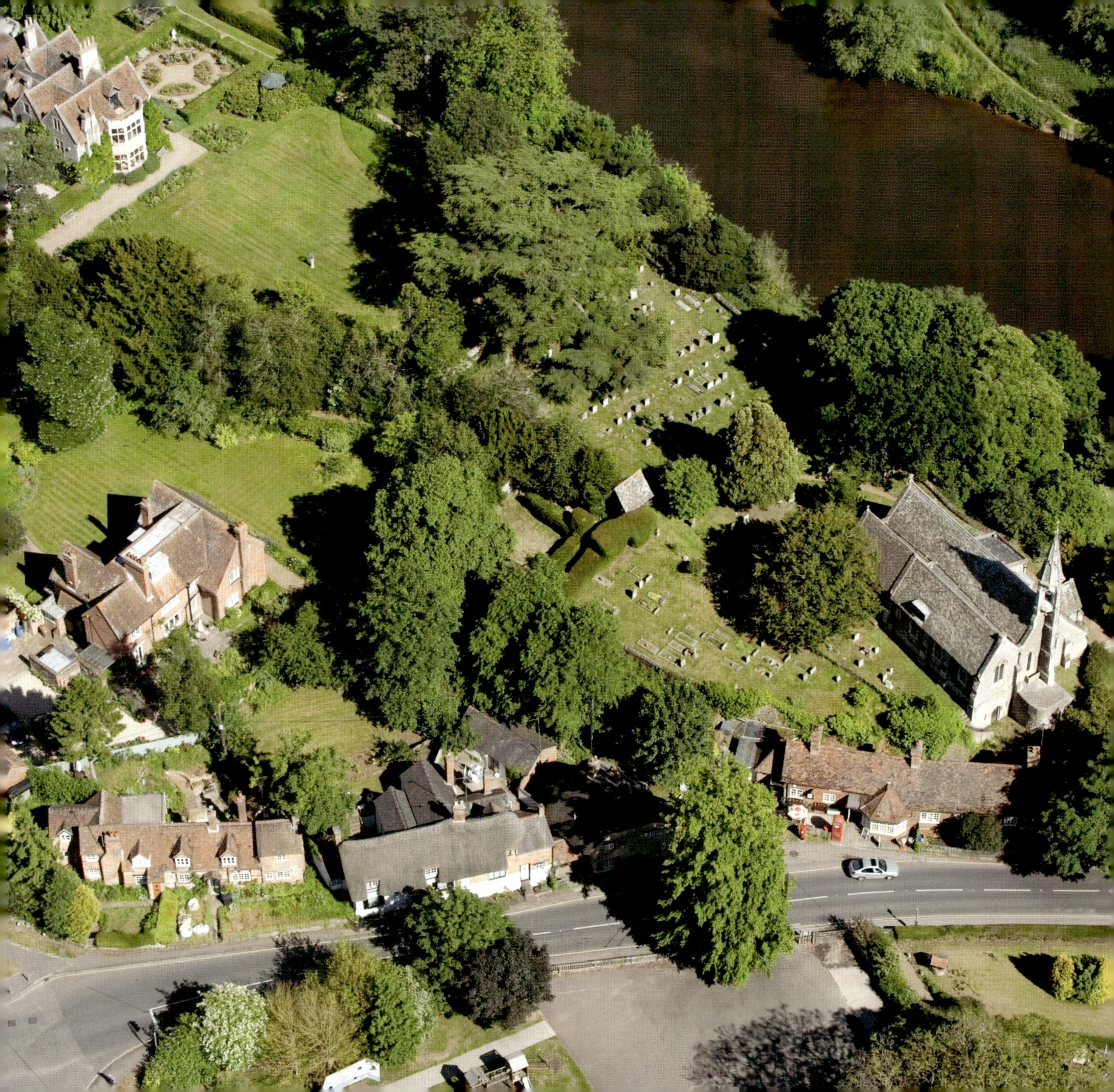

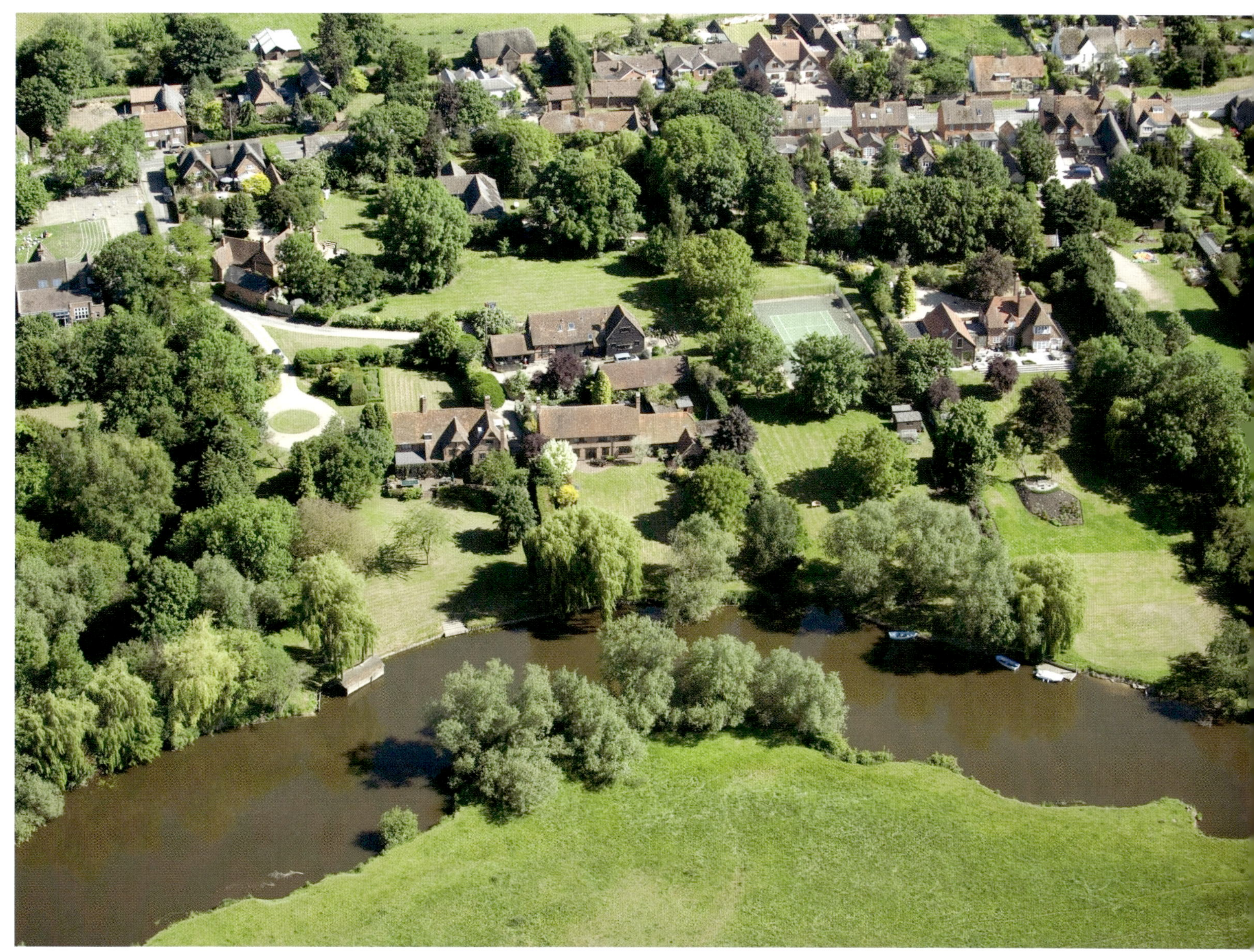

Left and above: The delightful village of Clifton Hampden lies on the north bank of the River Thames about three miles east of Abingdon. The parish church of St Michael and All Angels, parts of which date from 1180, was much rebuilt around 1844 by the renowned architect Sir Gilbert Scott.

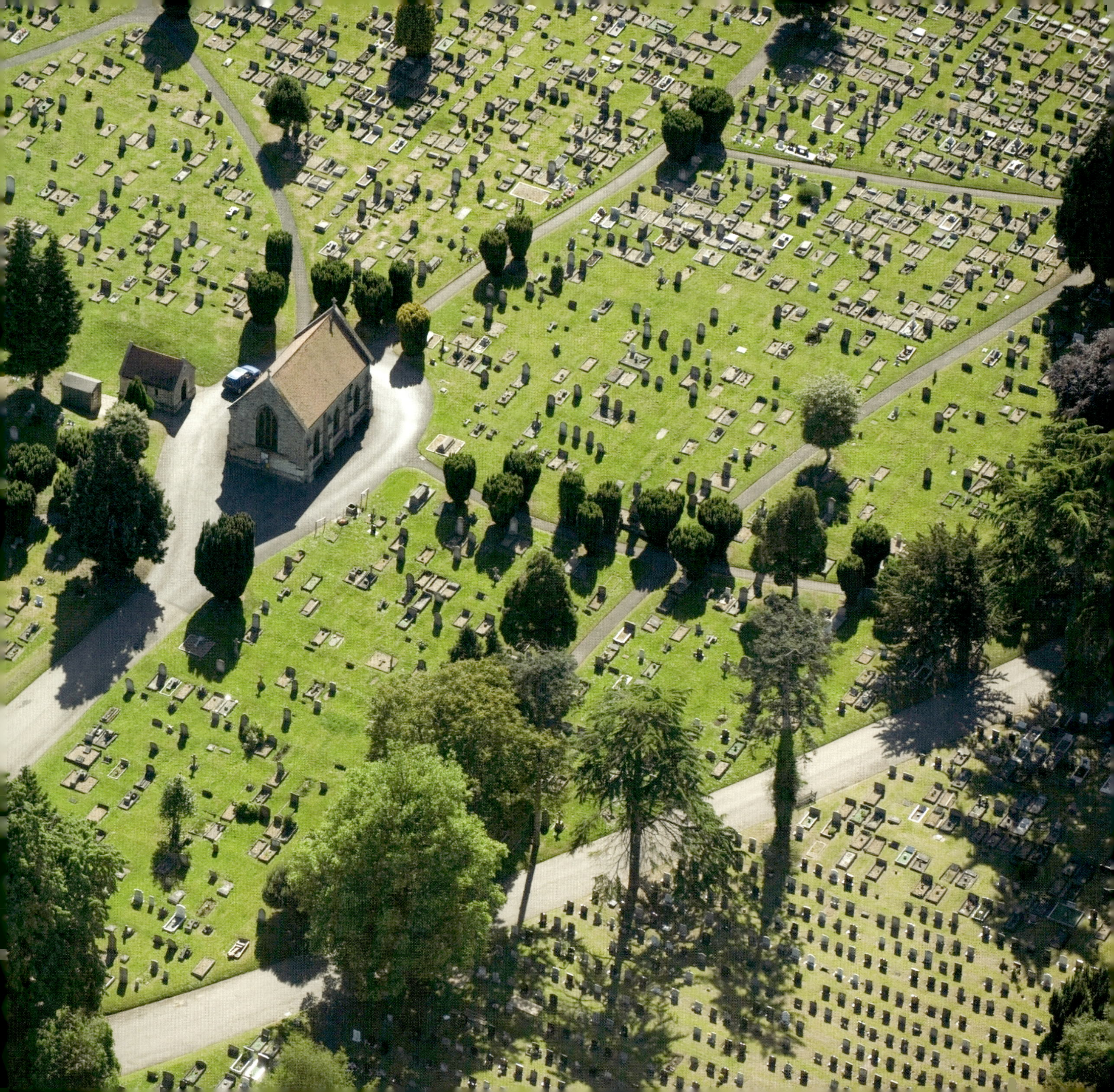

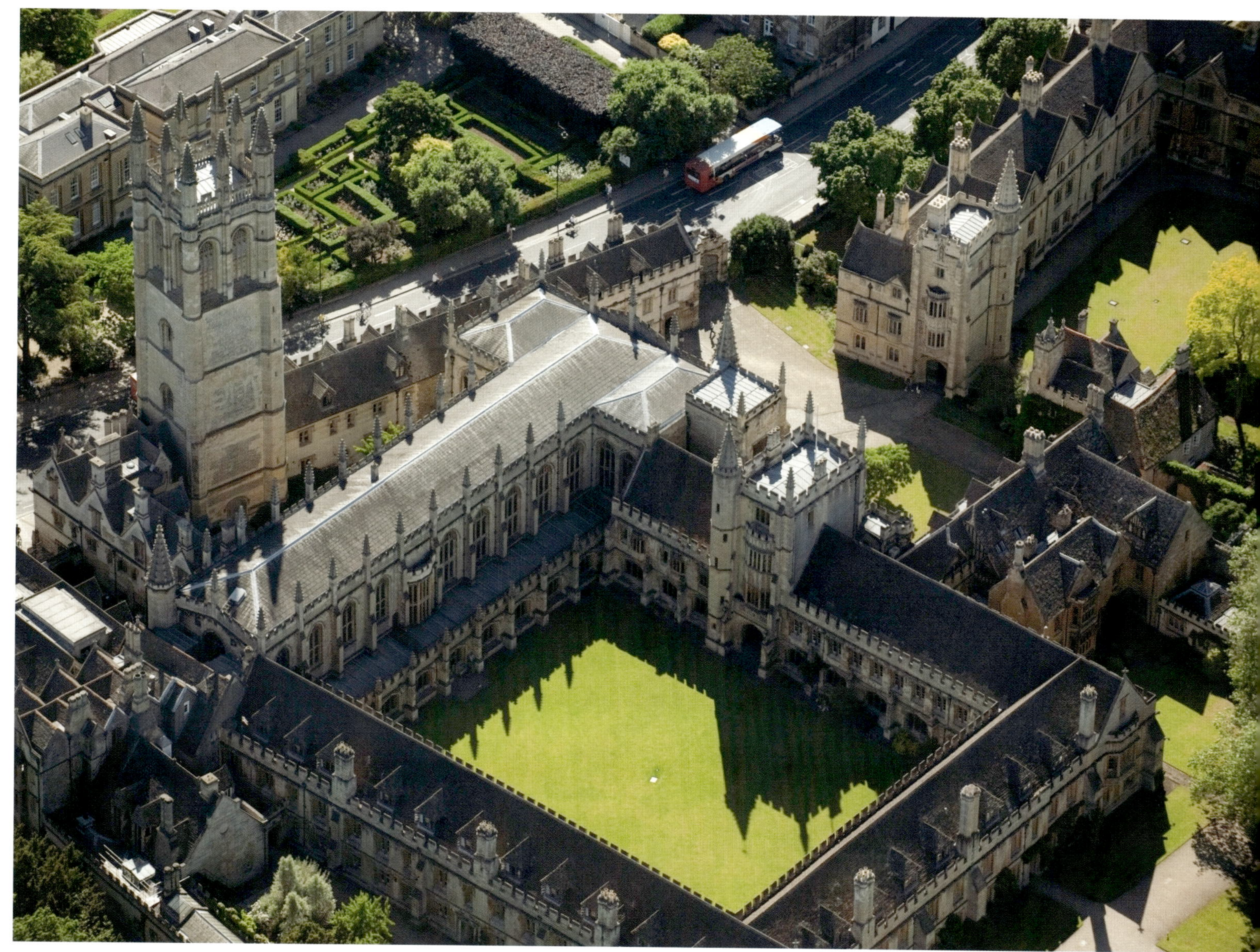

Left: East Oxford started to become a suburb of Oxford City in the mid-nineteenth century. Today the Victorian Churchyard of Saints Mary and John provides an important green public space in an urban setting within its sanctified grounds.

Above: Magdalen College, Oxford, was founded in 1458 as Magdalen Hall. It is one of the constituent colleges of the University of Oxford and is regarded by many as the most beautiful.

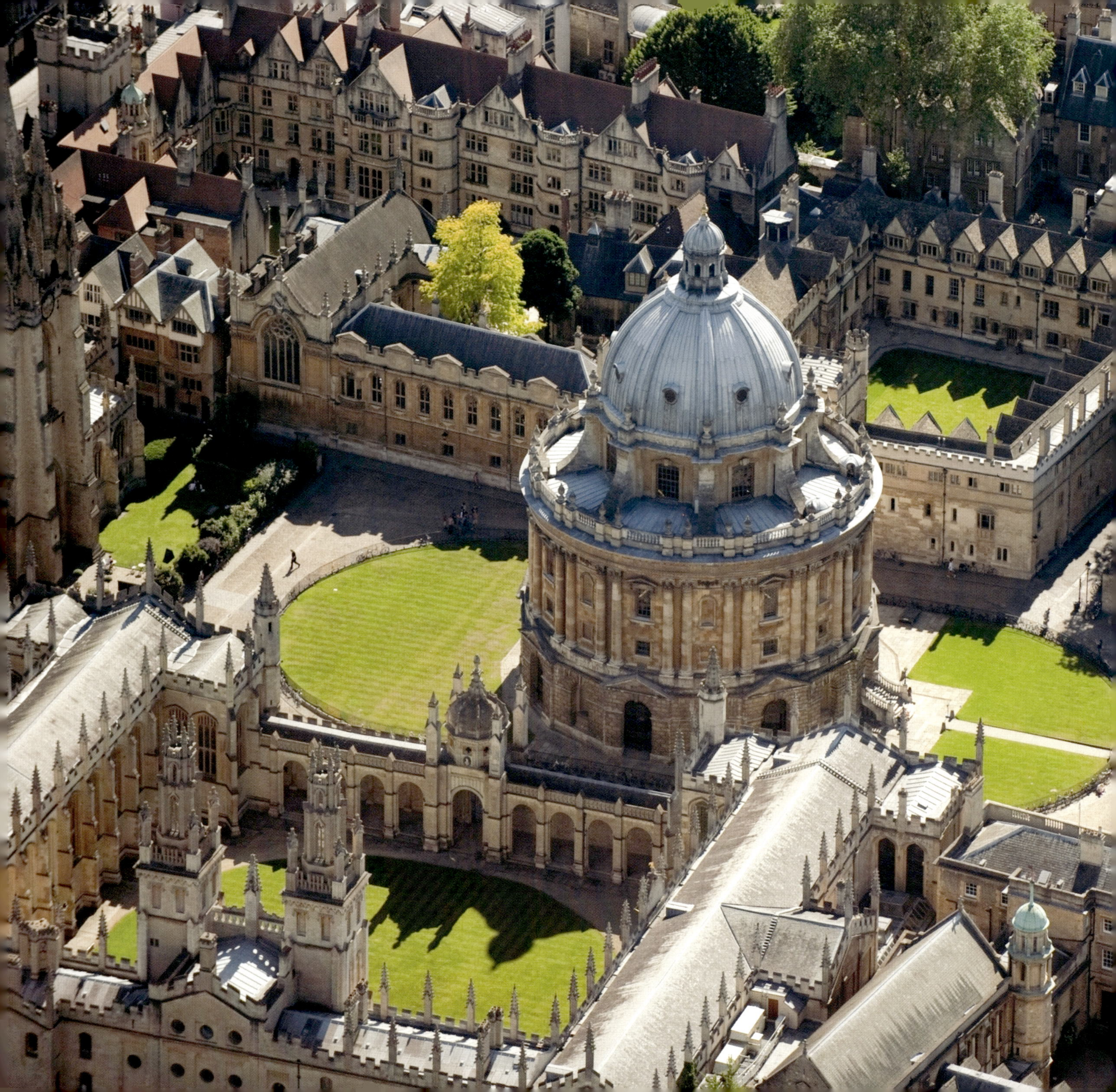

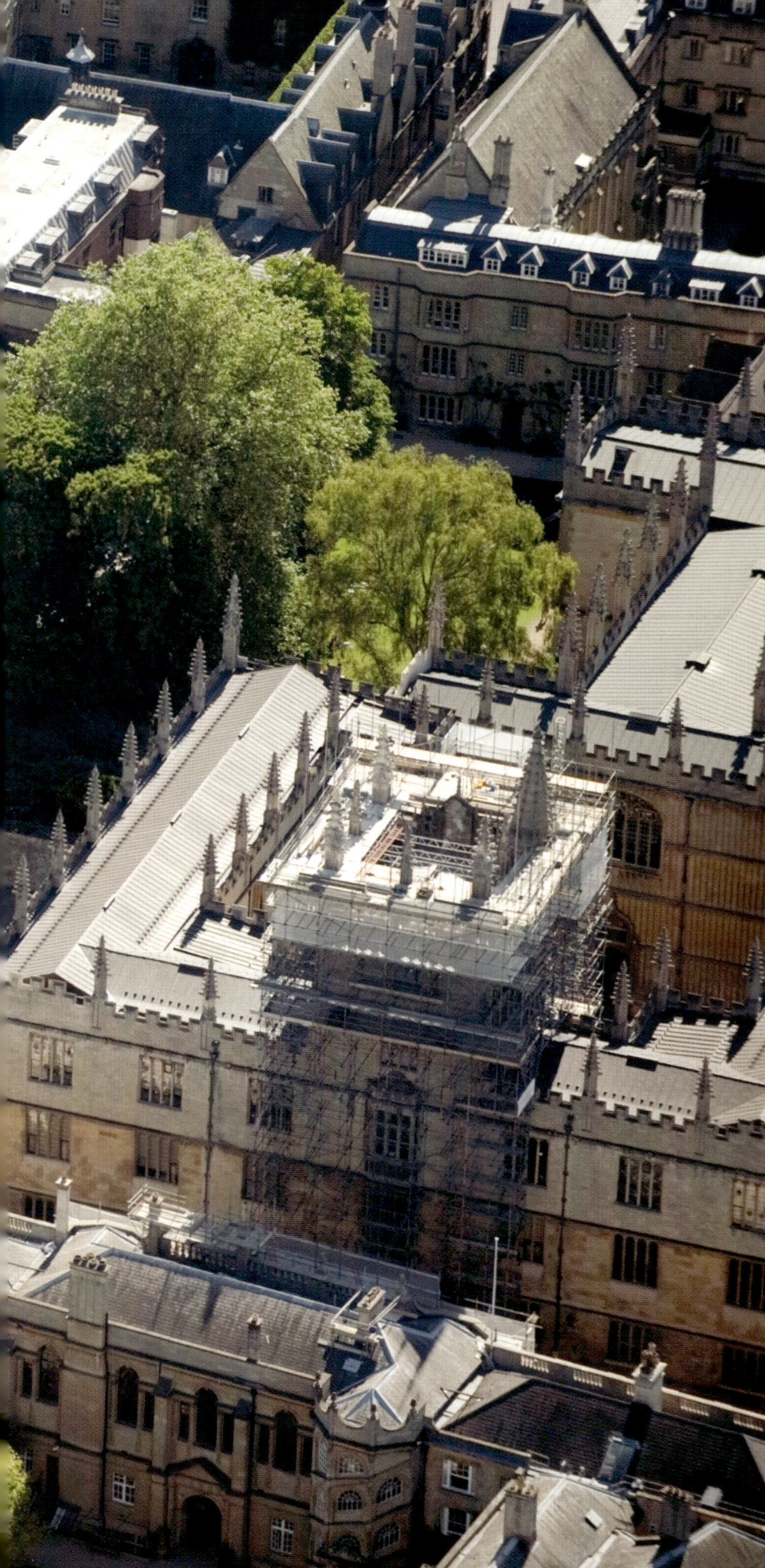

Radcliffe Square sits in the centre of the city of Oxford surrounded by historic Oxford University college buildings. It is named after John Radcliffe, a student of the university who became royal physician to William and Mary. He made a large fortune, and left a significant legacy to the University and his college (University College), which is nearby in the High Street to the south. The centrepiece of the square is the circular and imposing Radcliffe Camera, a library paid for by John Radcliffe's legacy. It is part of the Bodleian Library, the main building of which is situated immediately to the north of the square. The two buildings are connected by an underground tunnel and there are many books stored under the square. There used to be a small underground railway to transport books between the Radcliffe Camera and the main Bodleian site.

Looking down into Broad Street, Oxford. The Sheldonian Theatre, (centre, right), was built from 1664 to 1668 after a design by Christopher Wren for the University of Oxford. The building is named after Gilbert Sheldon, Chancellor of the university at the time and the project's main financial backer. It is used for music concerts, lectures and university ceremonies, but not for drama. The building with the imposing columned portico is the Clarendon Building, built in 1711–13 to the designs of Nicholas Hawksmoor.

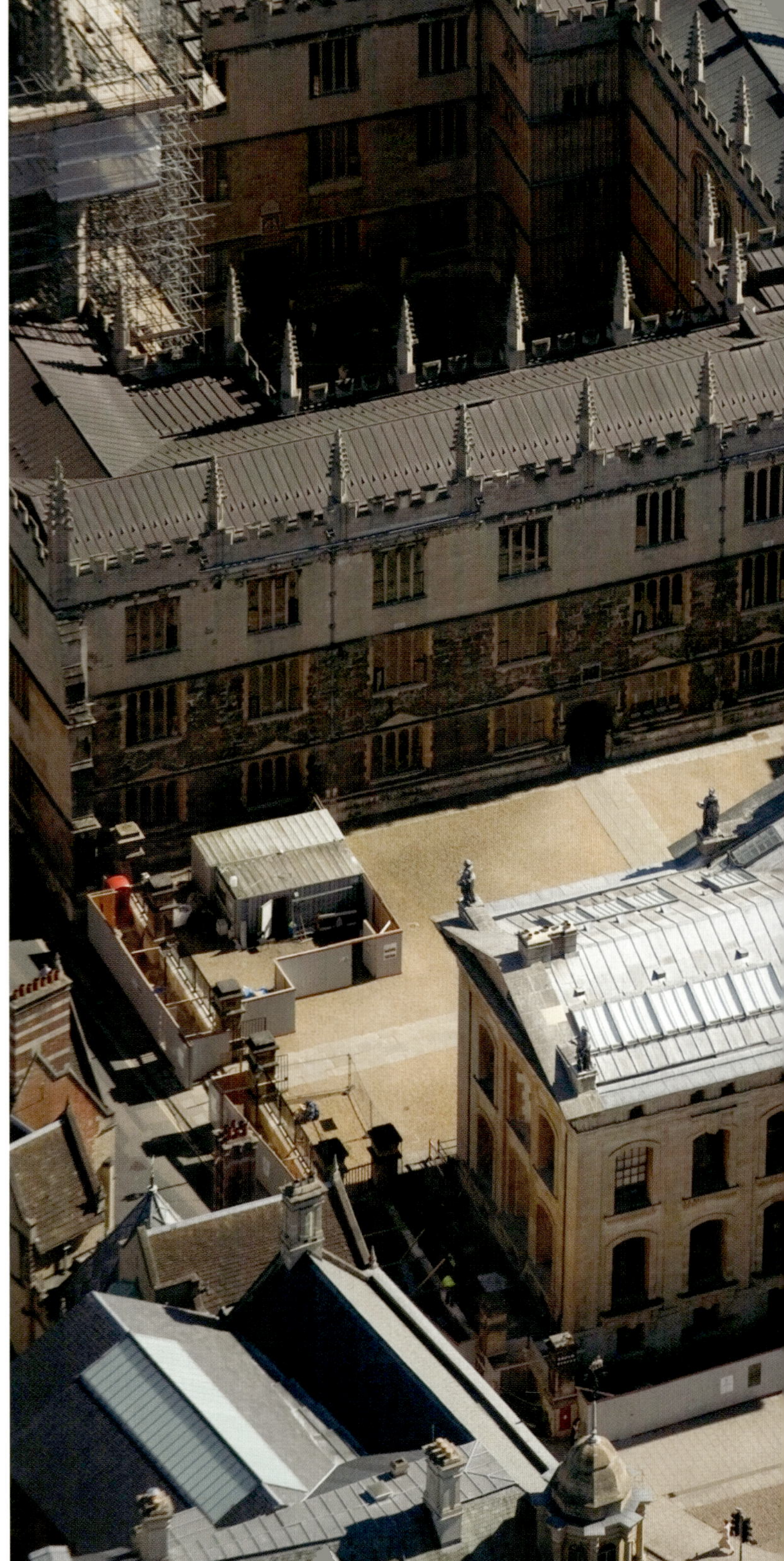

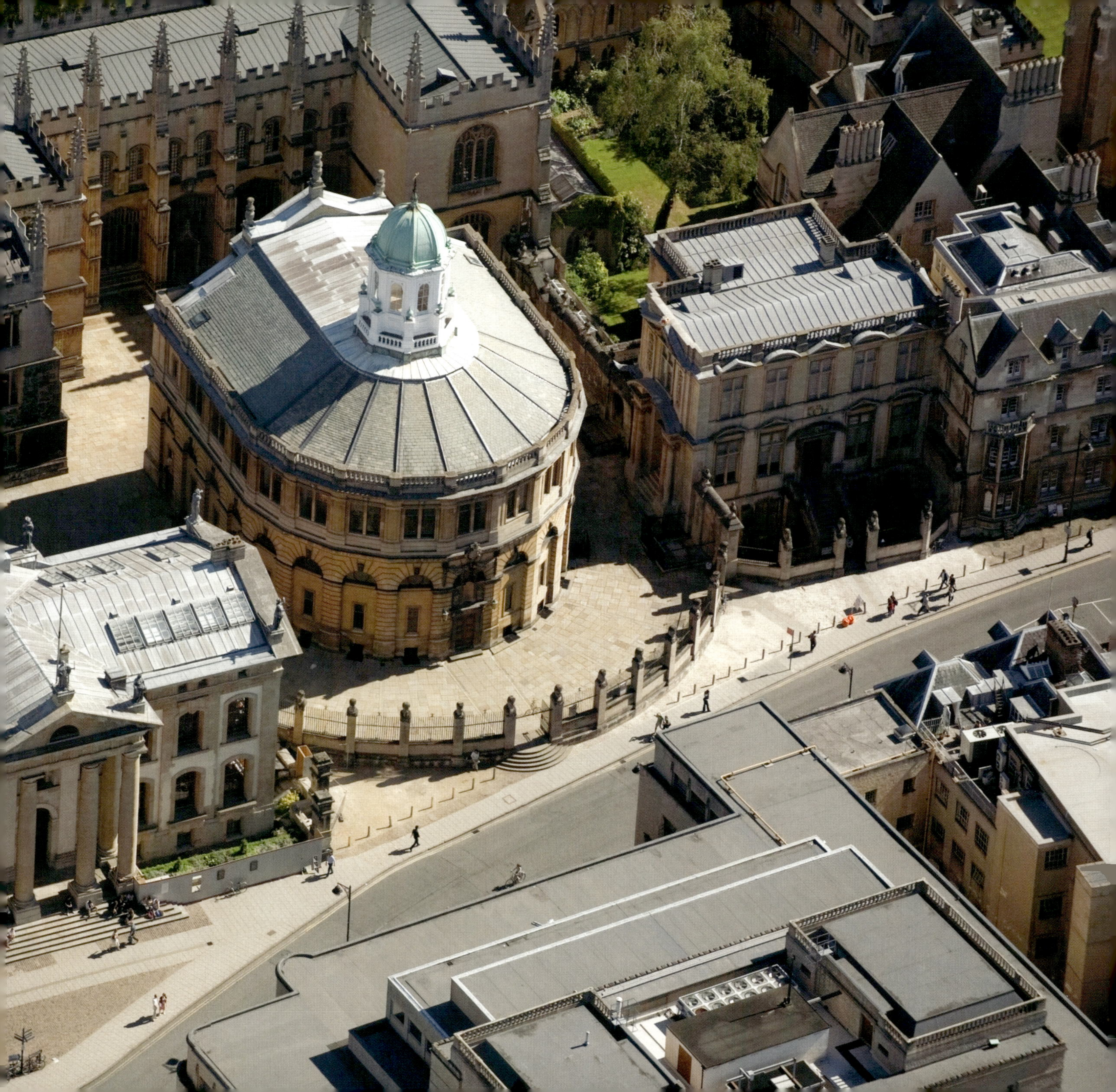

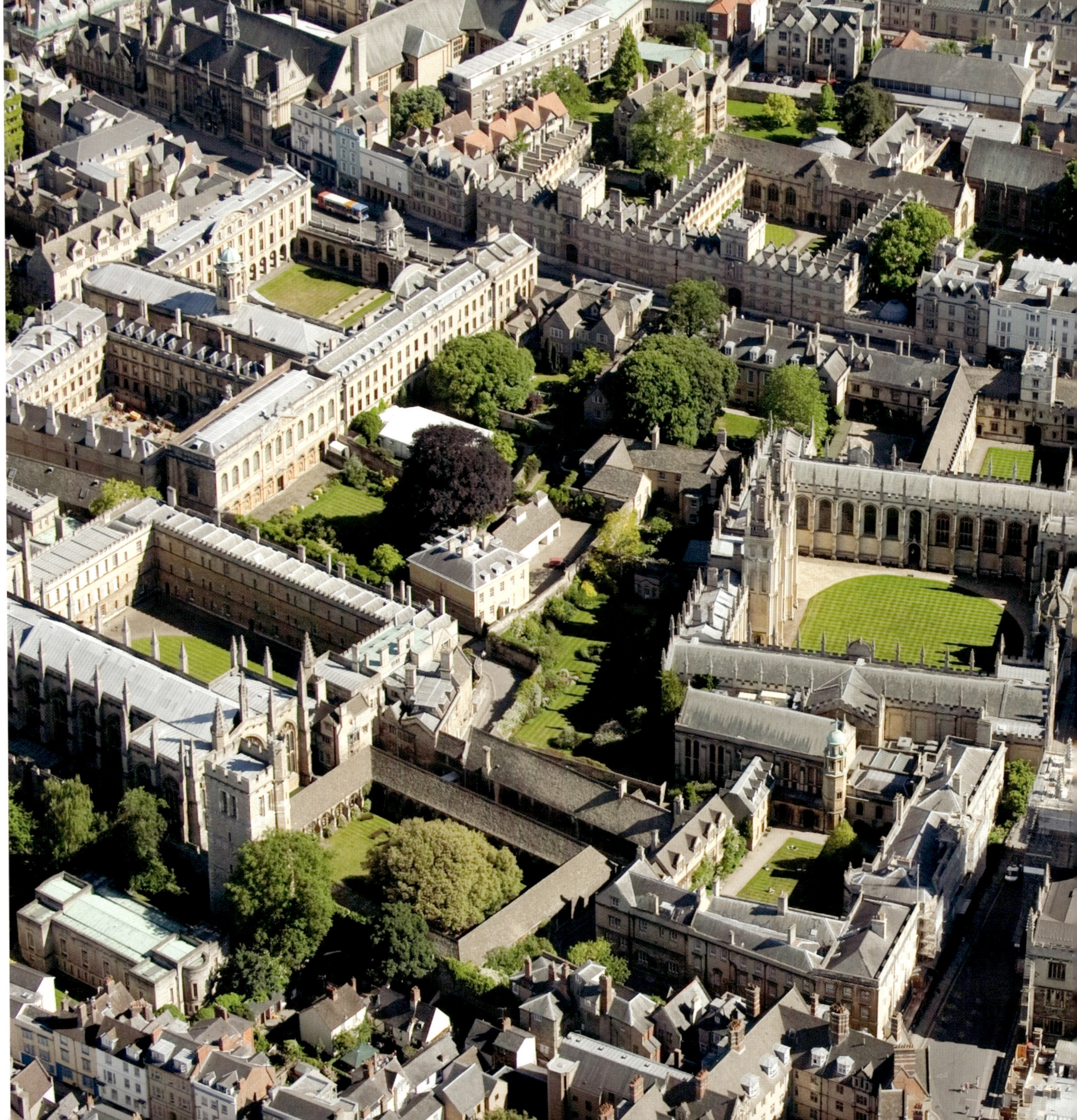

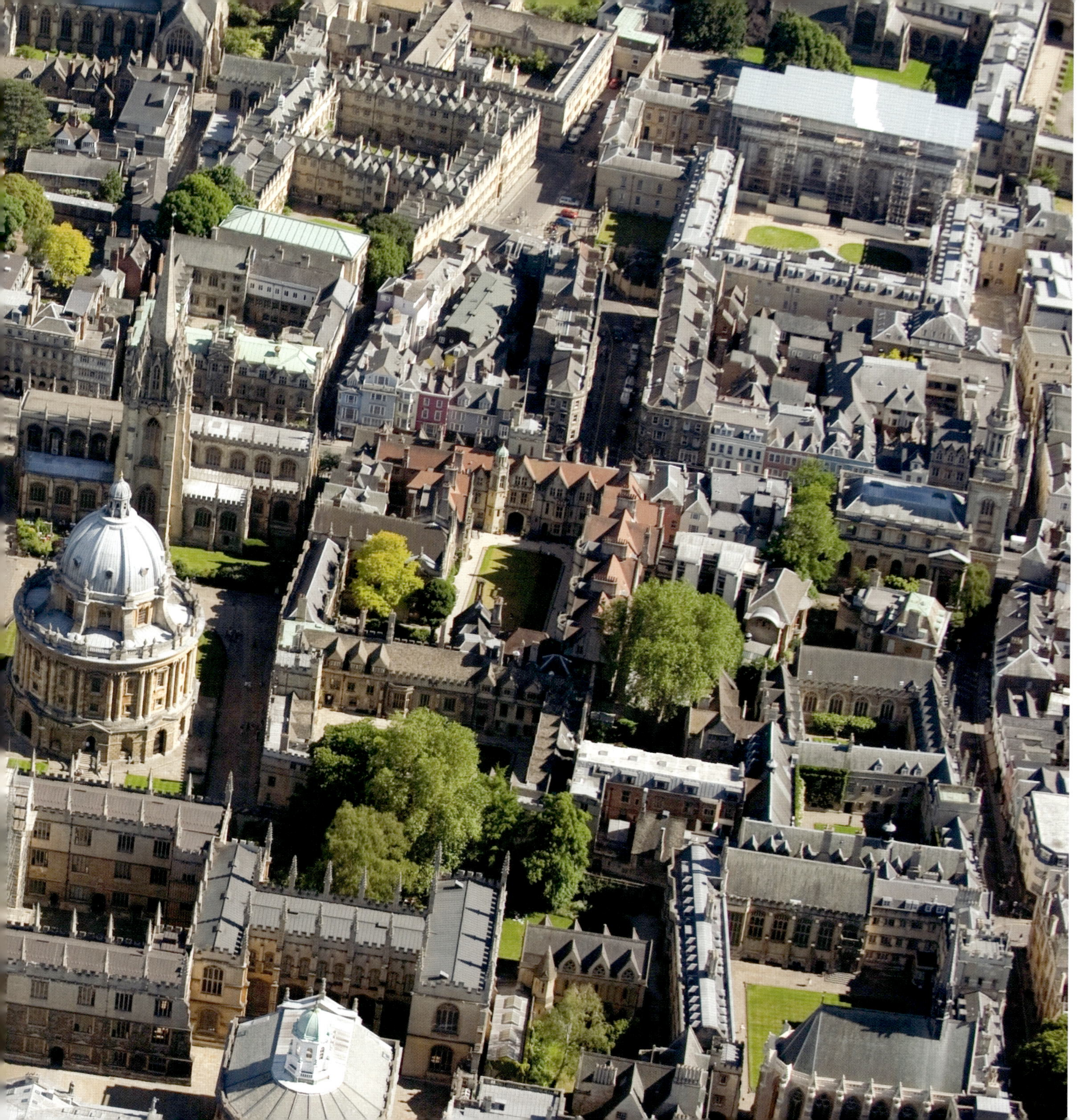

Previous page: A magnificent view across the city taking in many of the Colleges which comprise the University of Oxford. Centre is the Radcliffe Camera.

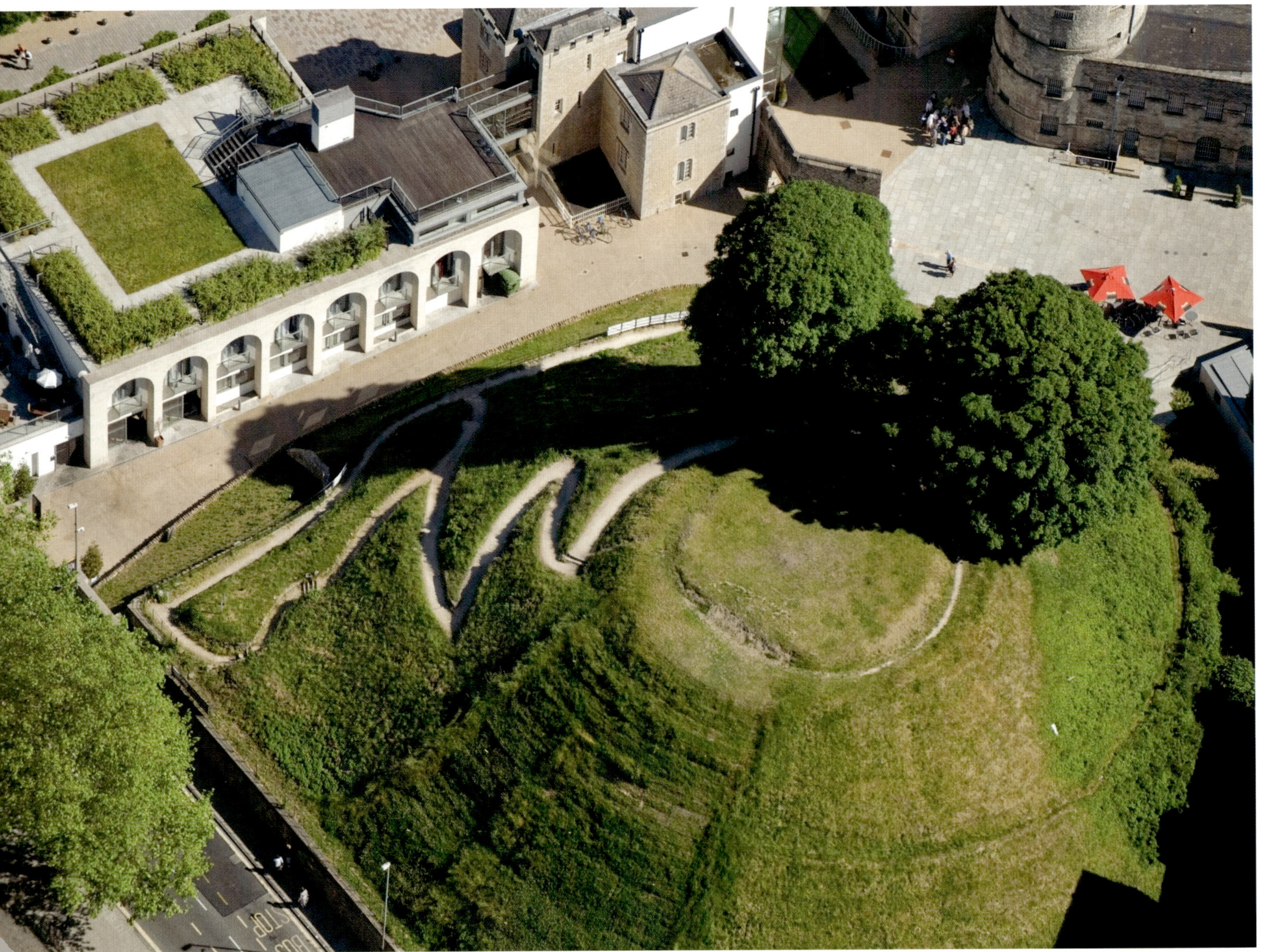

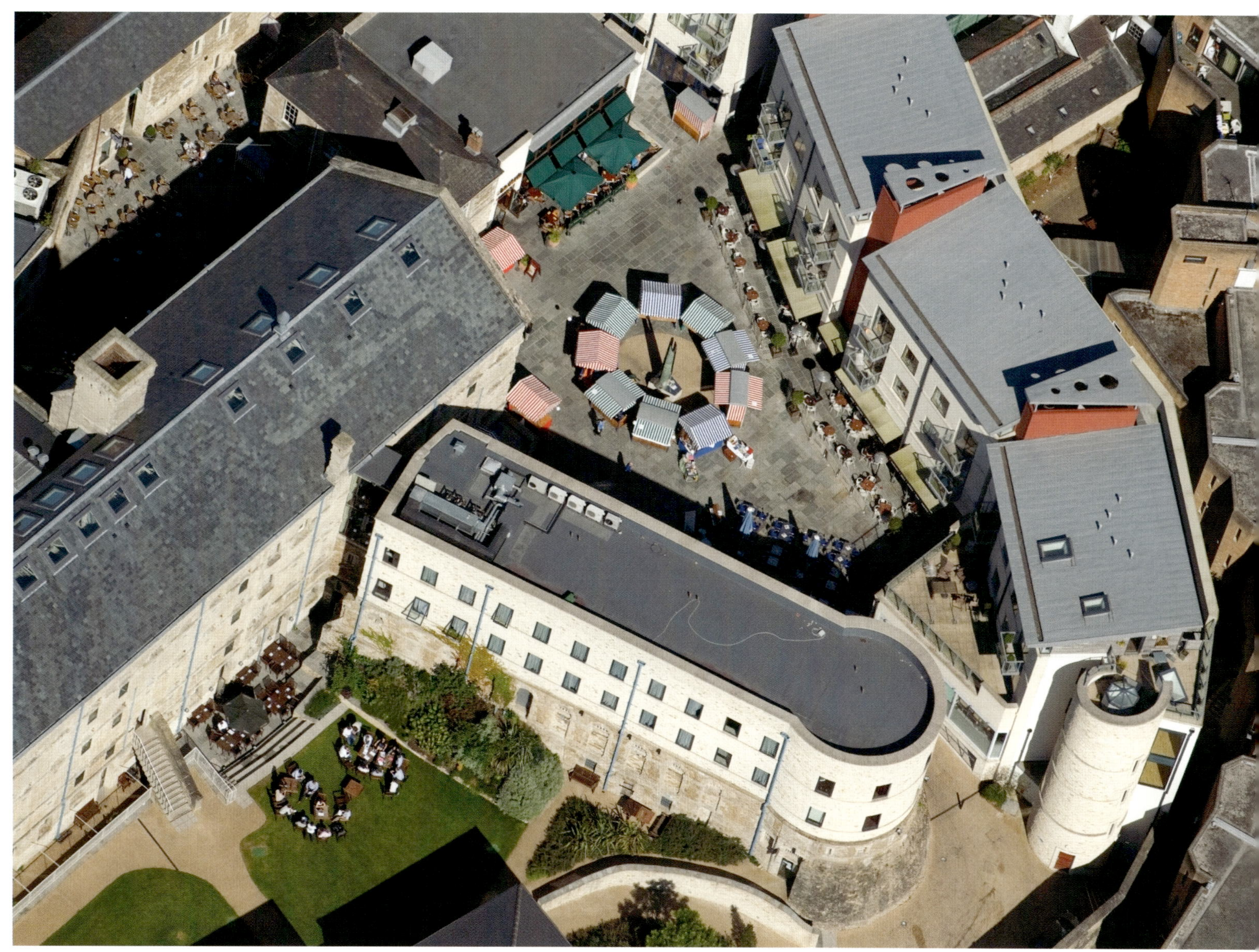

Left: Oxford castle, located in Oxford city centre, was built by a Norman baron, Robert D'Oyly, in 1071 shortly after the Norman Conquest in 1066. It was originally an earth mound with a wooden keep on the top.

Above: Market Square below Oxford castle, surrounded by the former Oxford Prison, now a hotel.

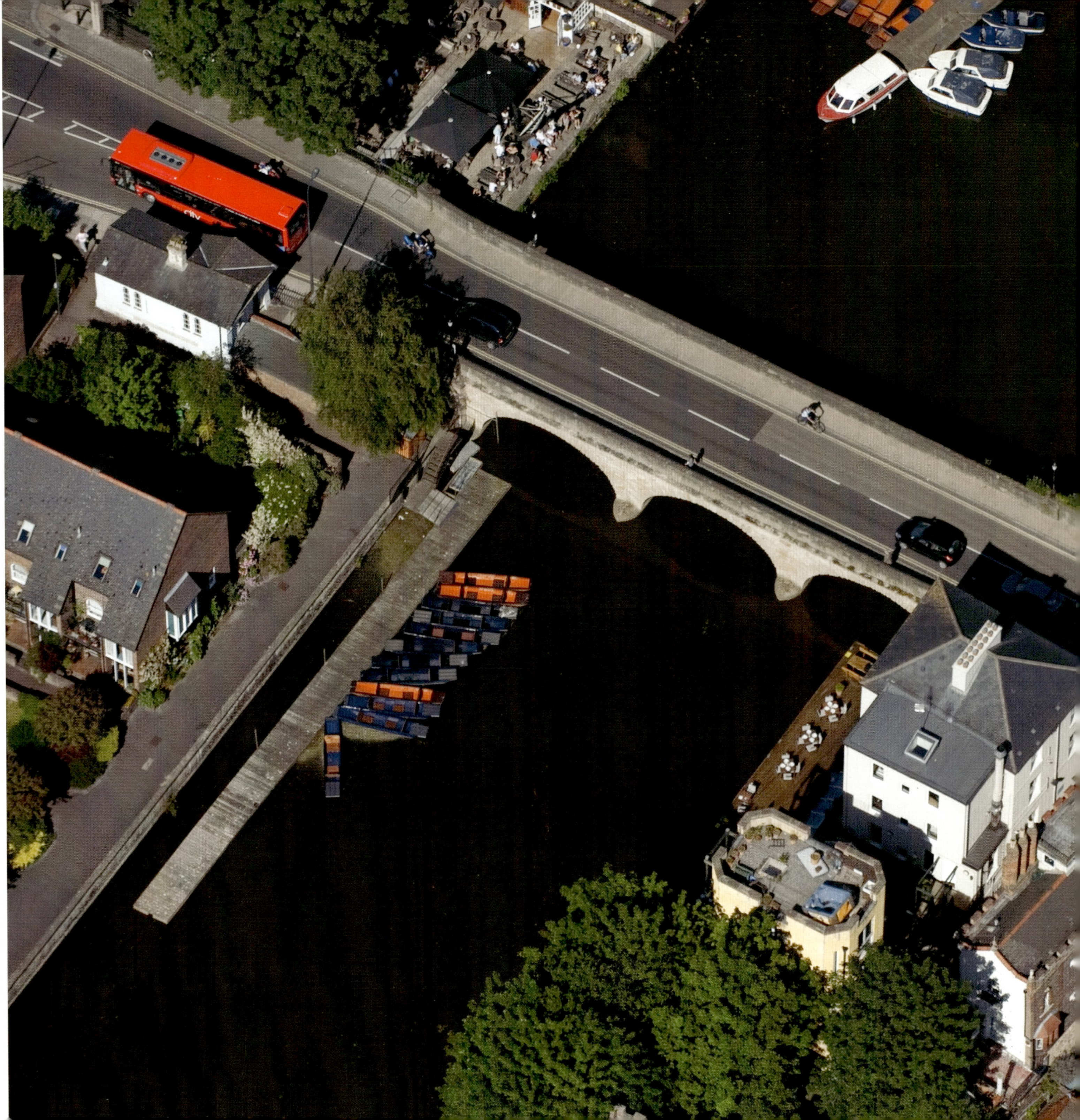

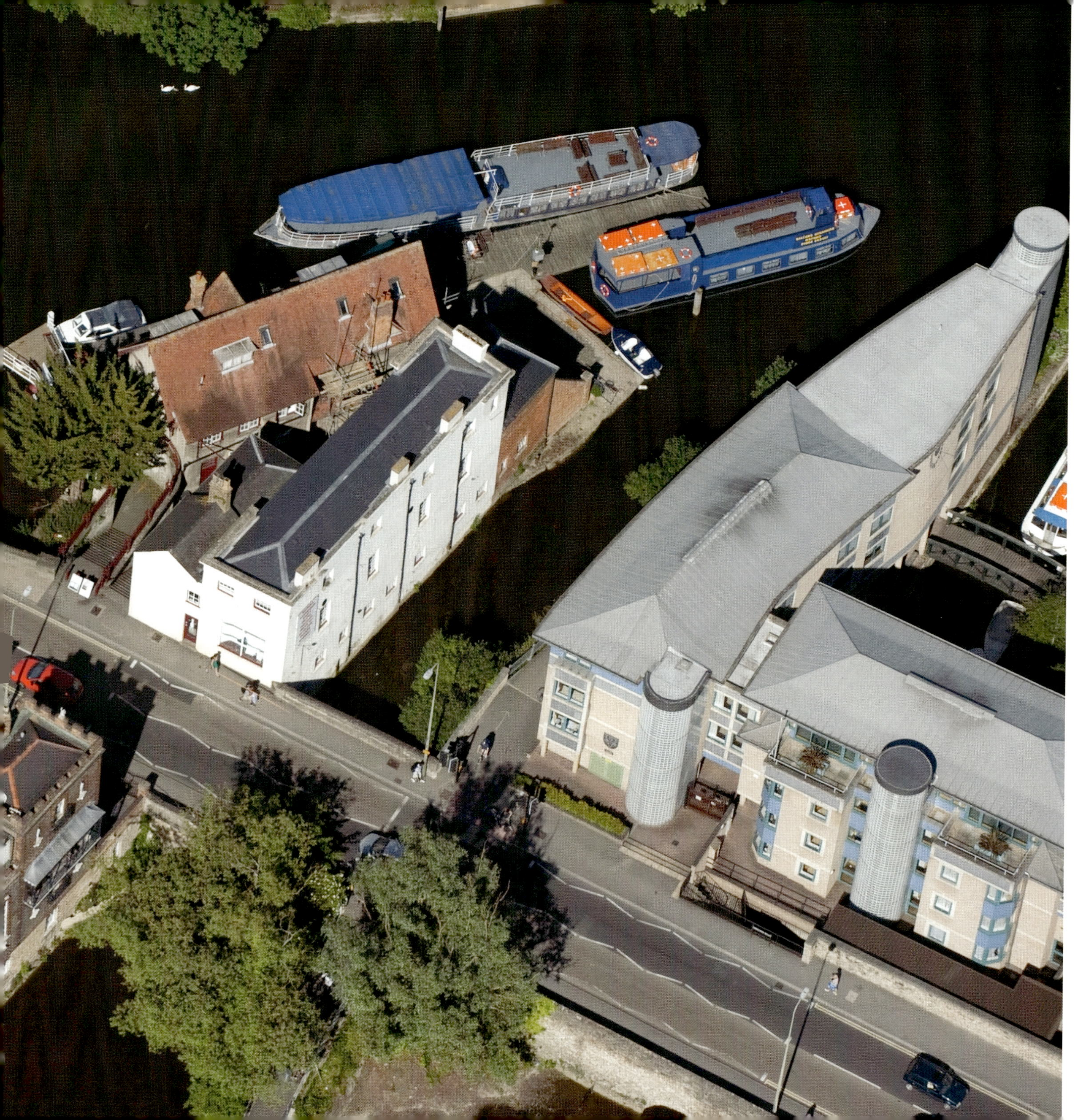

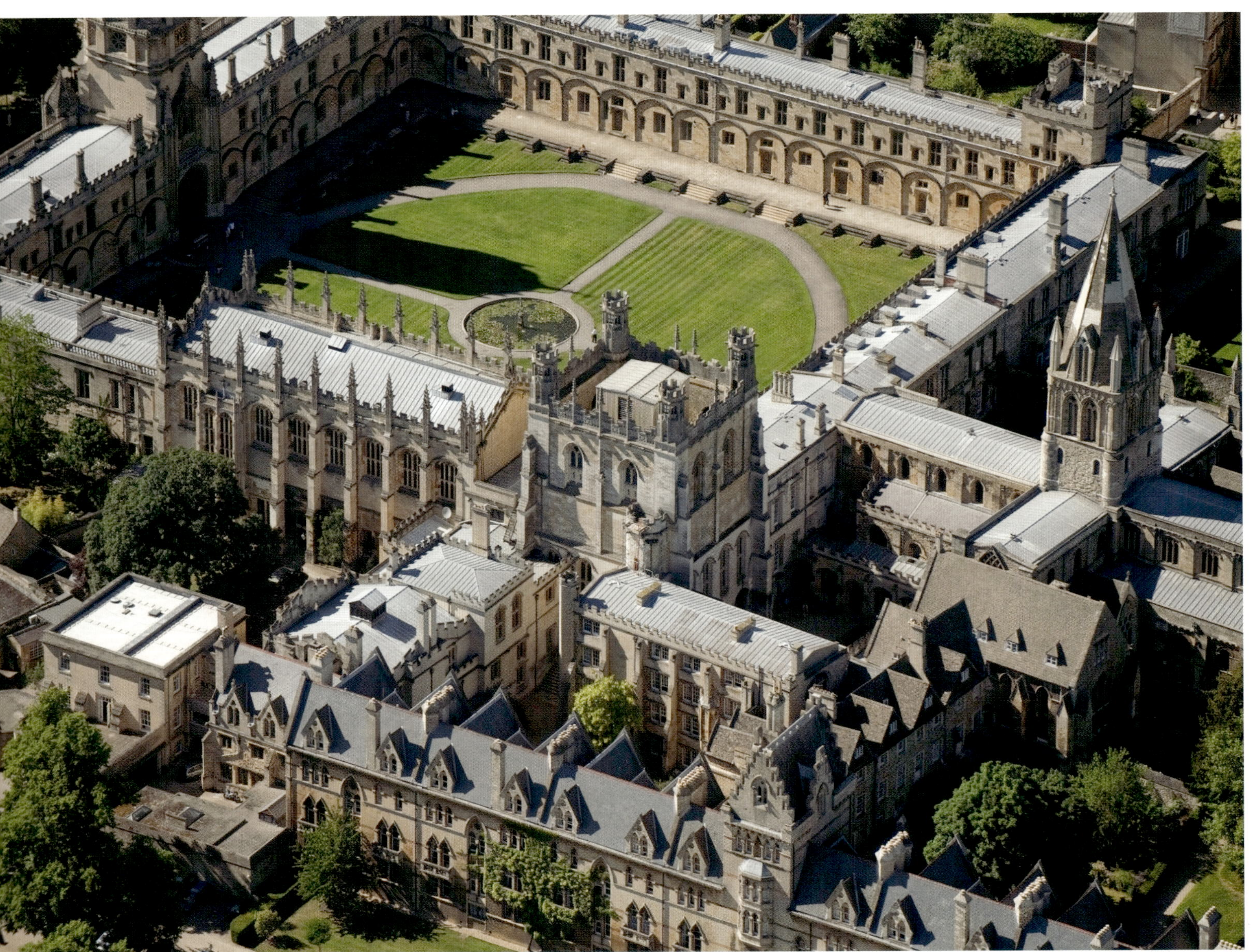

Previous page: Folly Bridge carries the Abingdon Road out of Oxford to the south over the River Thames, here known as the Isis. Punts are tied up close to the bridge, and the famous Salters Steamers are moored upstream.

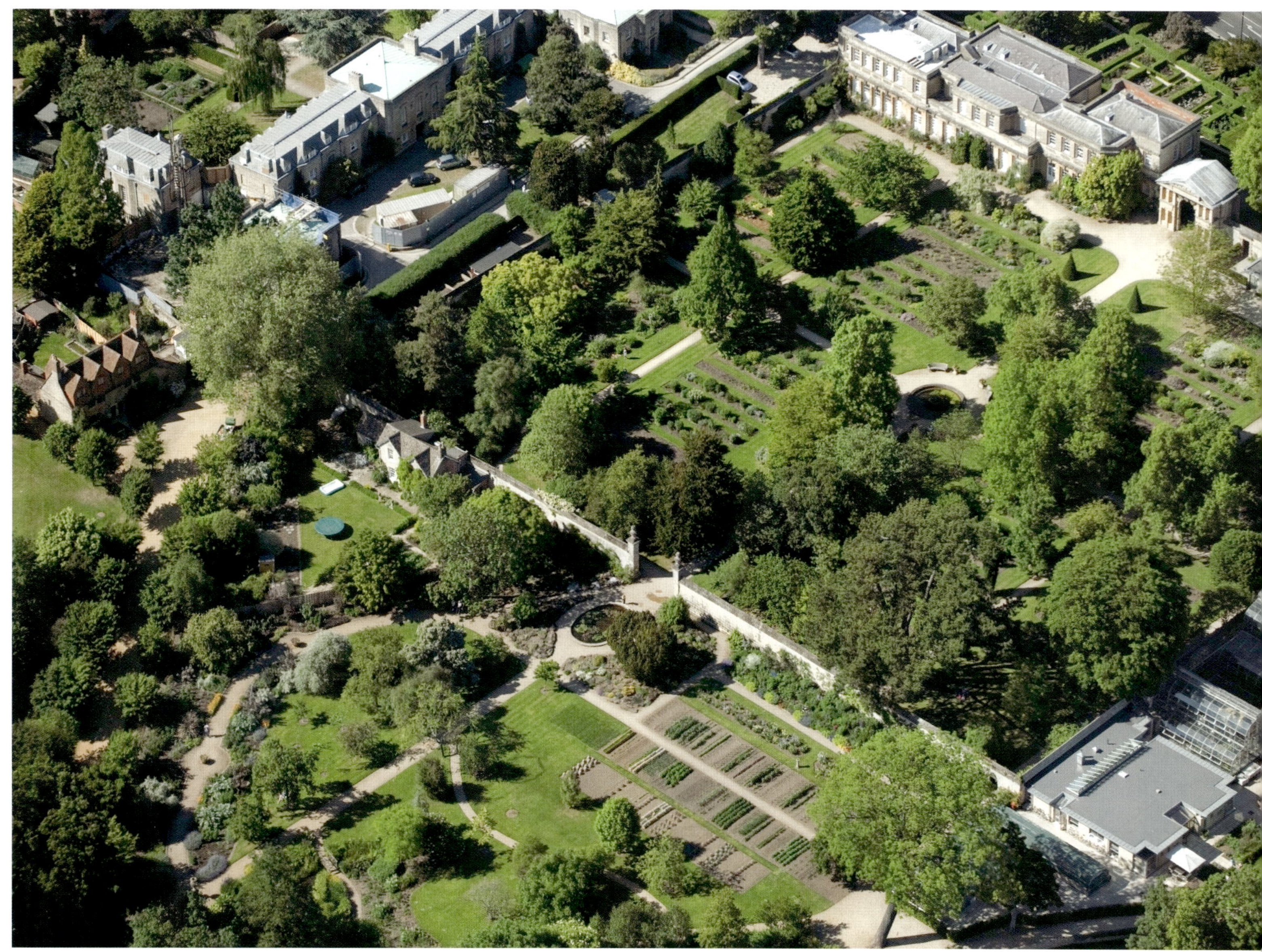

Left: Christ Church is one of the largest colleges within Oxford University. It is also the cathedral church of the diocese of Oxford, namely Christ Church Cathedral.

Above: University of Oxford Botanic Garden is the oldest botanic garden in Great Britain. It was founded in 1621 as a physic garden growing plants for medicinal research.

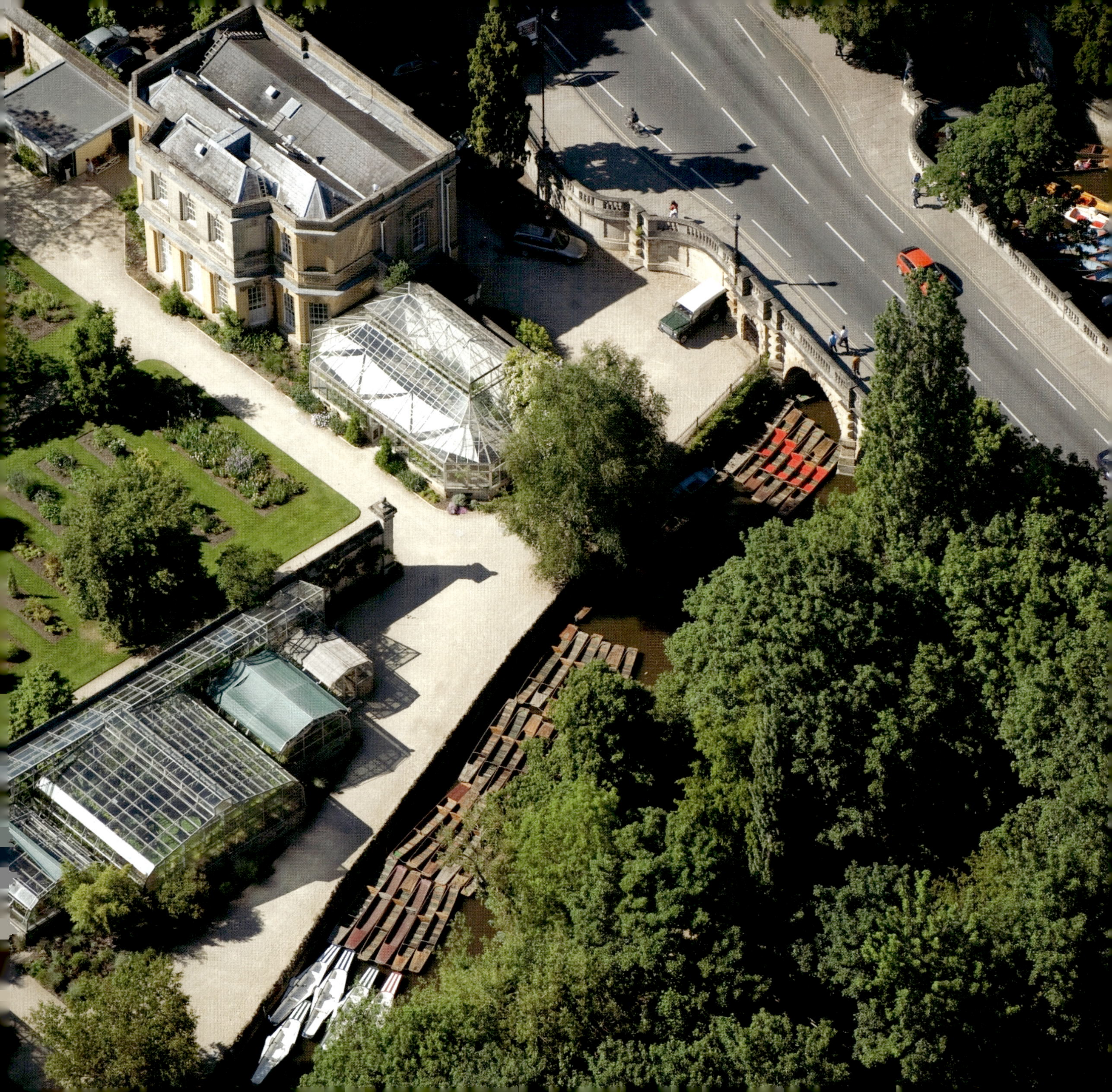

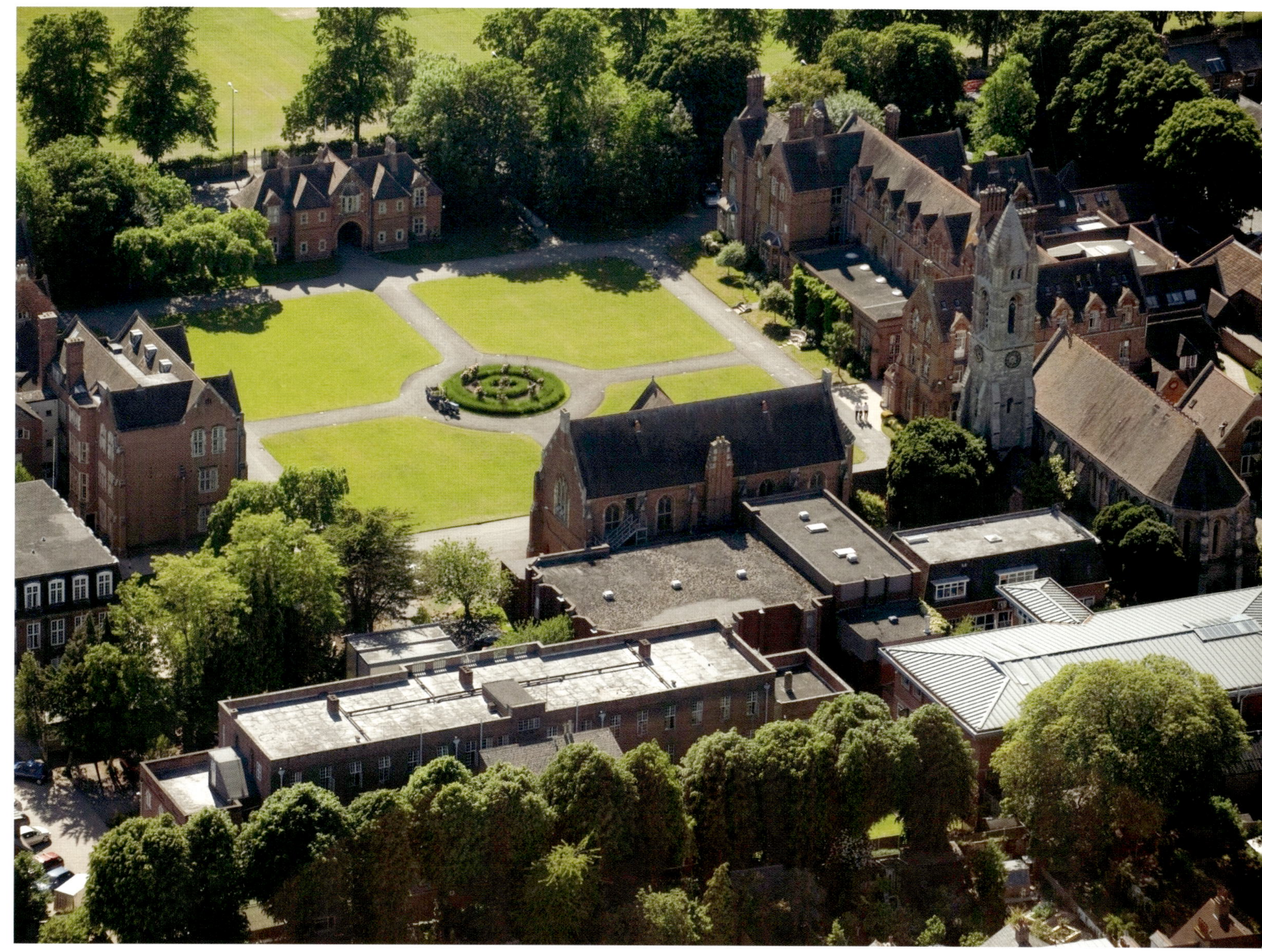

Left: Punts at Magdalen Bridge which spans the divided stream of the River Cherwell. It lies next to Magdalen College, whence it gets its (pronounced 'Mawdlin').

Above: St Edward's School (known as 'Teddies'), founded in 1863, is one of the top public schools in the country.

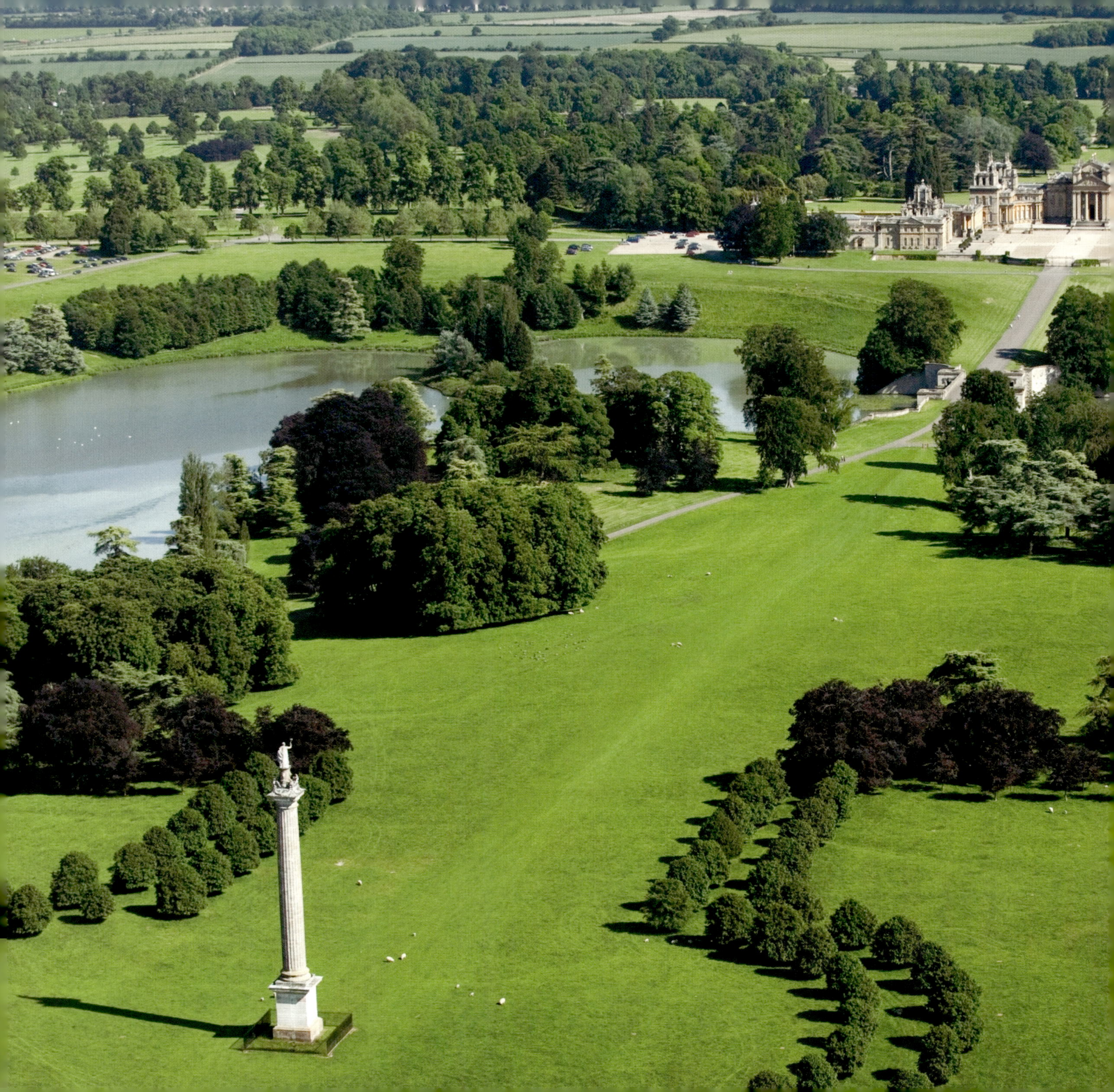

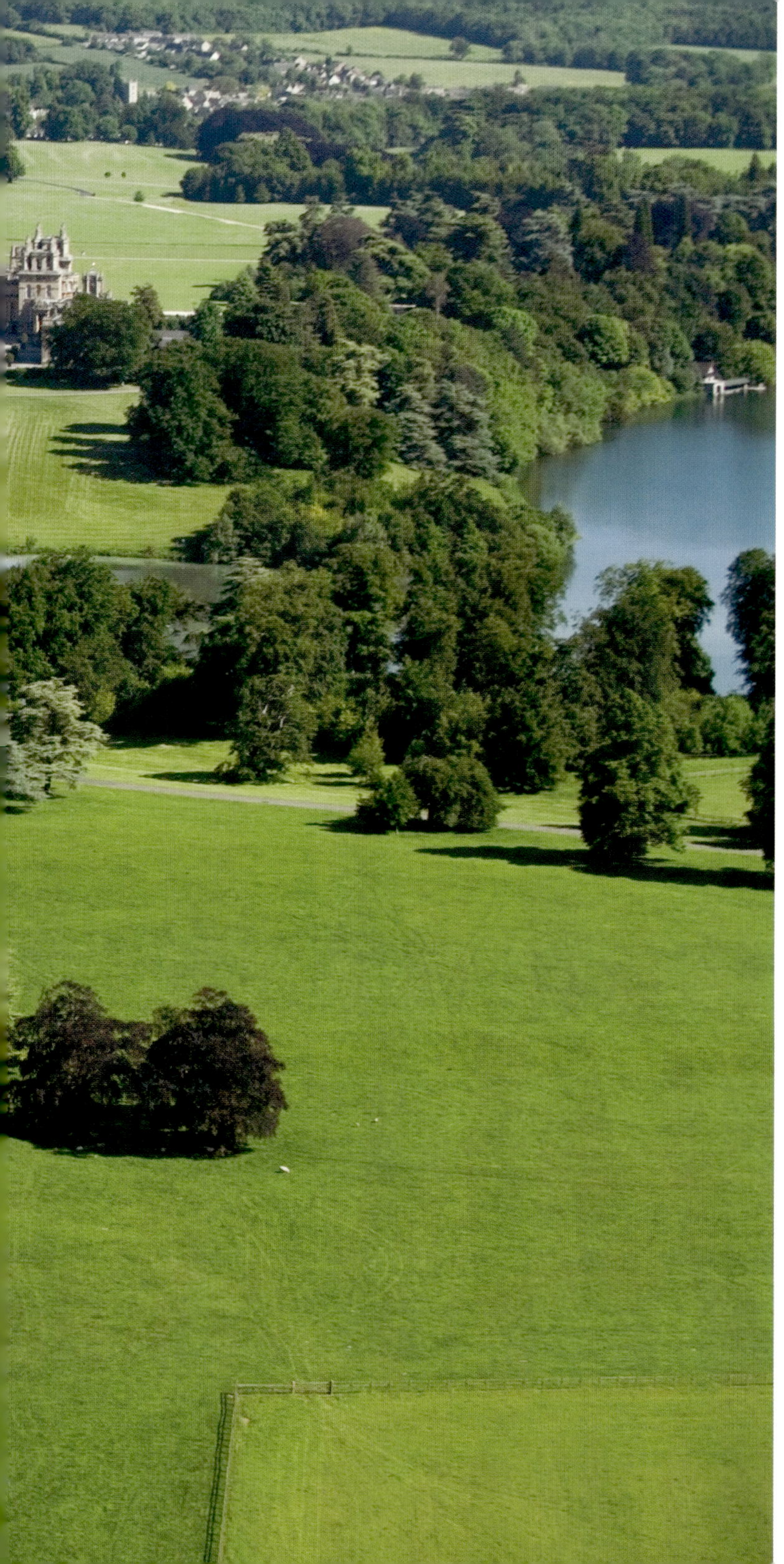

The magnificent Blenheim Palace is a unique example of English Baroque architecture. It is home to the 11th Duke and Duchess of Marlborough and the birthplace of Sir Winston Churchill. Open to the public, it is set in 2100 acres of beautiful parkland landscaped by 'Capability' Brown.

Situated in Woodstock, Blenheim is the only non-episcopal country house in England to hold the title 'palace'. One of England's largest houses, it was built between 1705 and 1724. It was recognised as a UNESCO World Heritage Site in 1987.

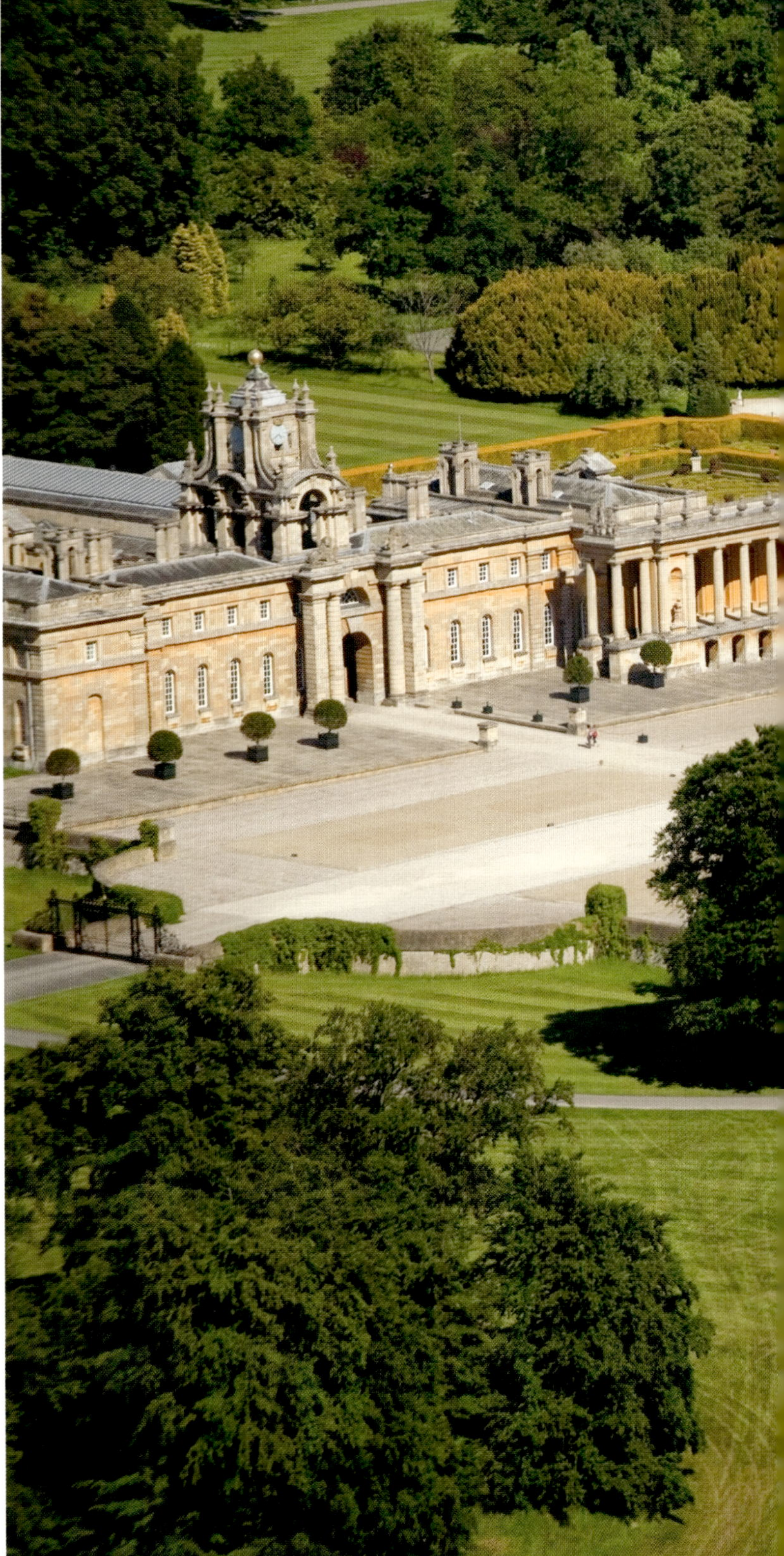

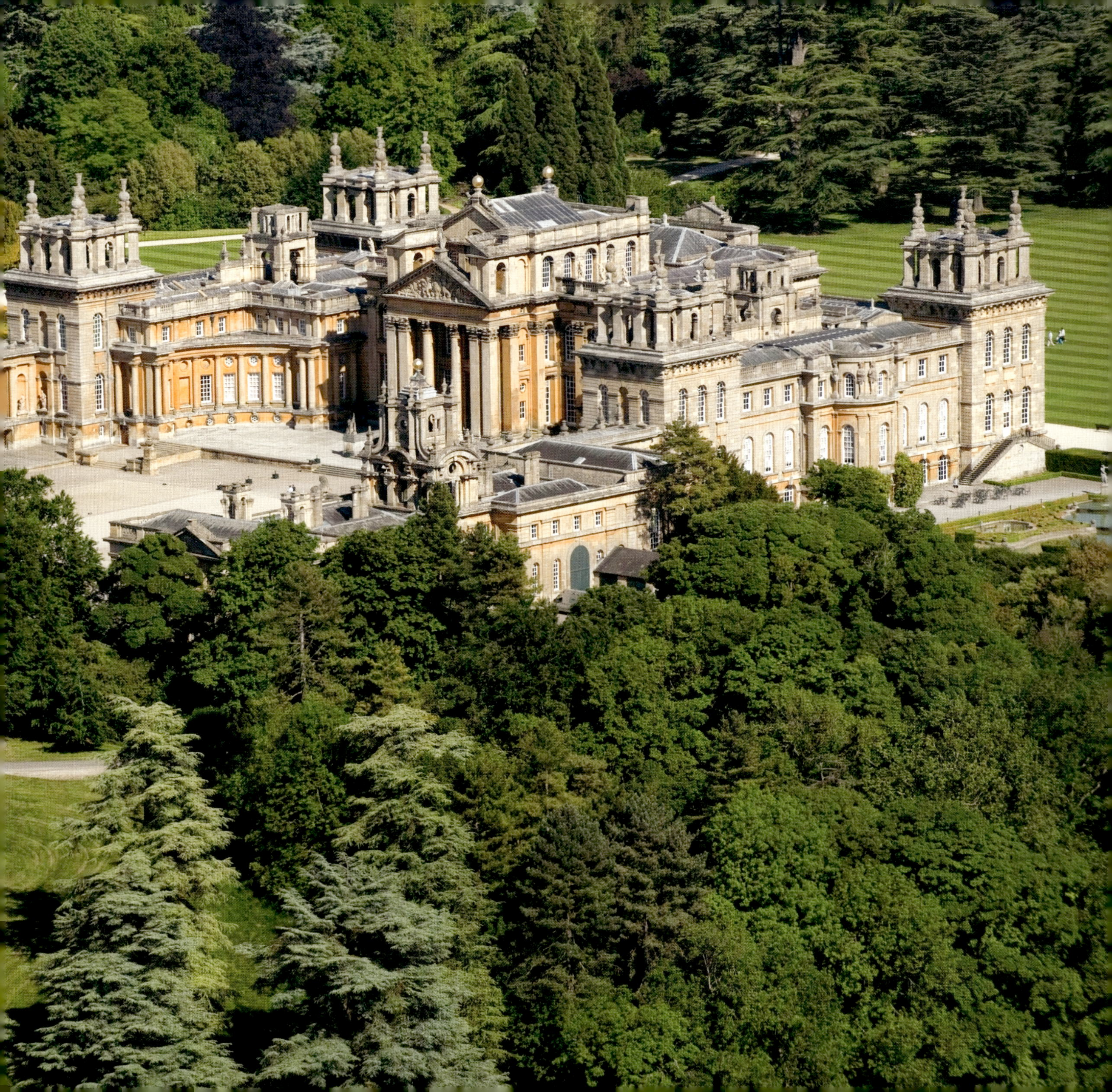

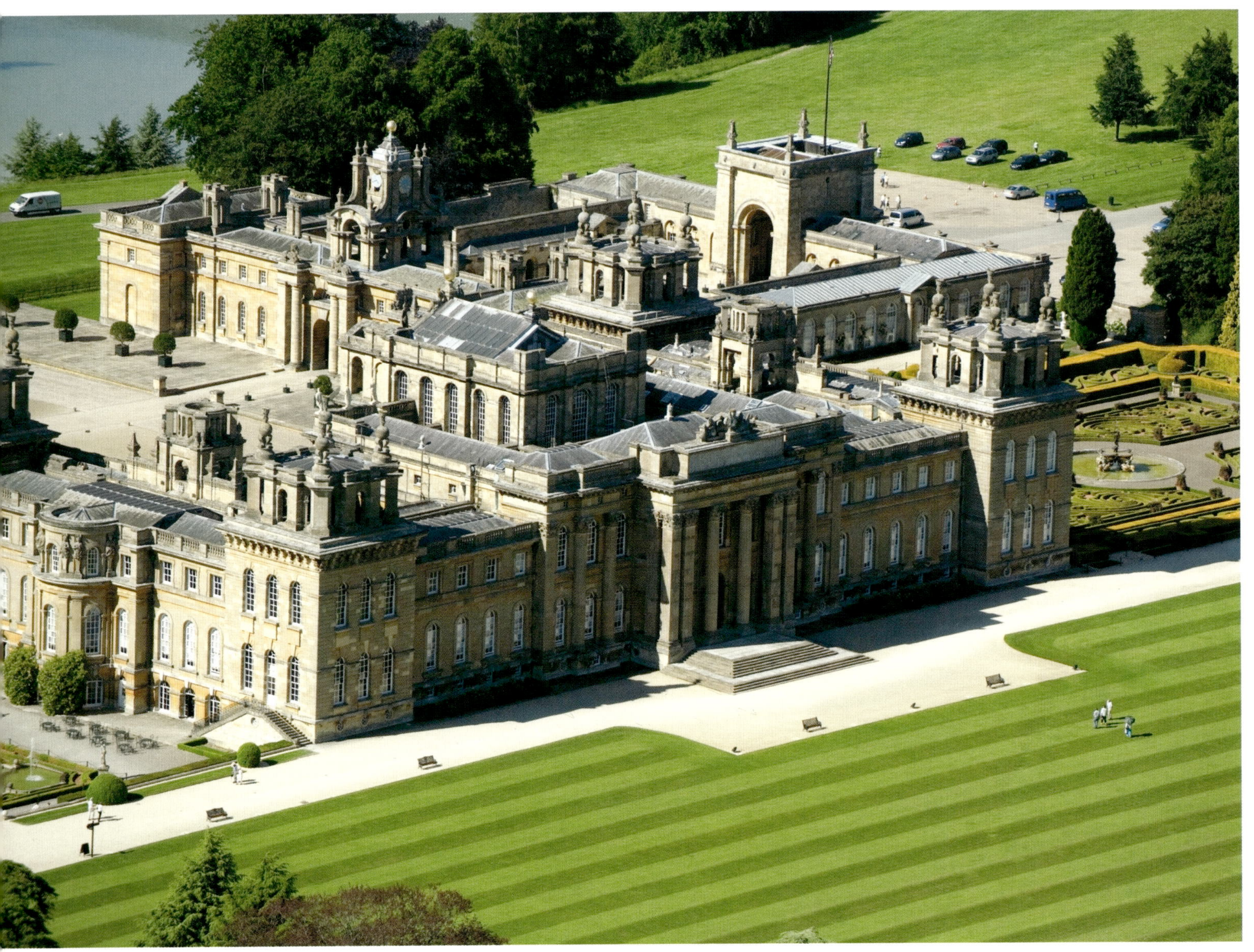

Above: The palace was originally a gift to John Churchill, the 1st Duke of Marlborough from a grateful nation in return for military triumph at the Battle of Blenheim.

Right: The Marlborough Maze is the world's second largest symbolic hedge maze, covering an area of just over an acre.

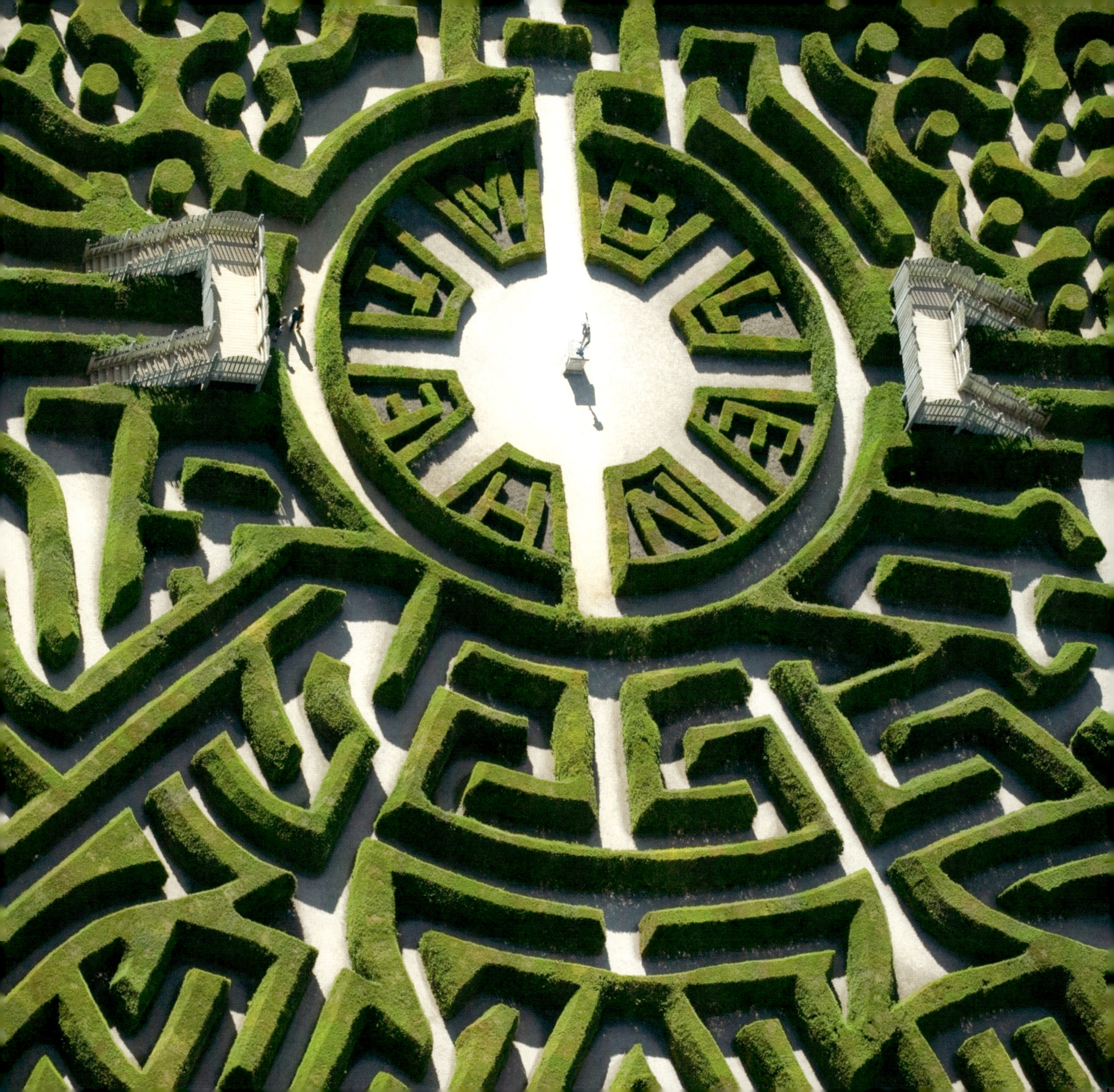

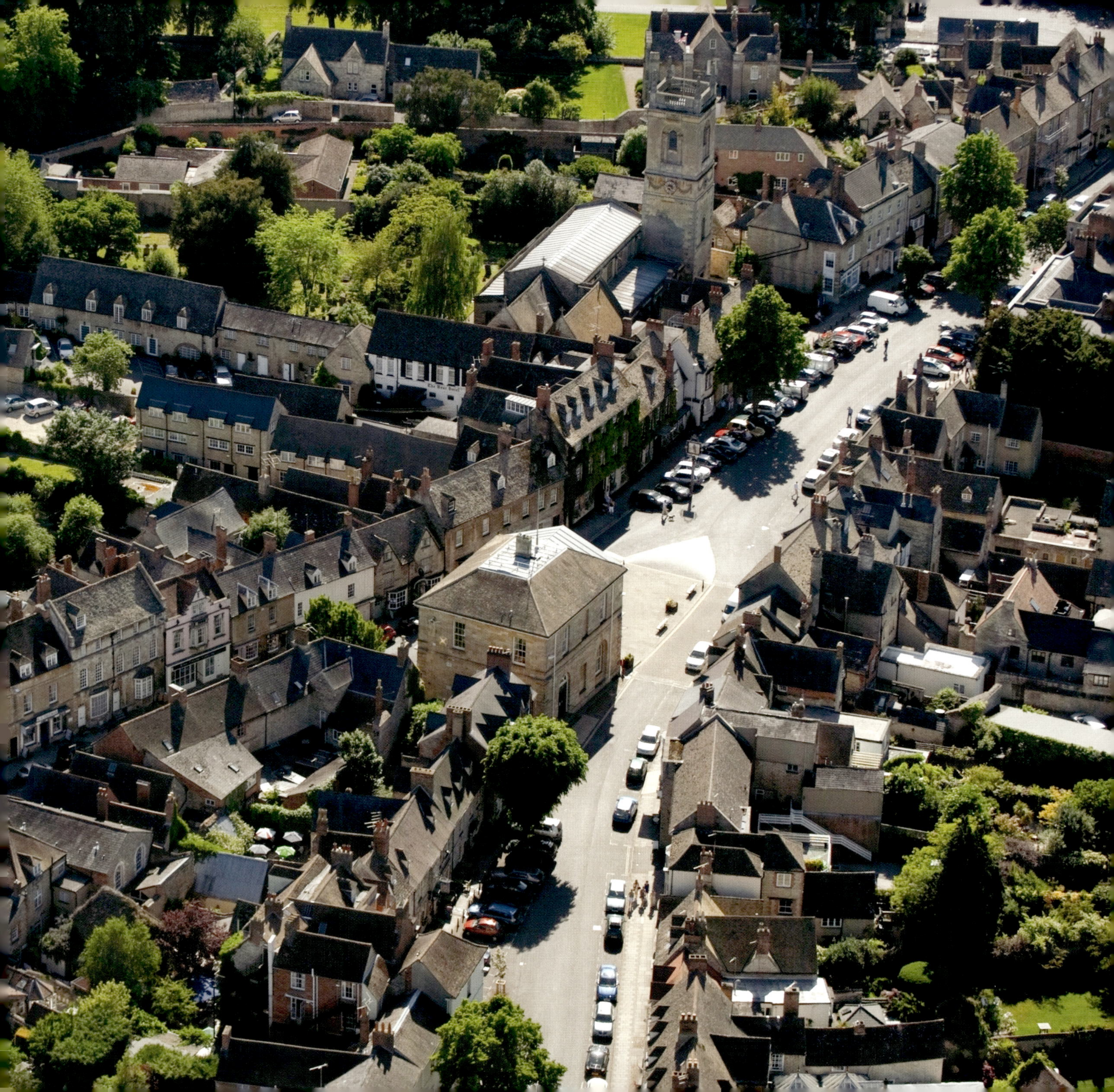

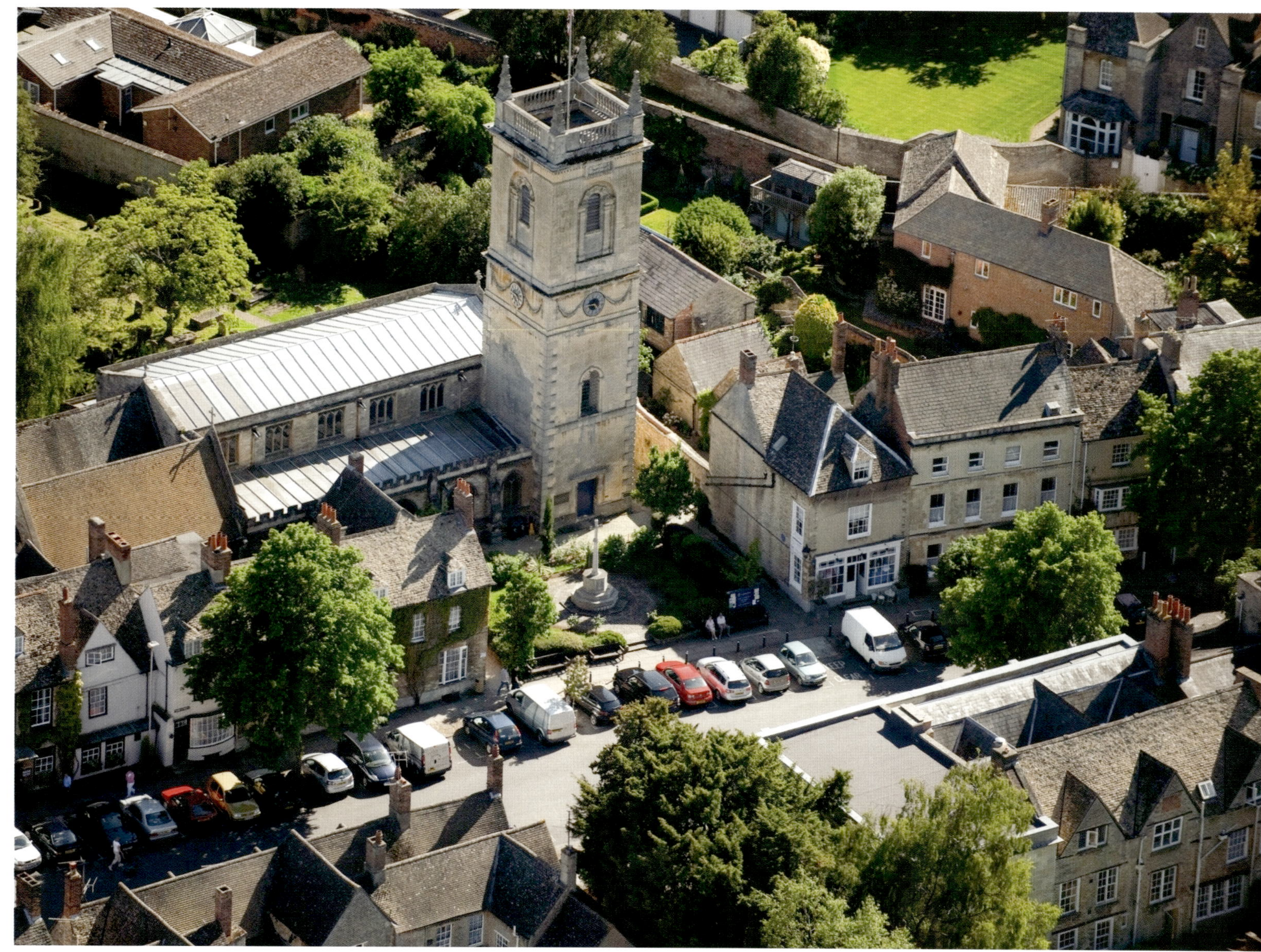

Left and above: Once famed for its glovemaking, Woodstock is now mainly given over to tourism due to its proximity to Blenheim Palace. These views look down into the town's centre. The large square building (centre in the left hand photograph) is the historic Town Hall. The parish church (dedicated to St Mary Magdalene) has a doorway of Norman origin. It features a musical clock which chimes every hour.

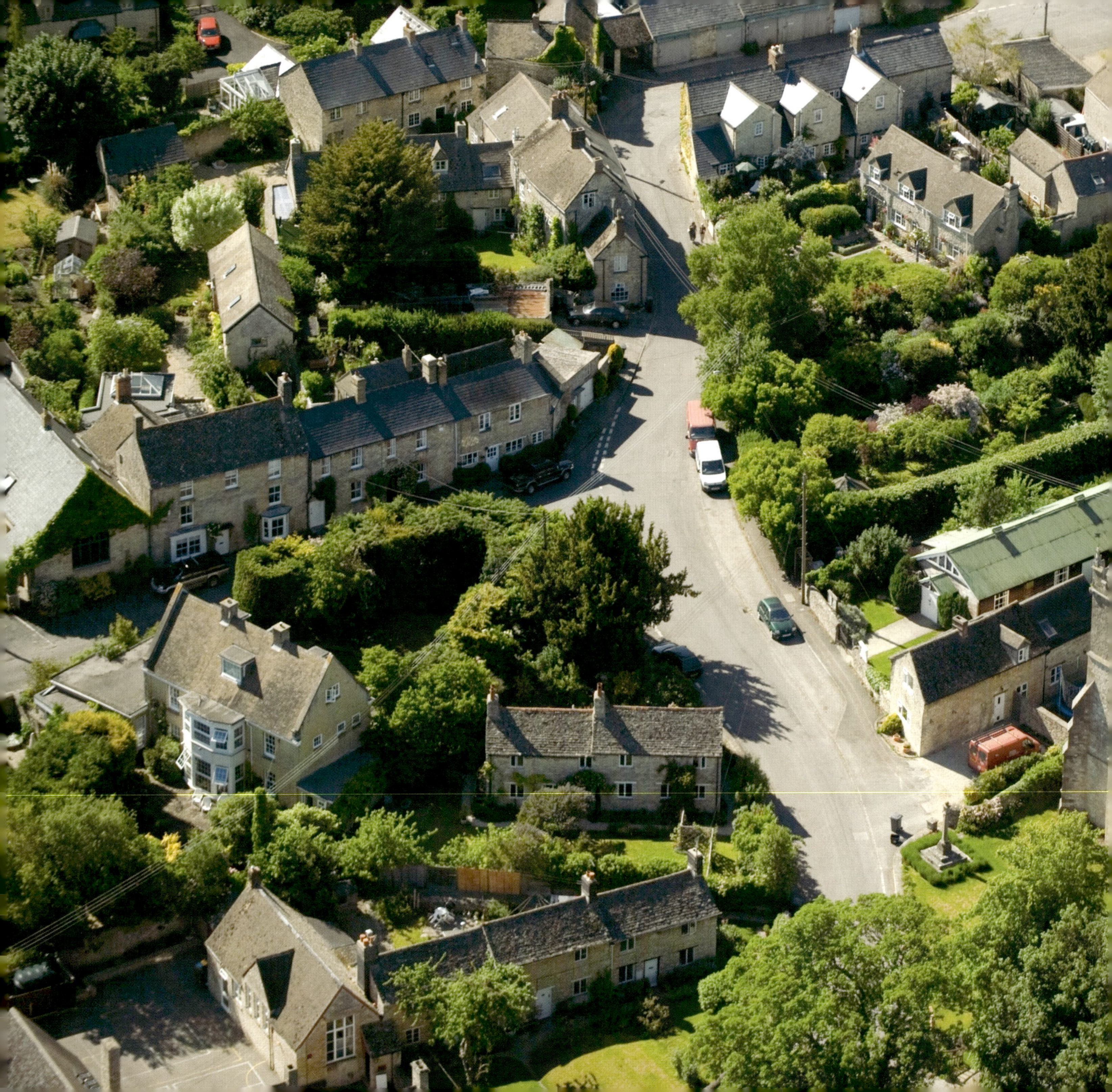

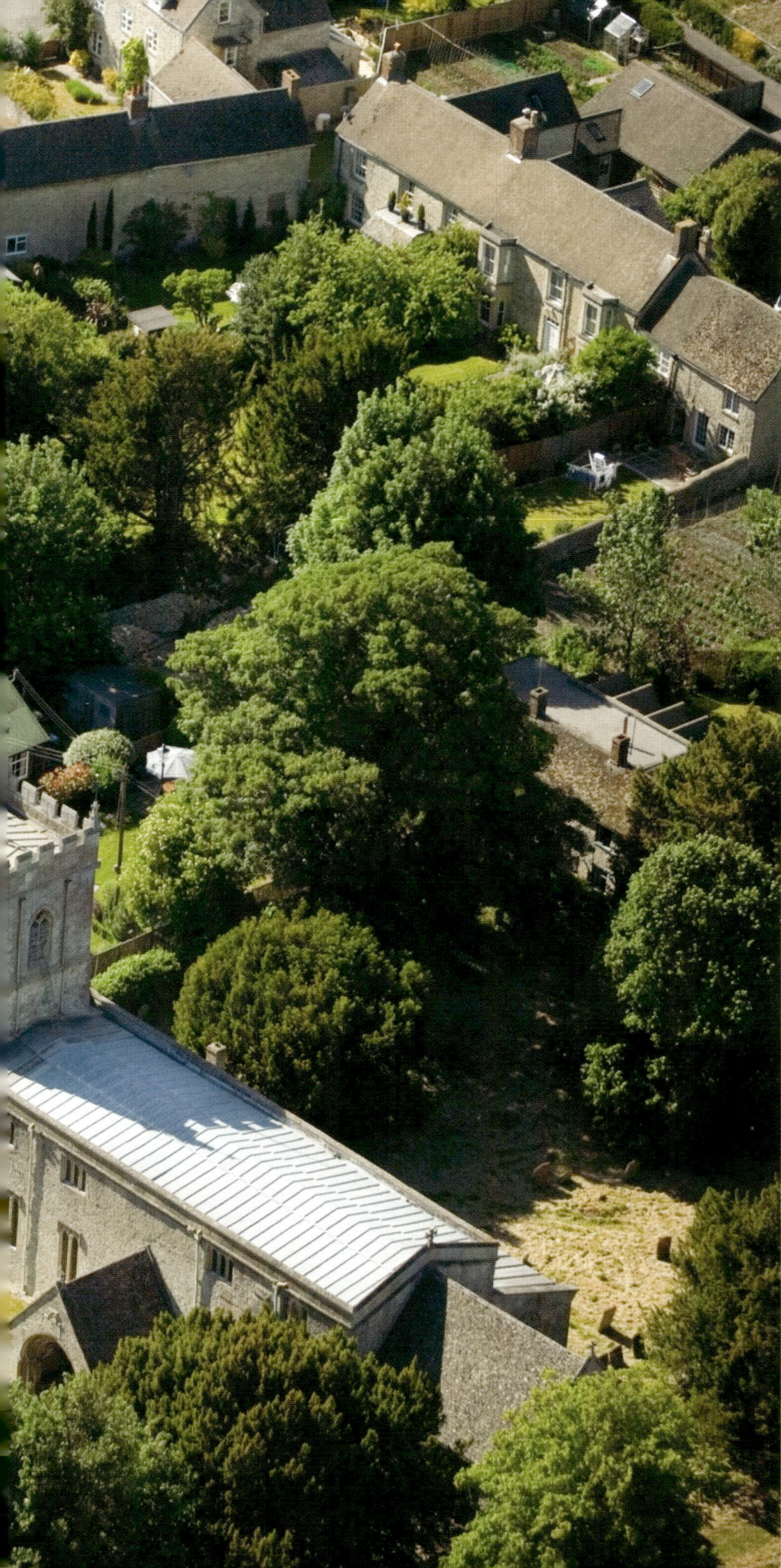

The small village of Wootton lies to the north of Woodstock. To distinguish it from another village of the same name in Oxfordshire – Wootton, Vale of White Horse – it is often referred to as Wootton-by-Woodstock.

Tackley lies beside the River Cherwell about 8 miles west of Bicester and 5 miles north of Kidlington. This pretty village consists of two neighbourhoods, Tackley itself, and Nethercott.

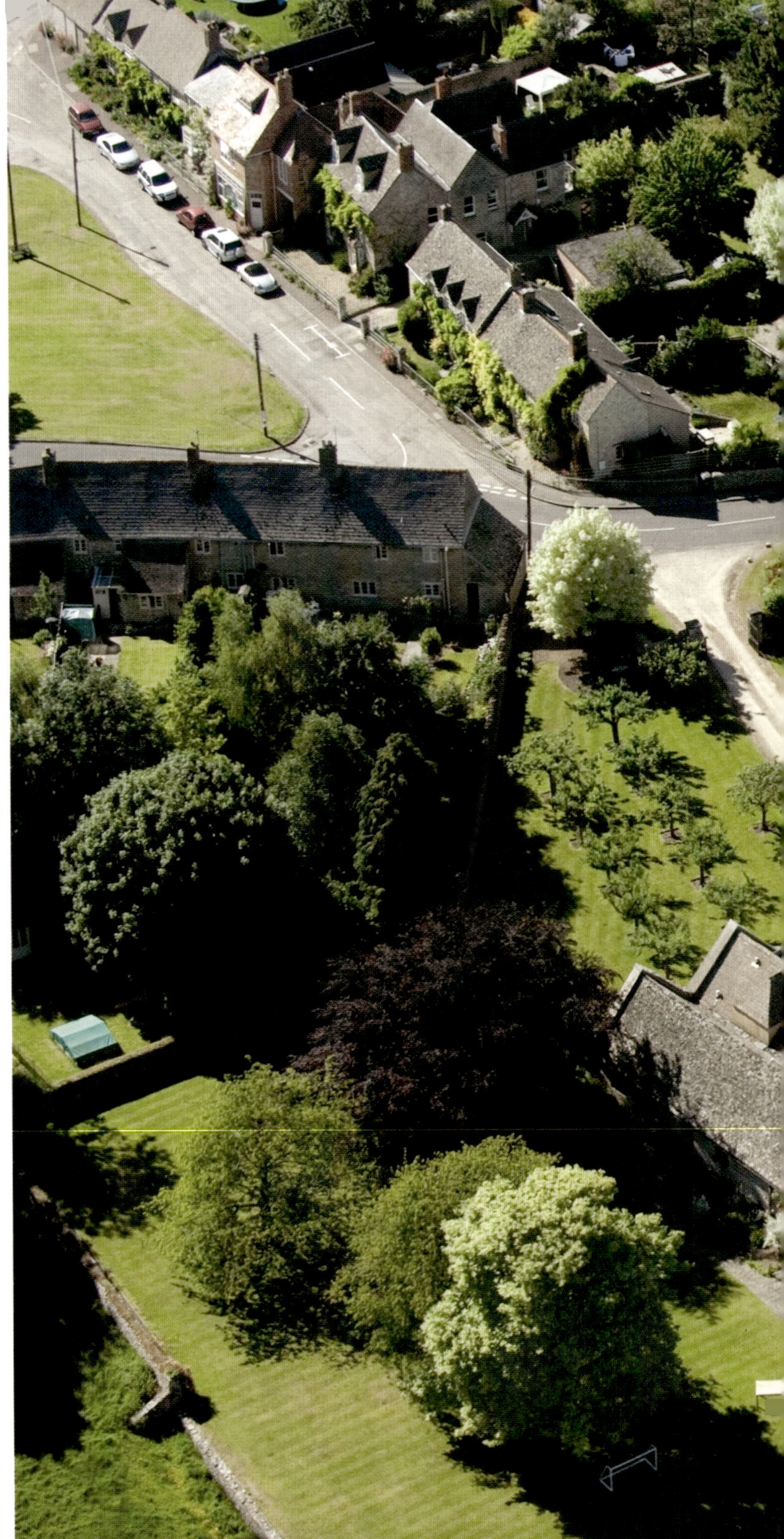

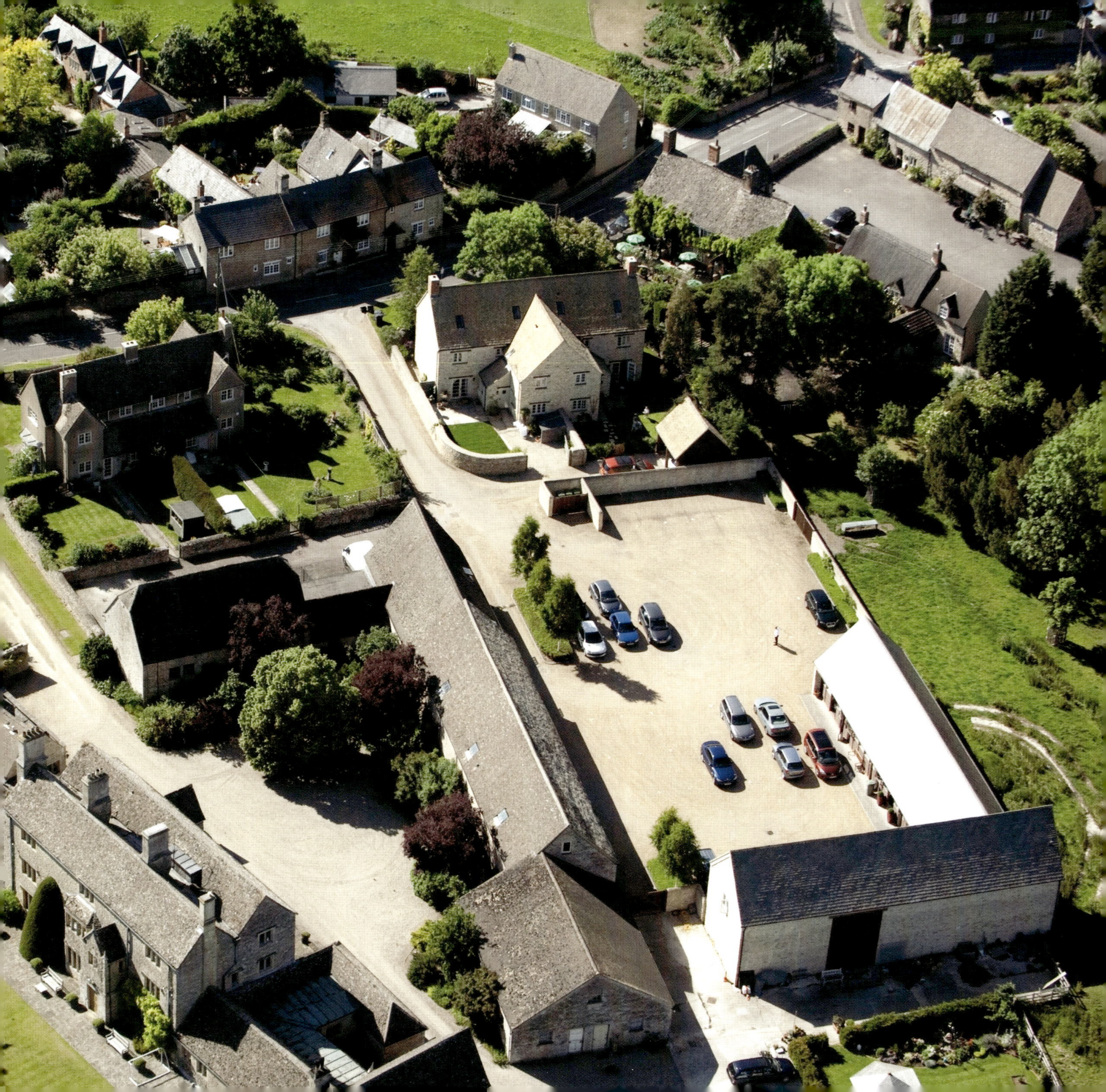

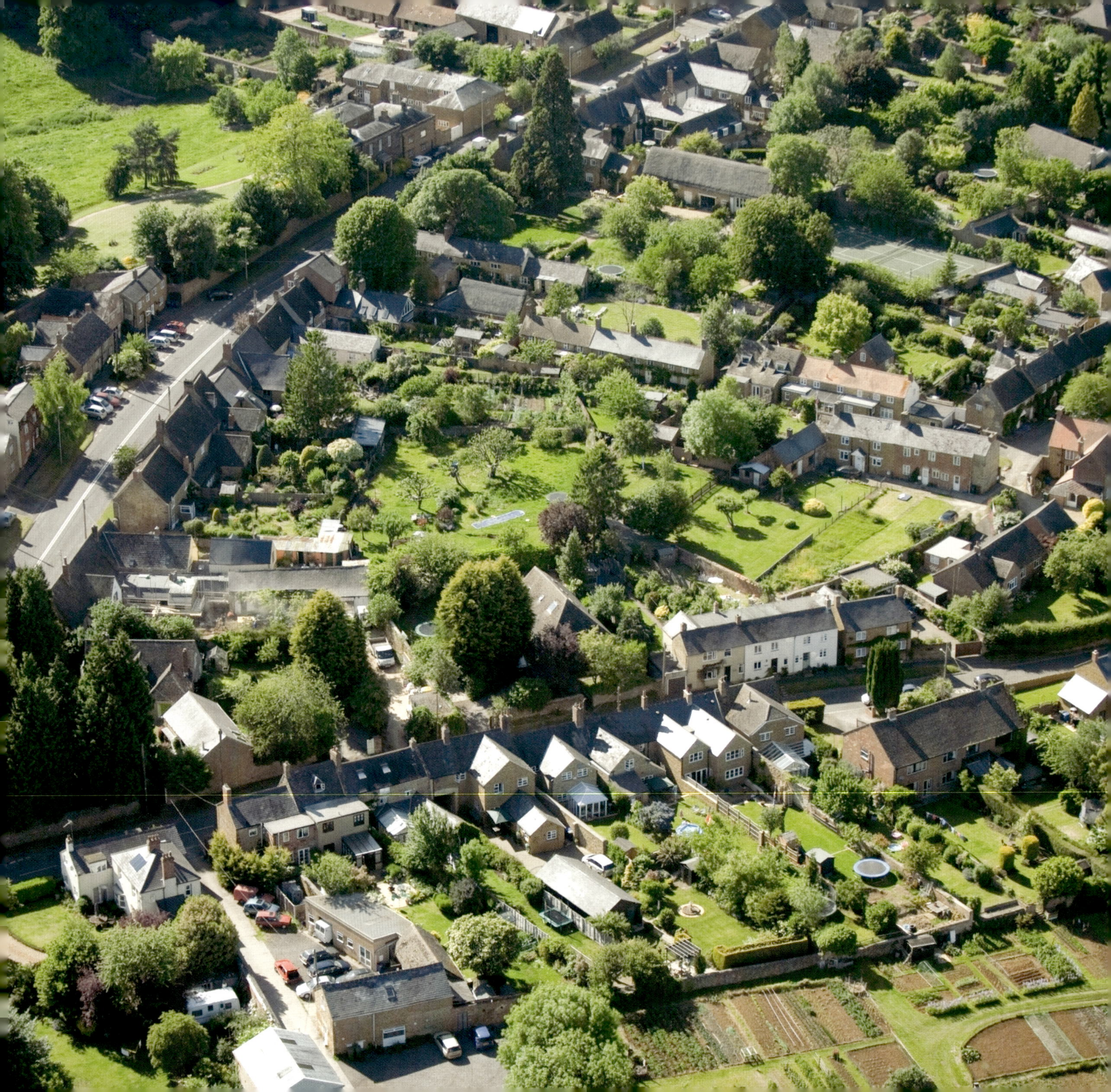

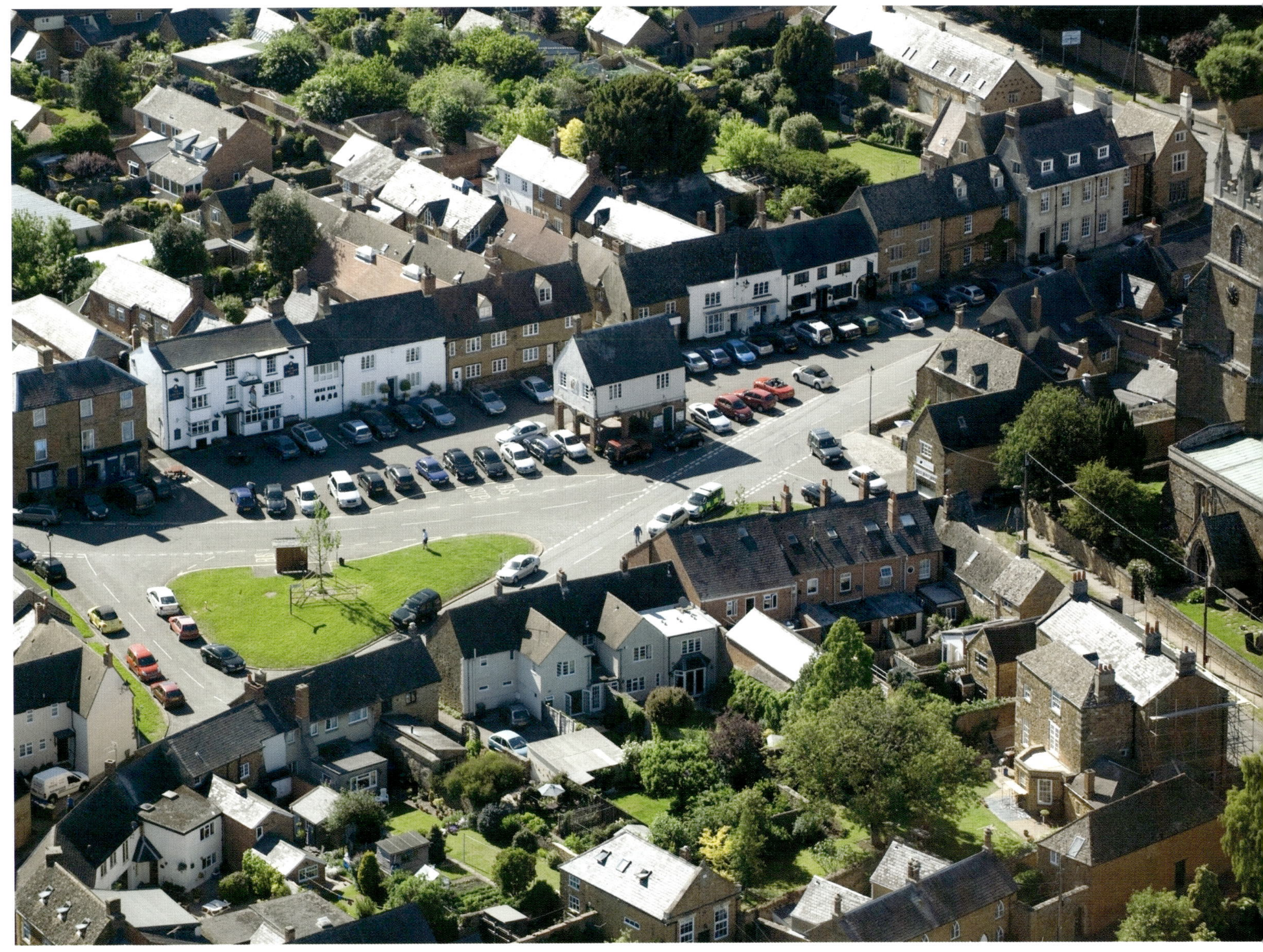

Left and above: Deddington lies between Oxford and Banbury. Sited at the edge of the Cotswolds, the honey-coloured local stone, provides the settlement with a characteristic atmosphere of warmth. The Town Hall, seen in the centre of the photograph above, stands on brick arches and over the years has served as a polling booth, courtroom and library.

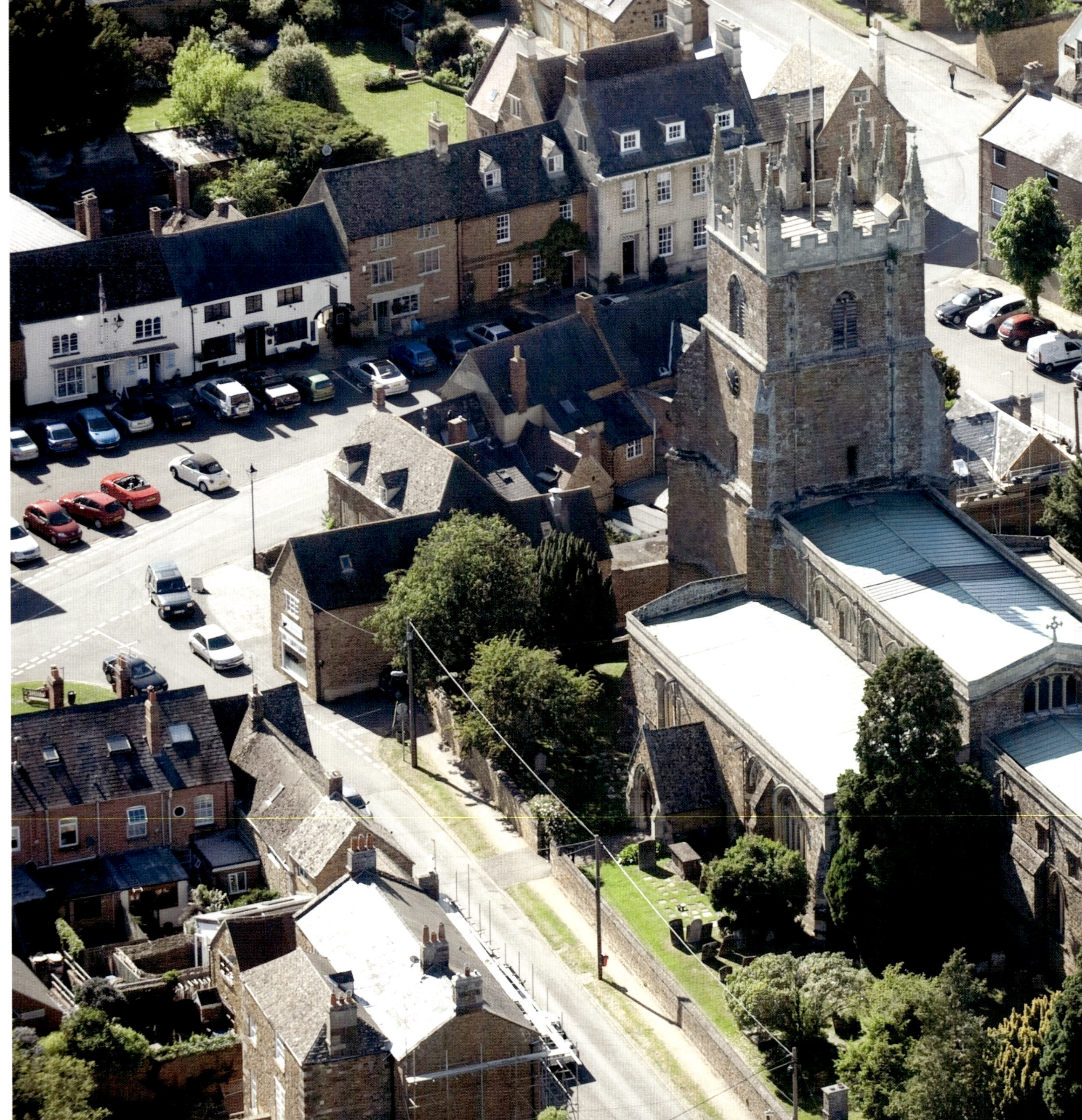

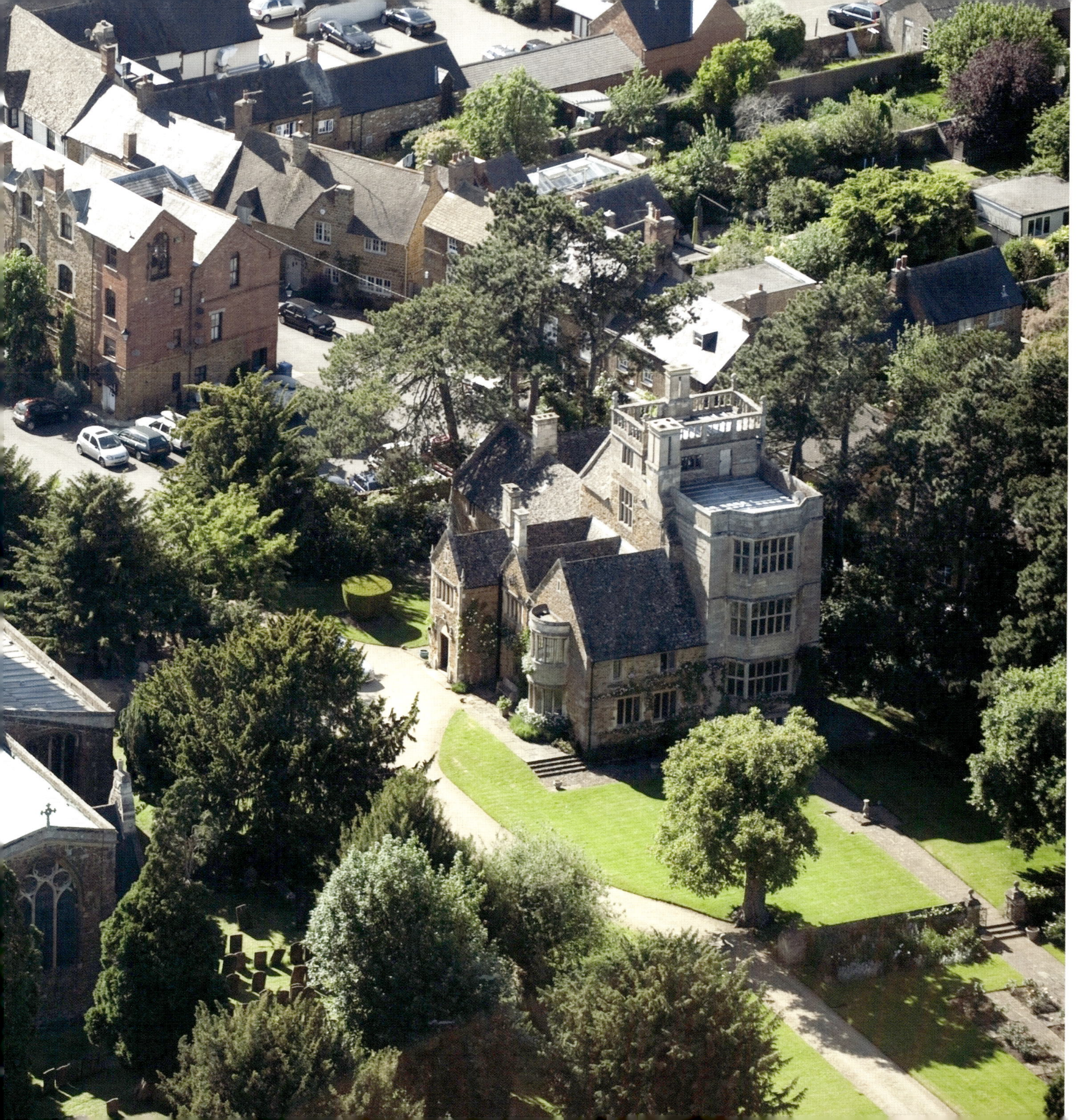

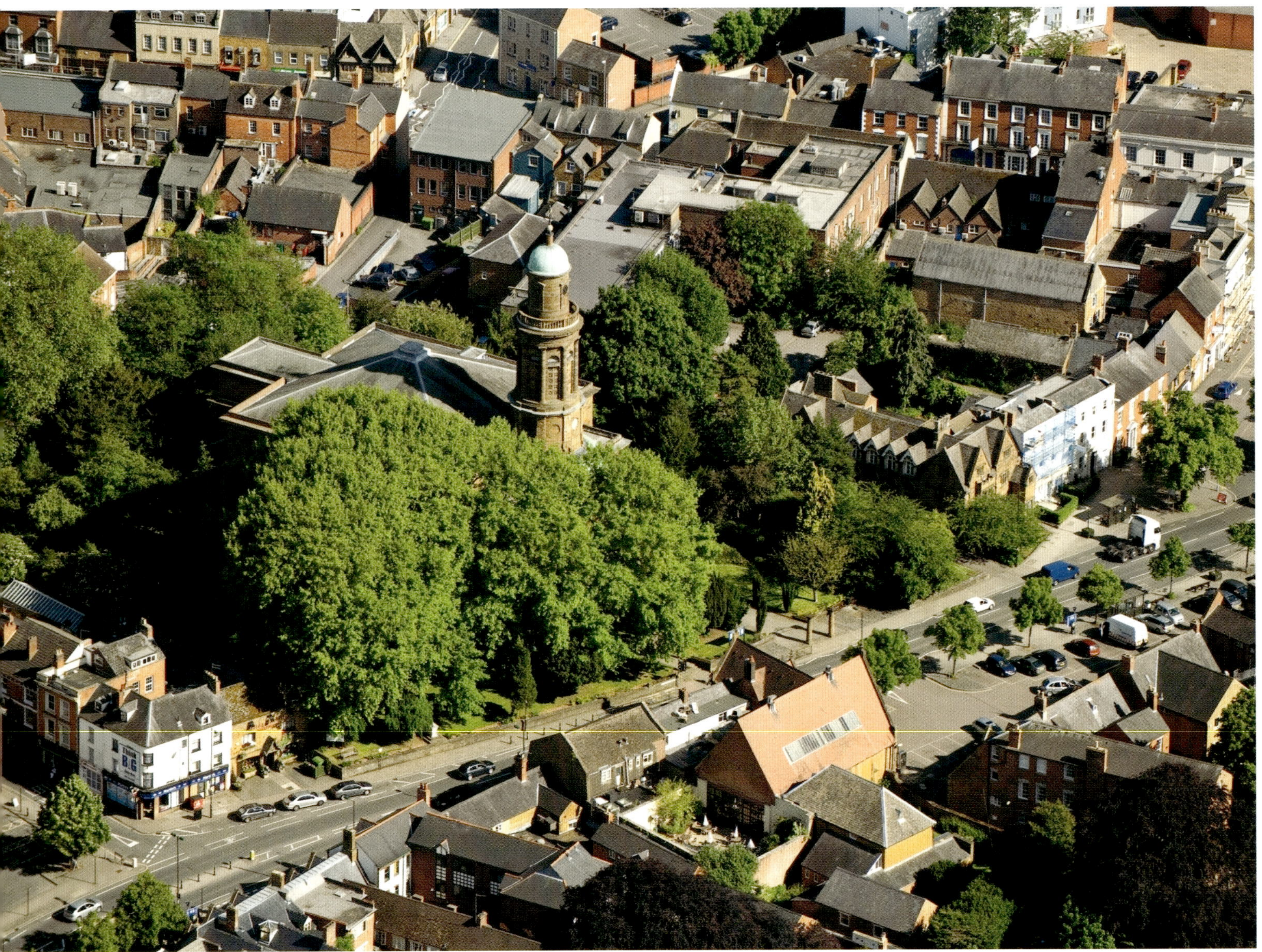

Previous page: Looking down on to Market Place and Church Street, Deddington.

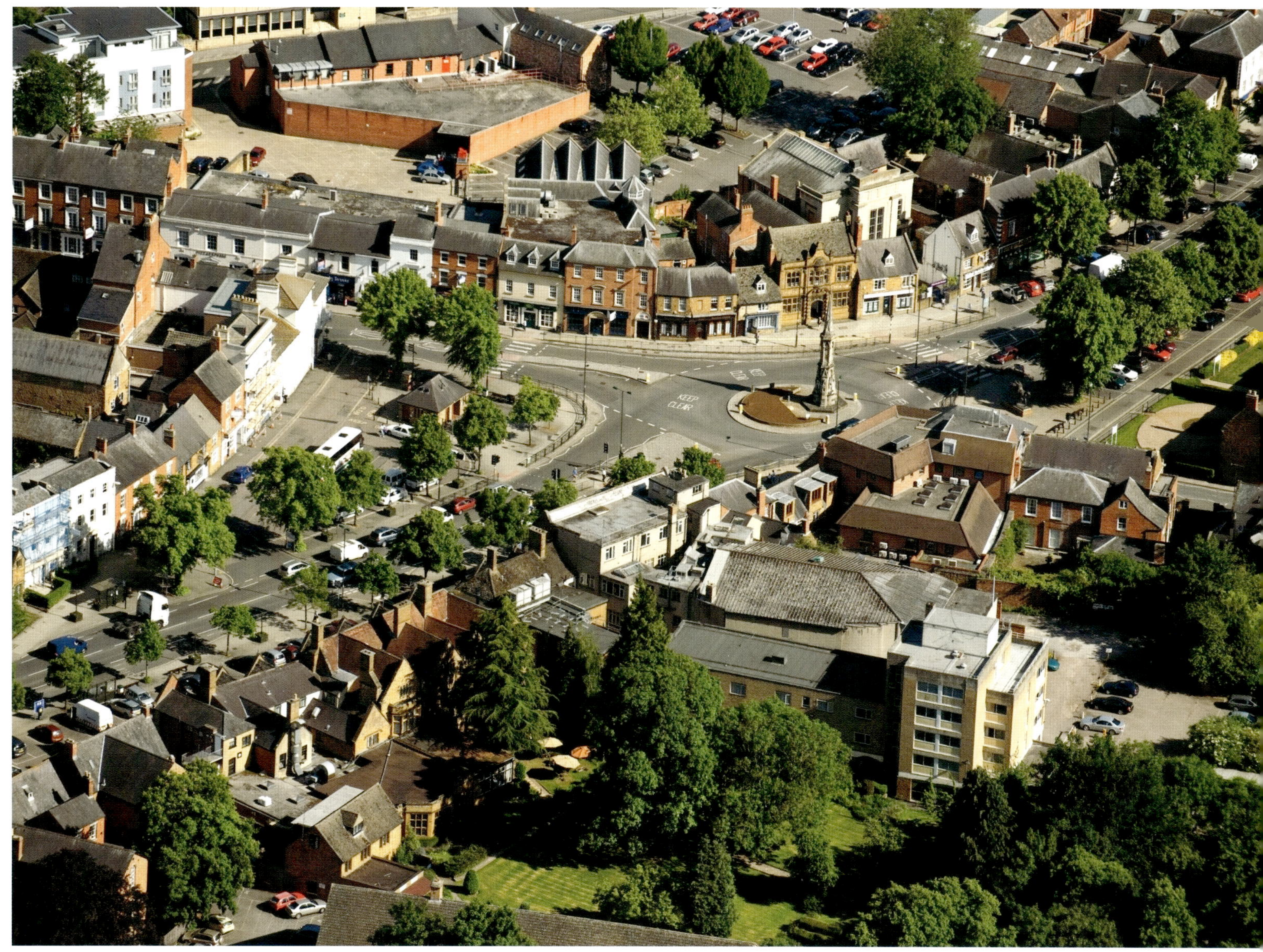

Left and above: Banbury is famed for the nursery rhyme relating to Banbury Cross. At one time Banbury had many crosses (High Cross, Bread Cross and White Cross), but these were destroyed by the Puritans. The town remained without a cross for another 250 years until the current Banbury Cross was erected in 1859 to commemorate the marriage of Queen Victoria's eldest daughter.

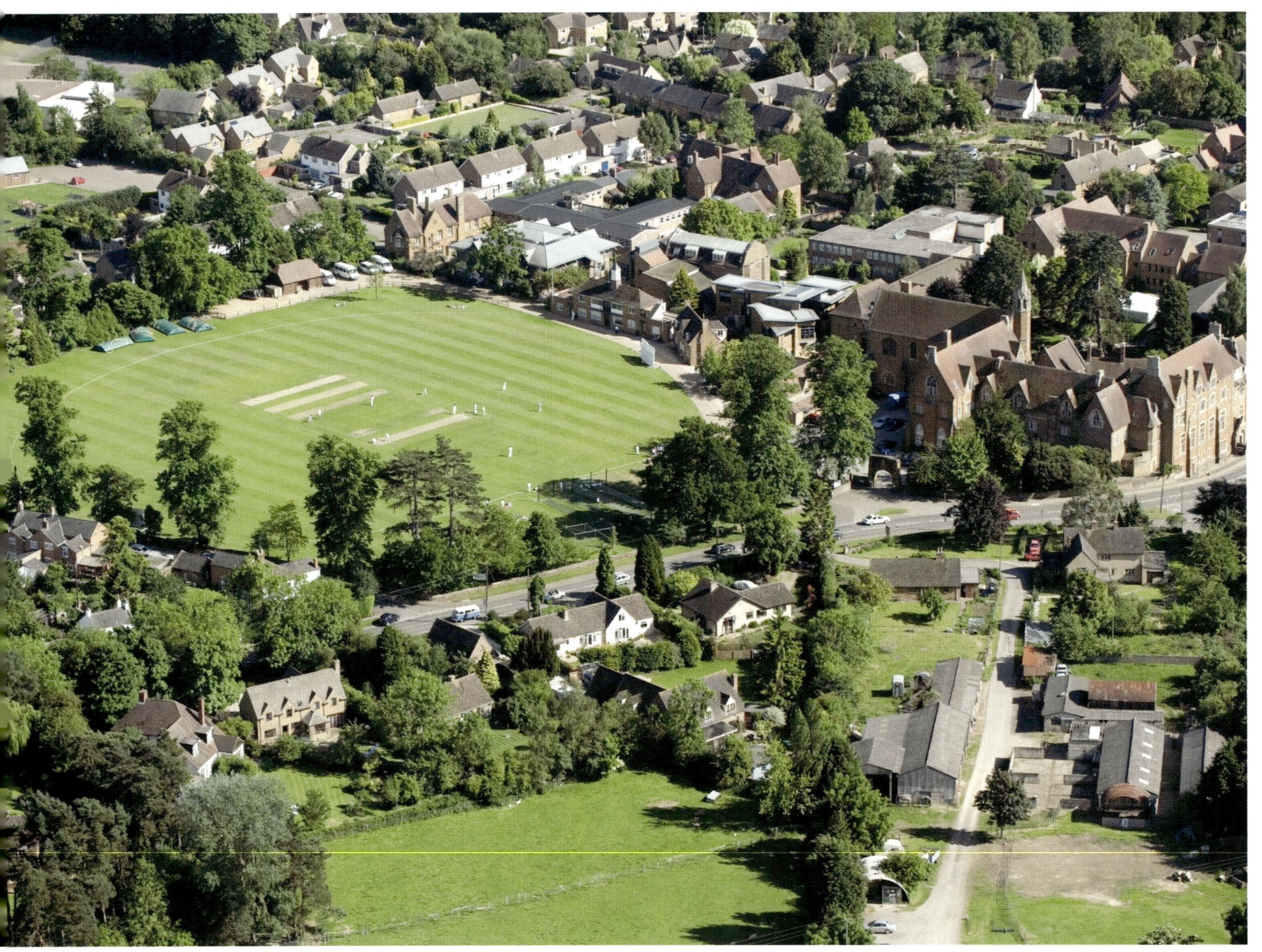

Above and right: Bloxham lies to the south-west of Banbury. Bloxham School, seen in the photograph above, is an independent school founded in 1860. St Mary's Church, seen right, is said to have the tallest spire in Oxfordshire, standing at 198 feet.

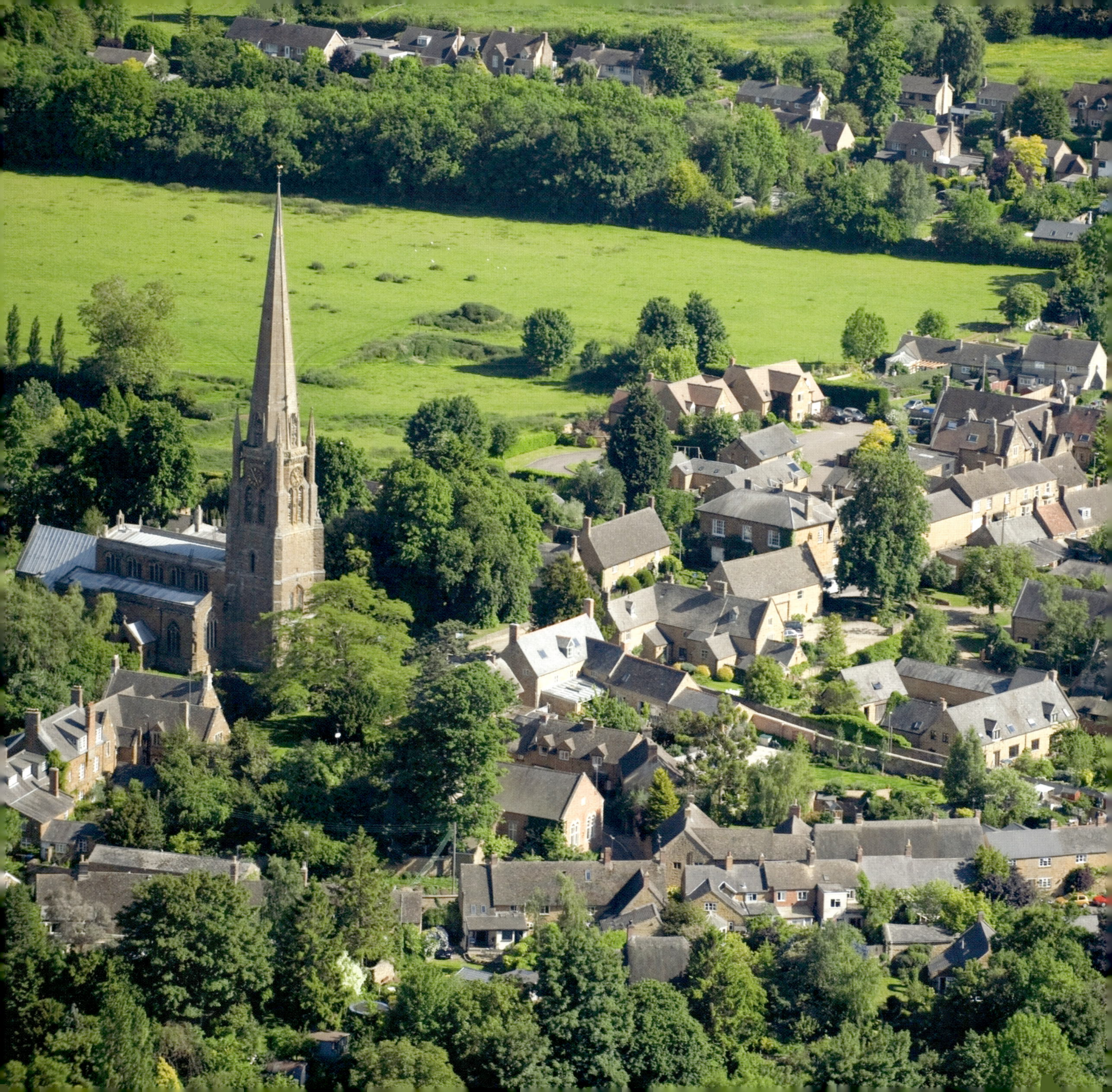

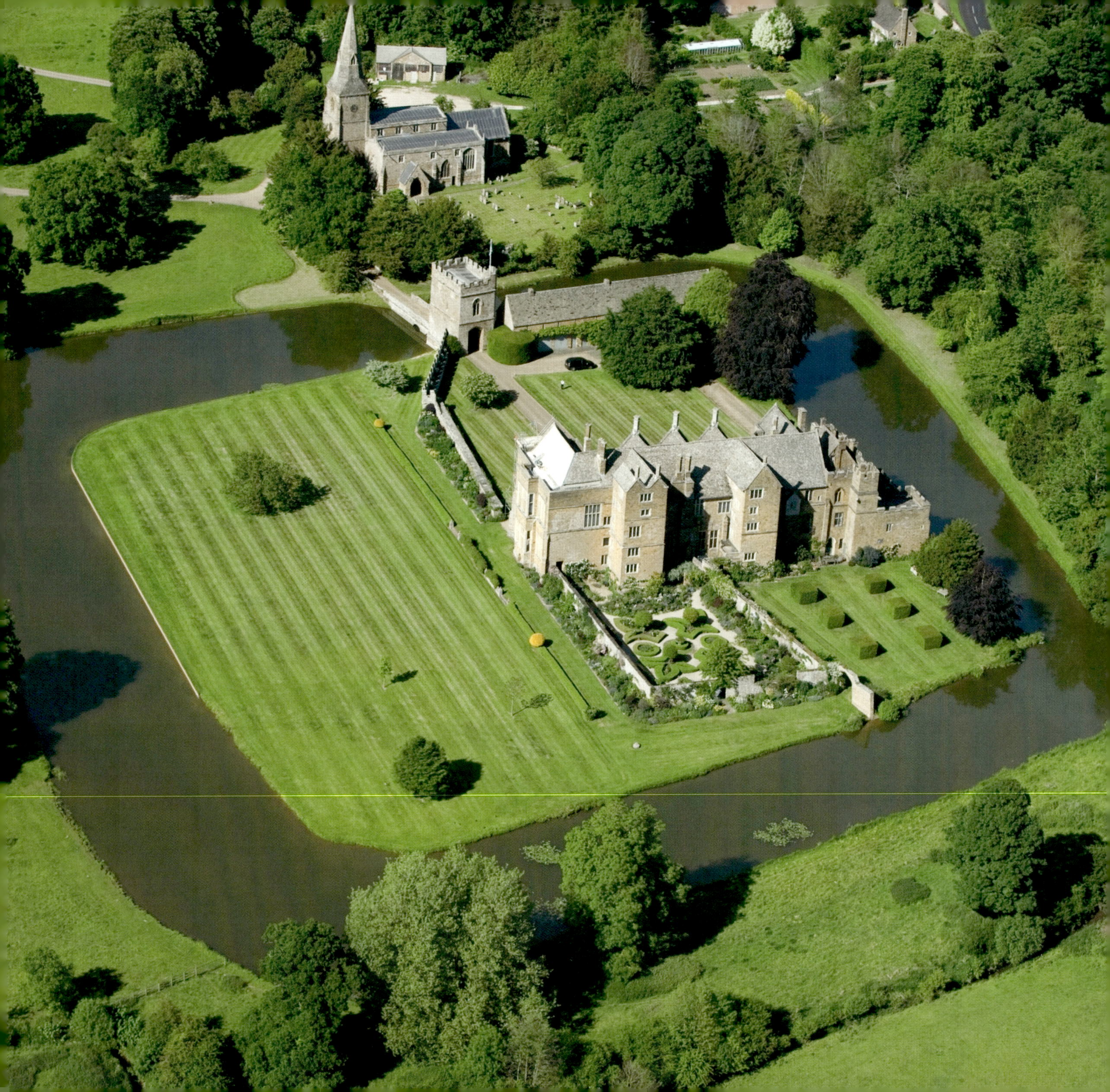

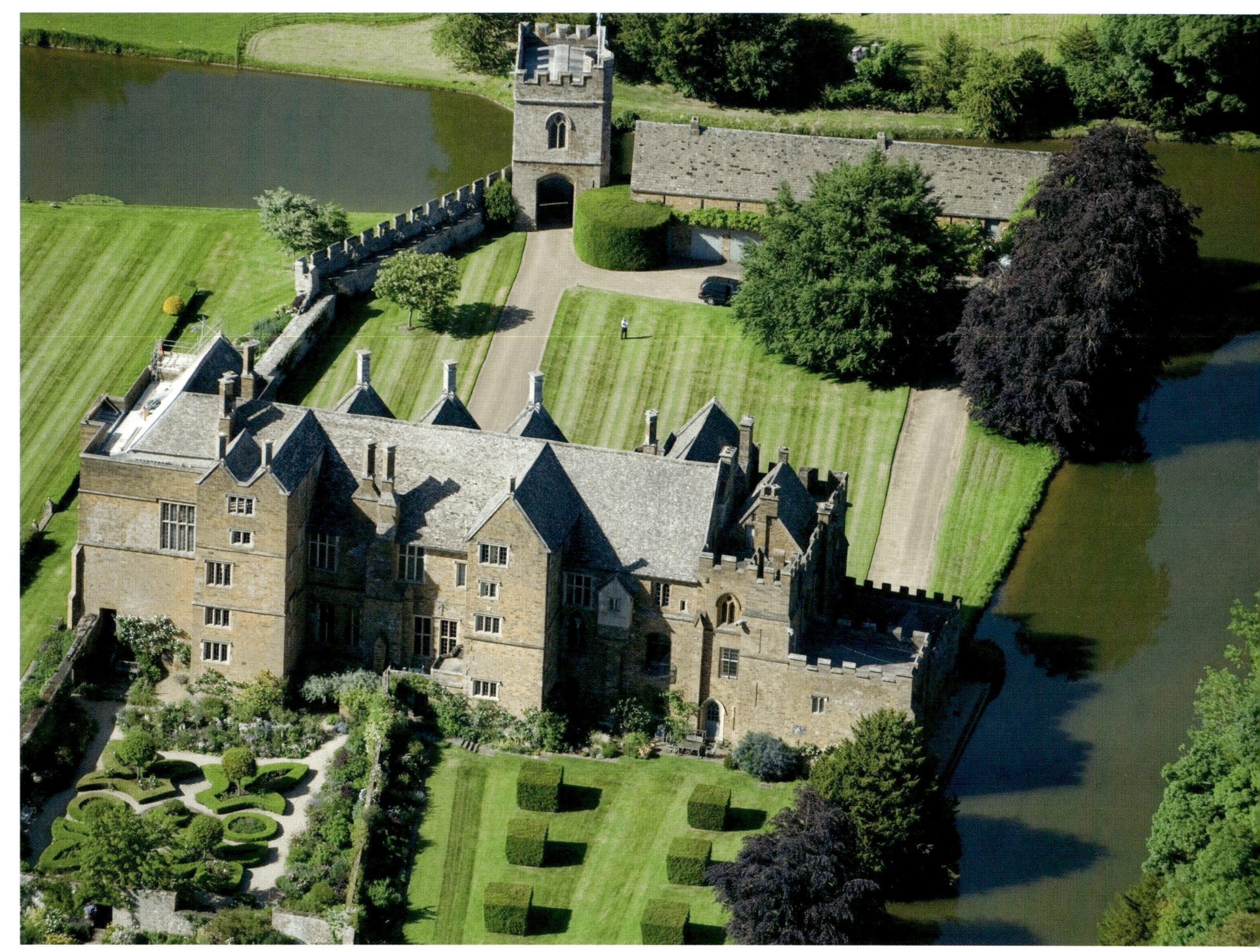

Left and above: Broughton Castle, near Banbury, is one of the best surviving examples of a medieval manor house in Britain. In the seventeenth century the castle came into the hands of William Fiennes, 1st Viscount Saye and Sele, and remains with that family today. It is open to the public at specific times during summer months.

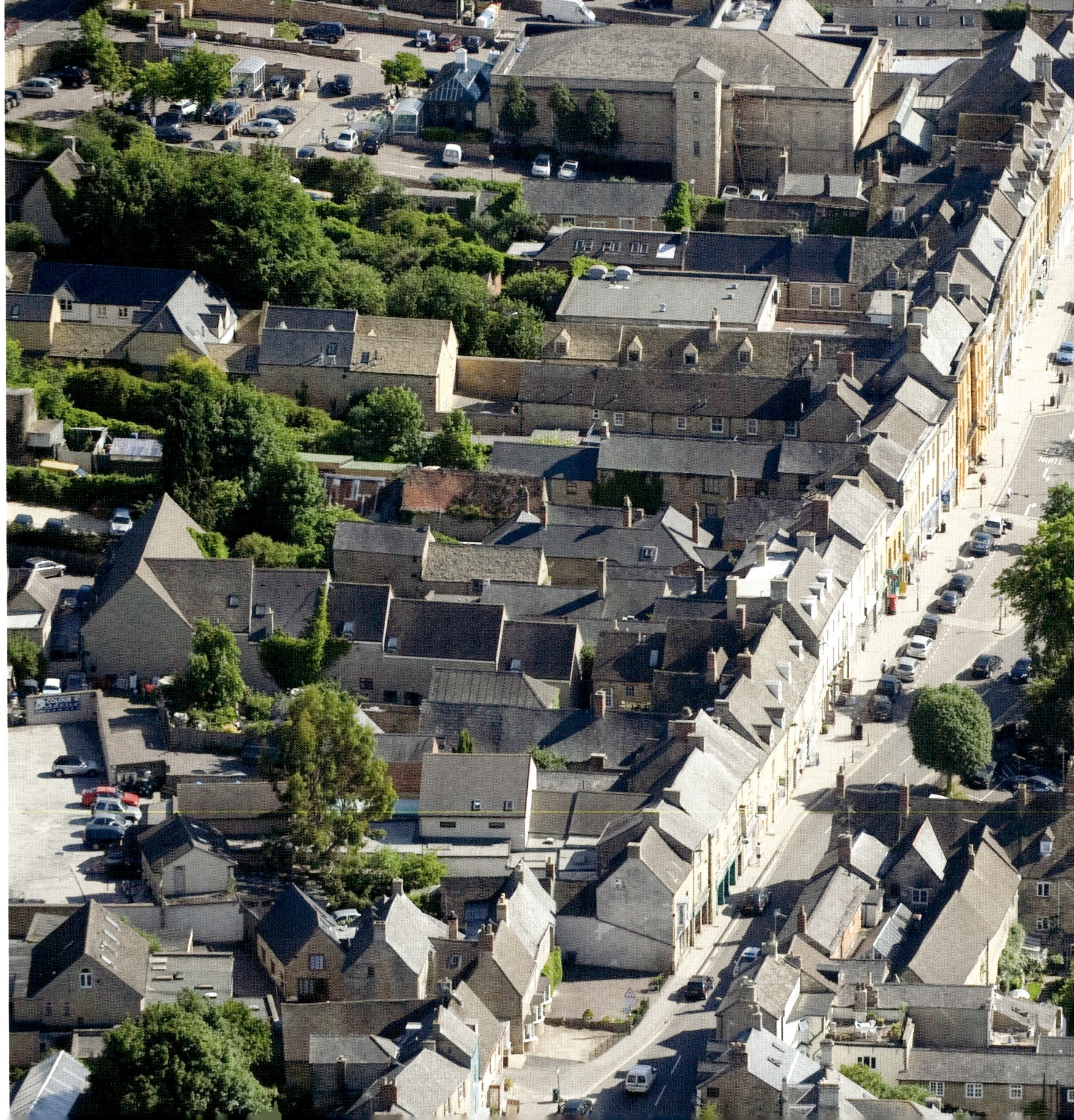

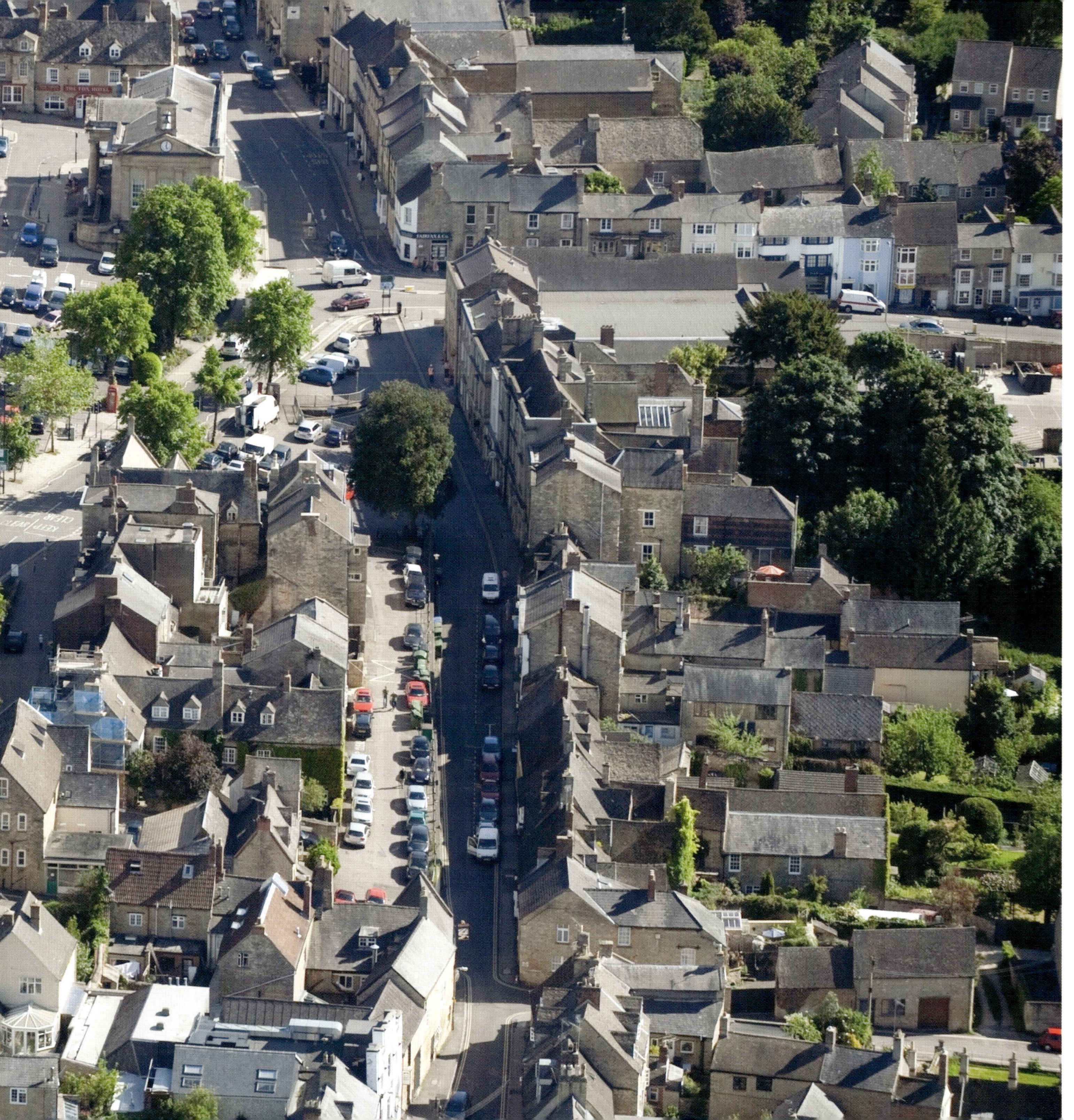

Previous page: Chipping Norton lies in the Cotswolds about 12 miles south-west of Banbury. In the Middle Ages wool production made this part of England one of the wealthiest areas in the country.

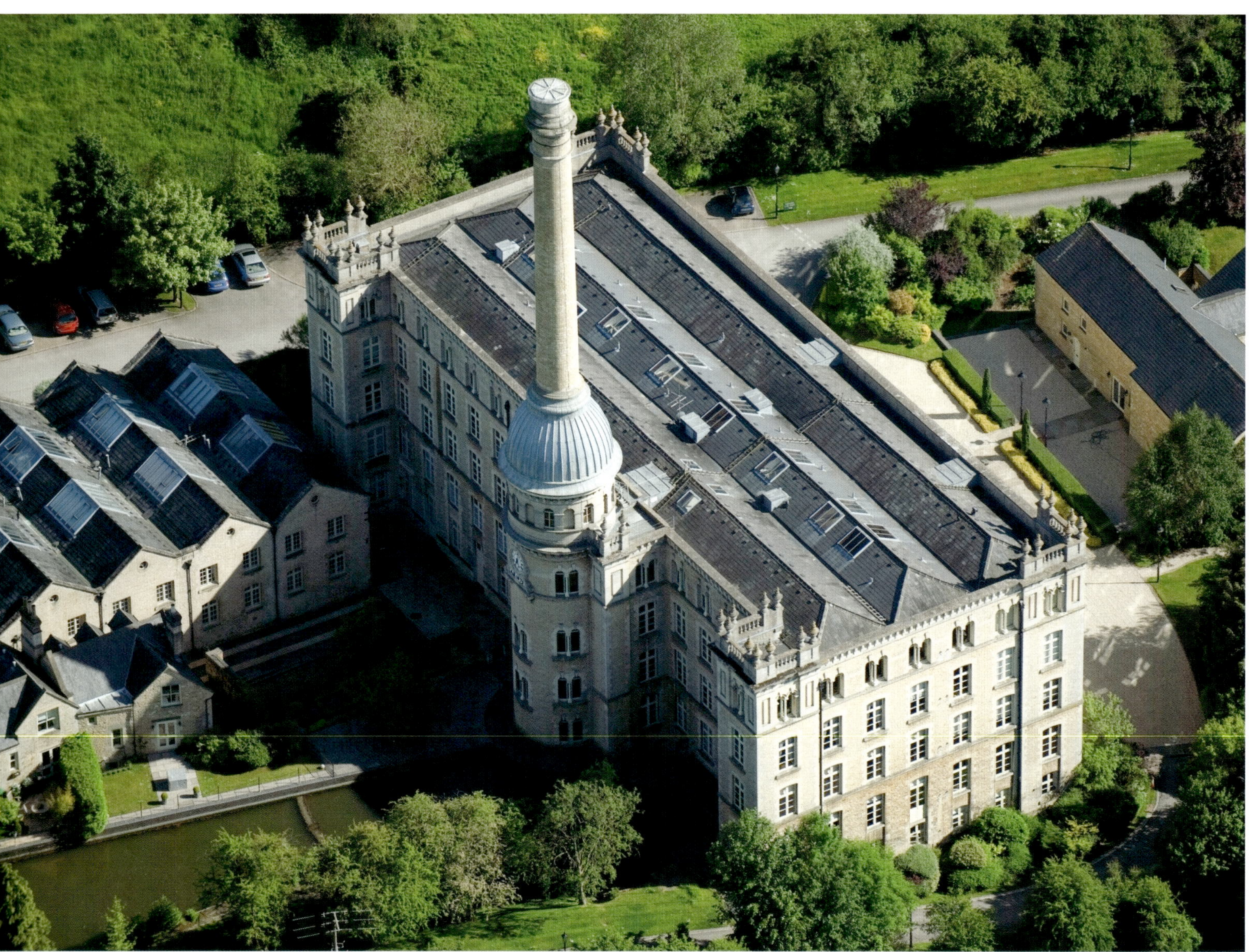

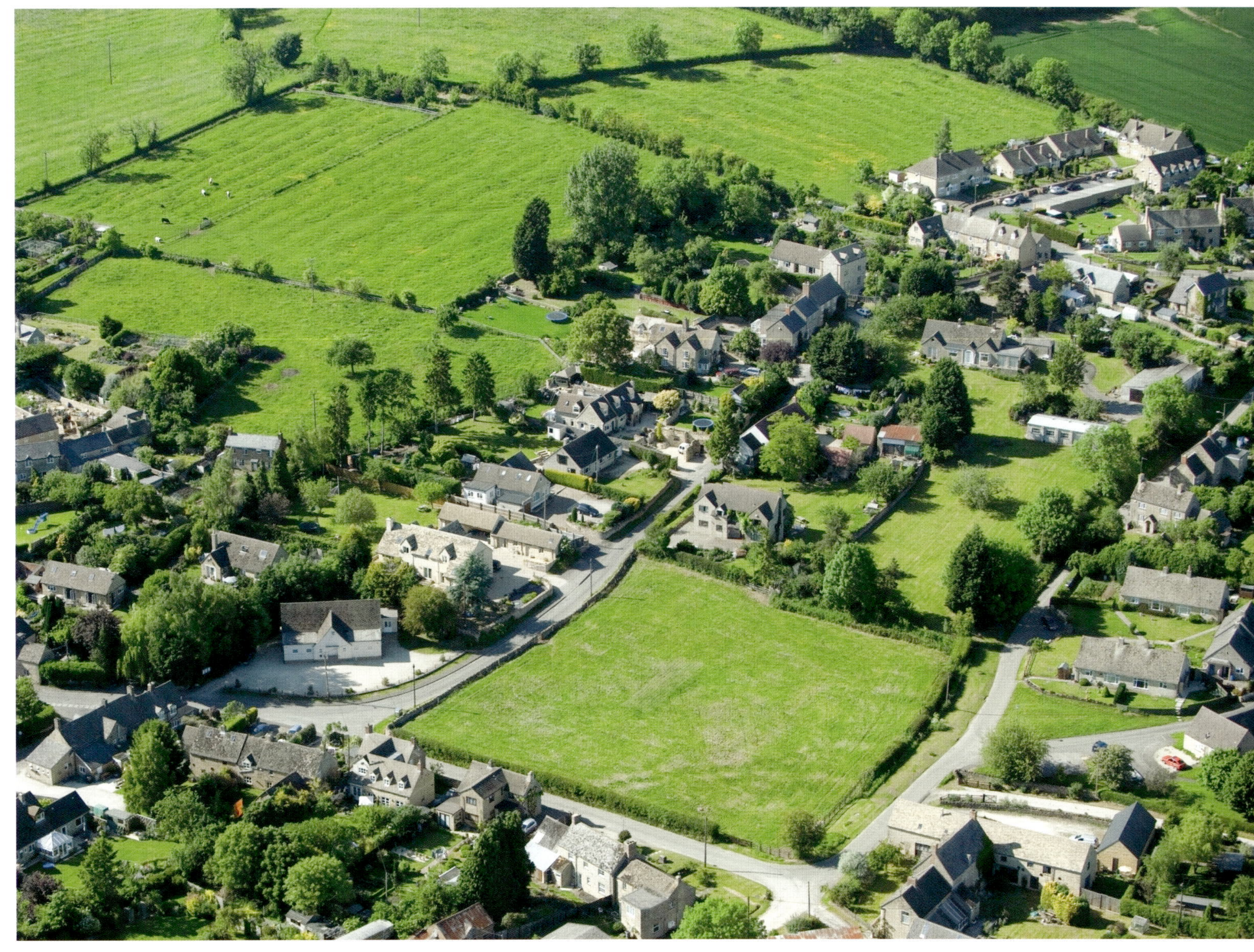

Left: Bliss & Sons Tweed Mill is situated just outside Chipping Norton. It was built around 1873, and remained as a woollen mill until the 1980s. It is now residential apartments.

Above: Salford is a tiny settlement lying to the west of Chipping Norton.

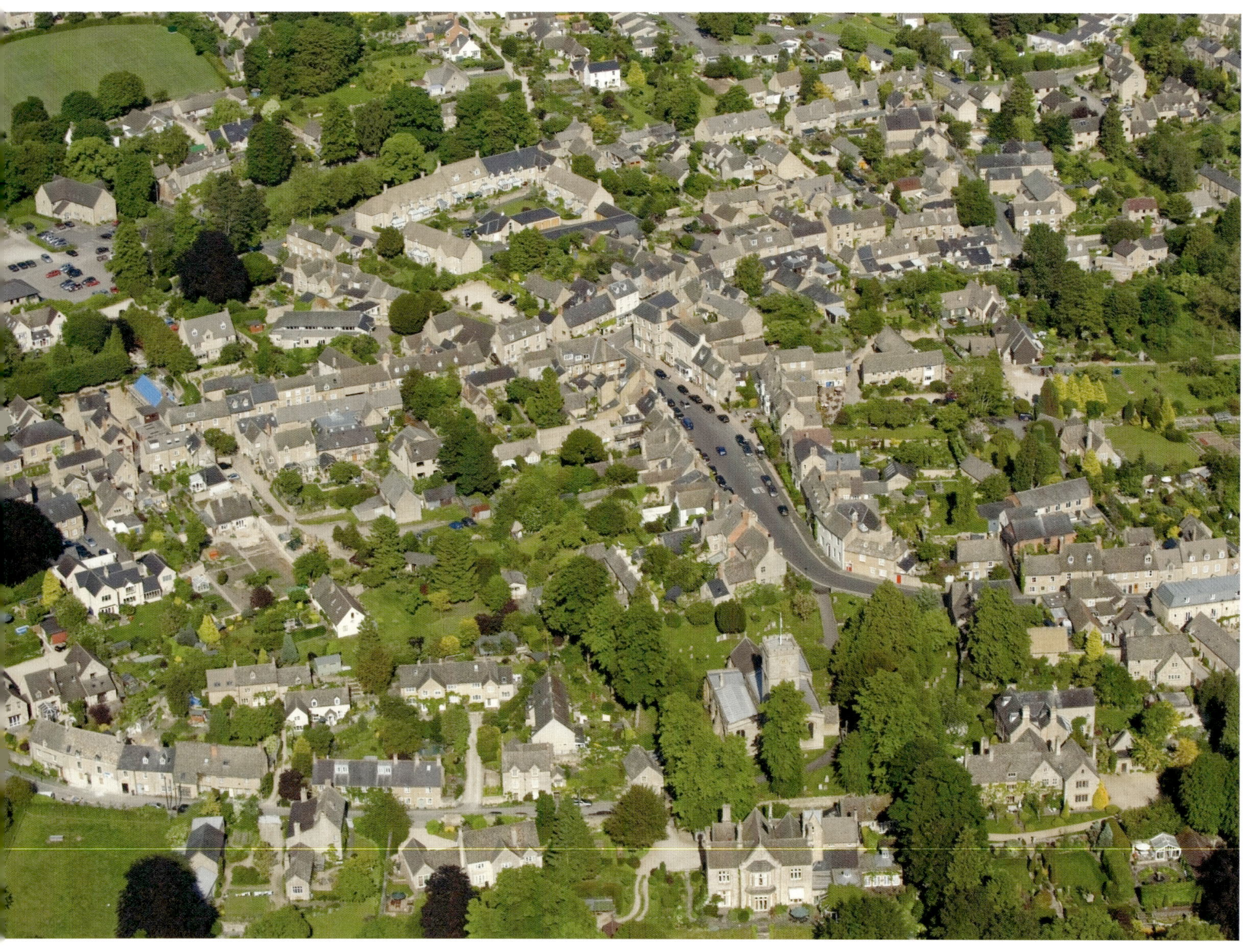

Above and right: Charlbury lies in the valley of the Evenlode river on the edge of the Wychwood Forest and the Cotswolds. Apart from its intrinsic attractiveness, rail links to Oxford and, via Stratford, to Birmingham make this a desirable area in which to live.

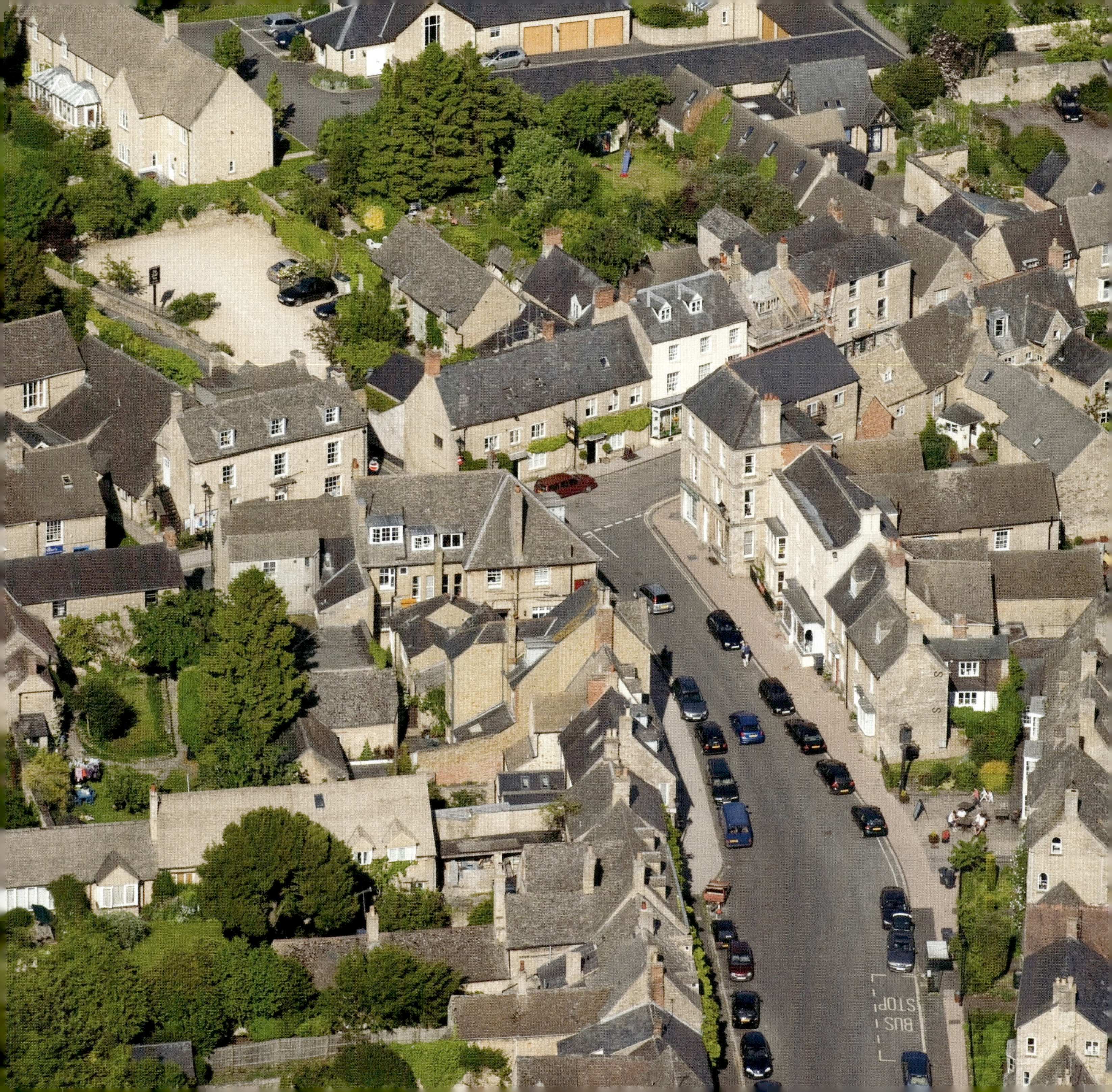

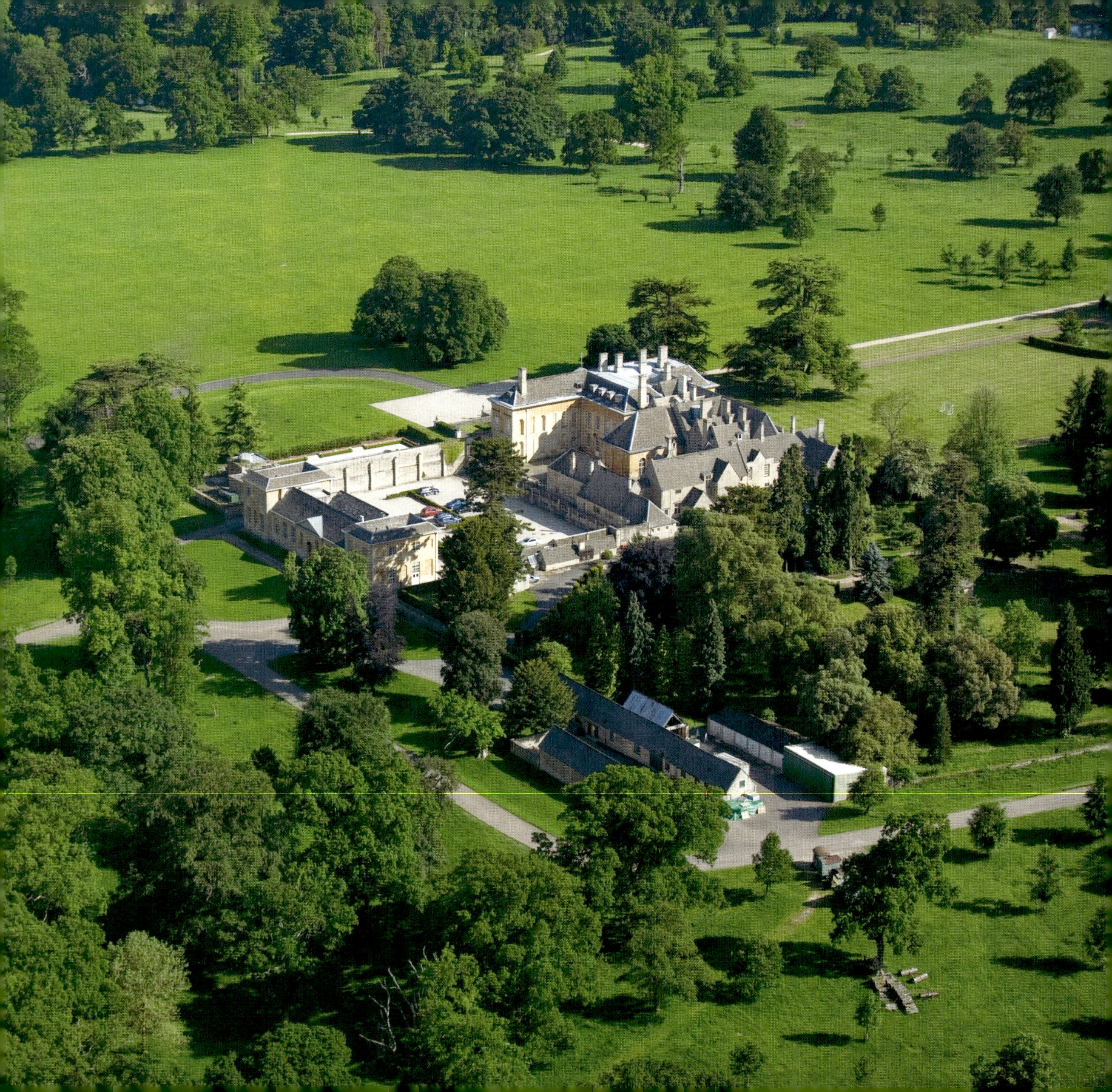

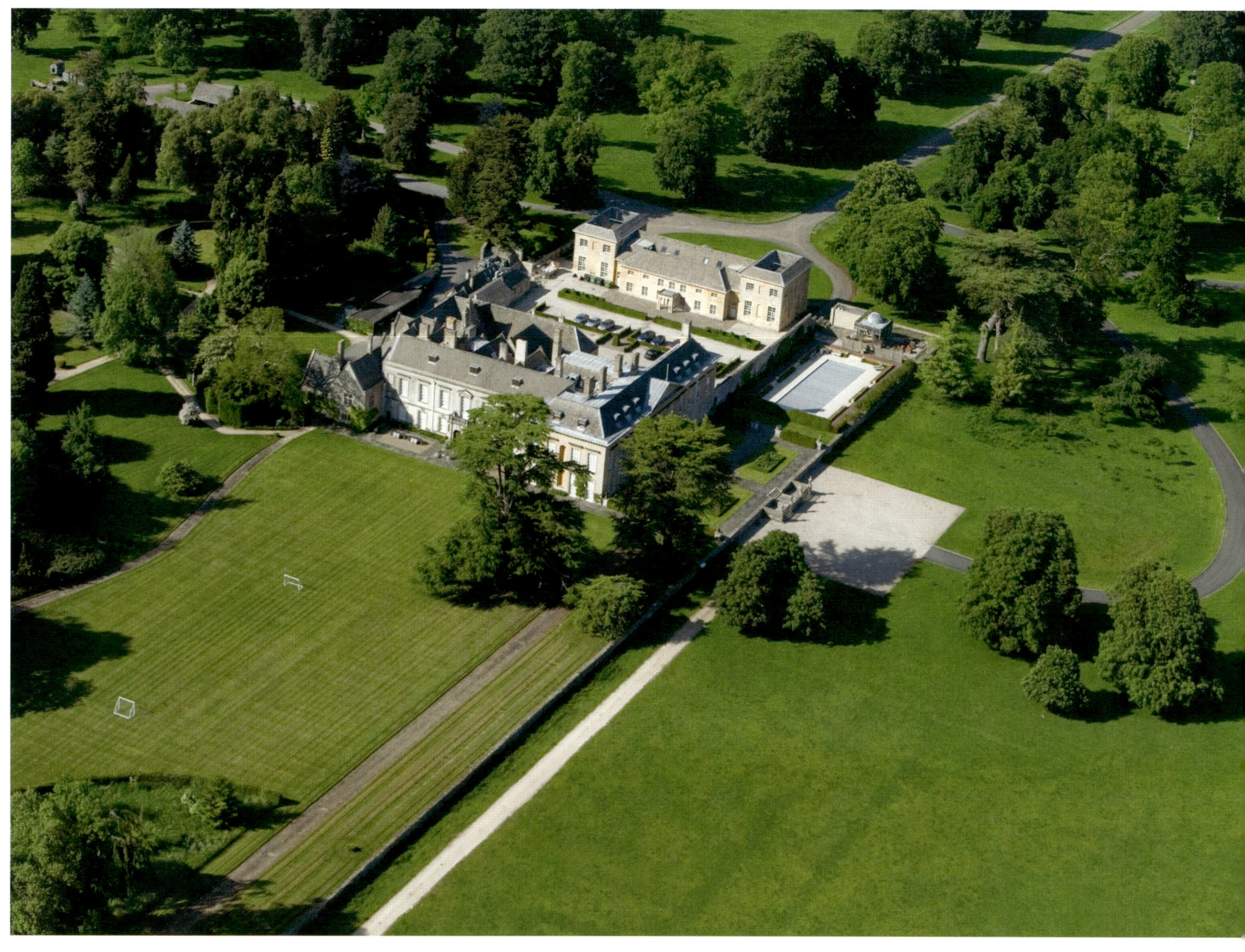

Left and above: Cornbury Park, near Charlbury, is the family home of Lord and Lady Rotherwick. The estate includes some 1700 acres of the most ancient forest in Britain today and is a protected environment for native wildlife. The annual Cornbury Festival is held here in July.

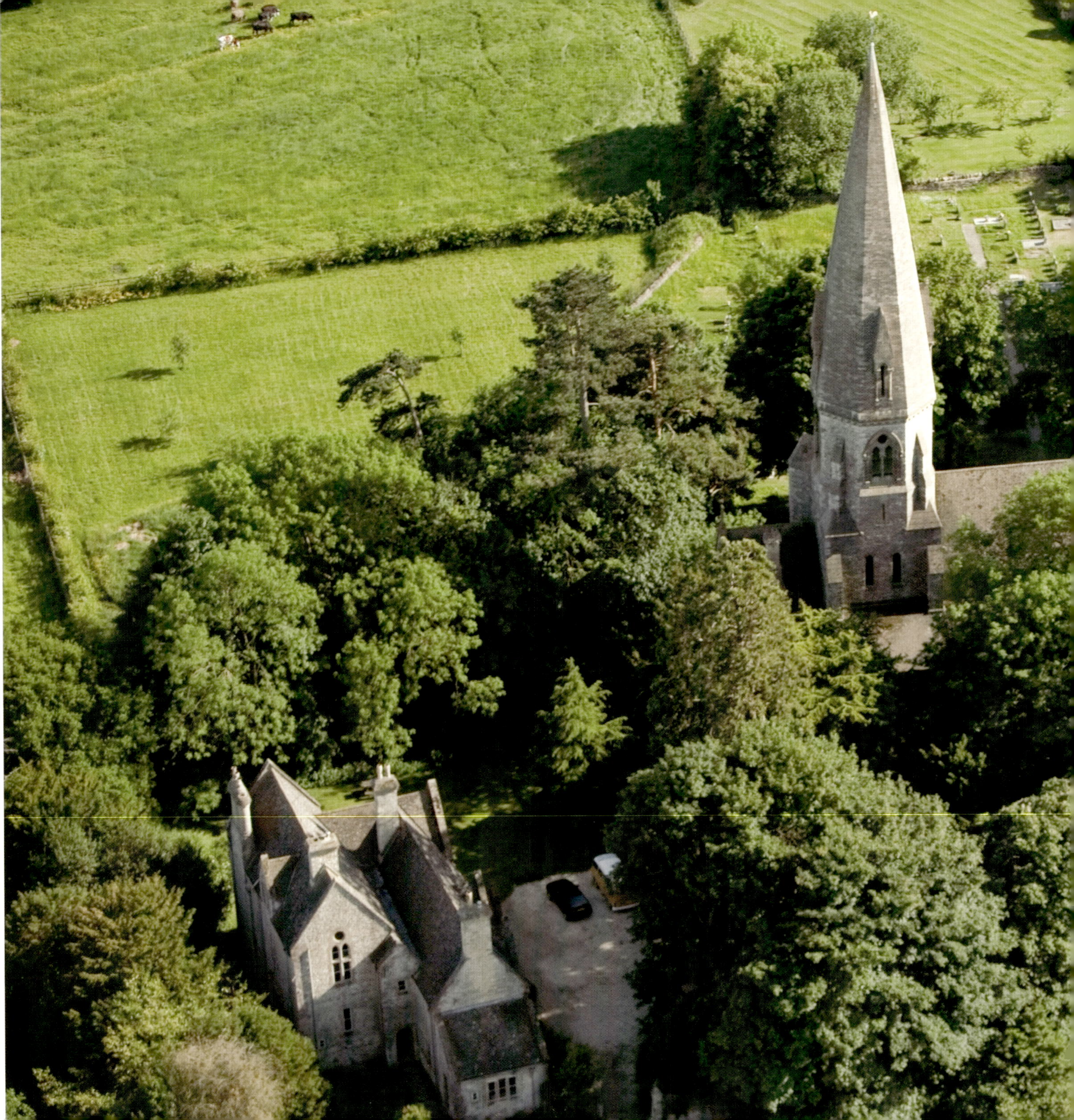

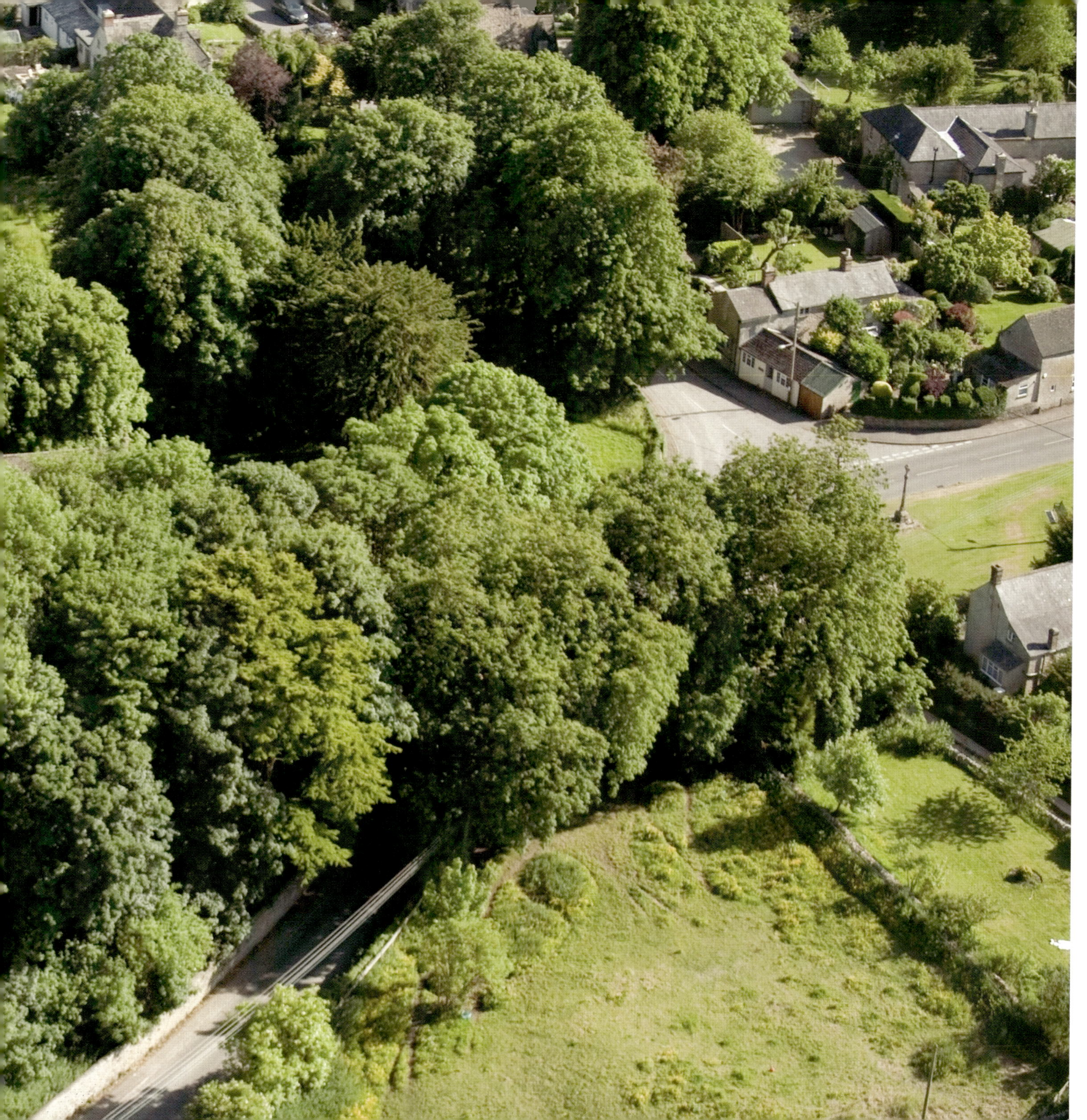

Previous page: Leafield is a village on the edge of the Cotswolds, 18 miles north-west of Oxford, in the middle of the triangle formed by the towns of Witney, Burford and Charlbury. The spire of the church of St Michael and All Angels dominates the skyline for miles around; originally reaching 145ft 6ins, but following damage and later rebuilding it is now somewhat shorter.

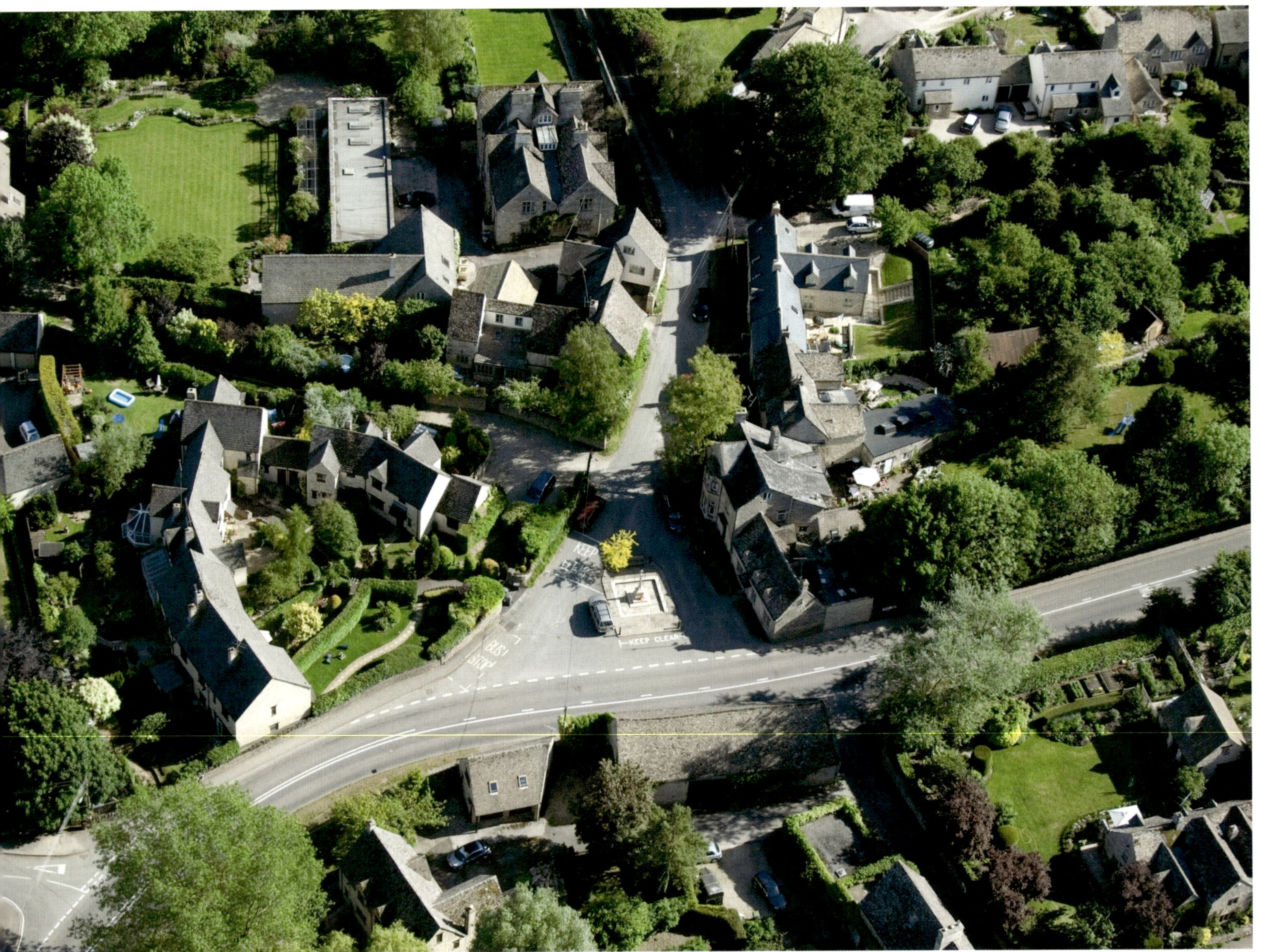

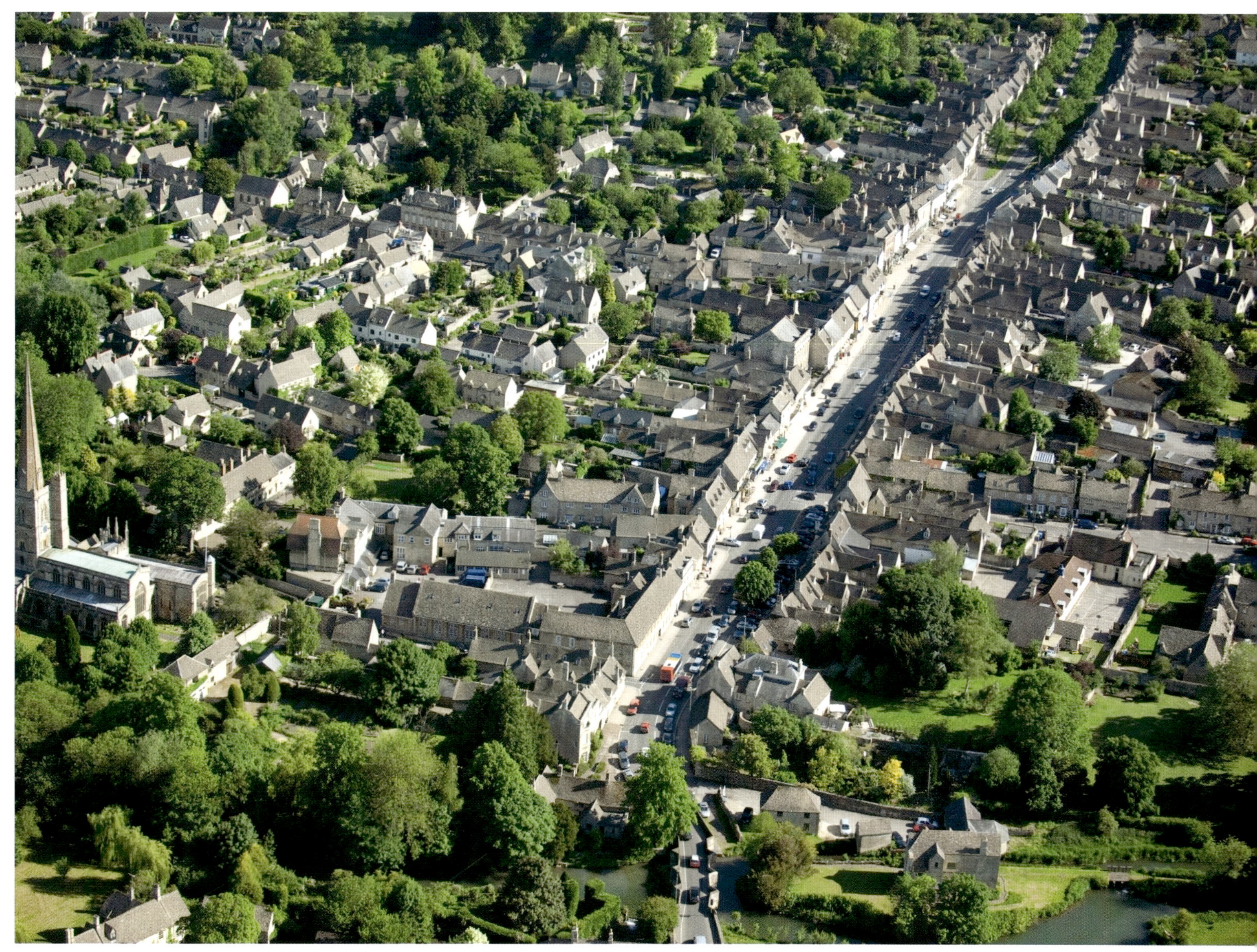

Left: Fulbrook is a typically attractive Cotswold village situated a short distance from Burford in the Windrush valley.

Above: Burford is known as the 'gateway to the Cotswolds'. Firmly on the tourist map it boasts a wide variety of bespoke shops, among them many antique emporiums.

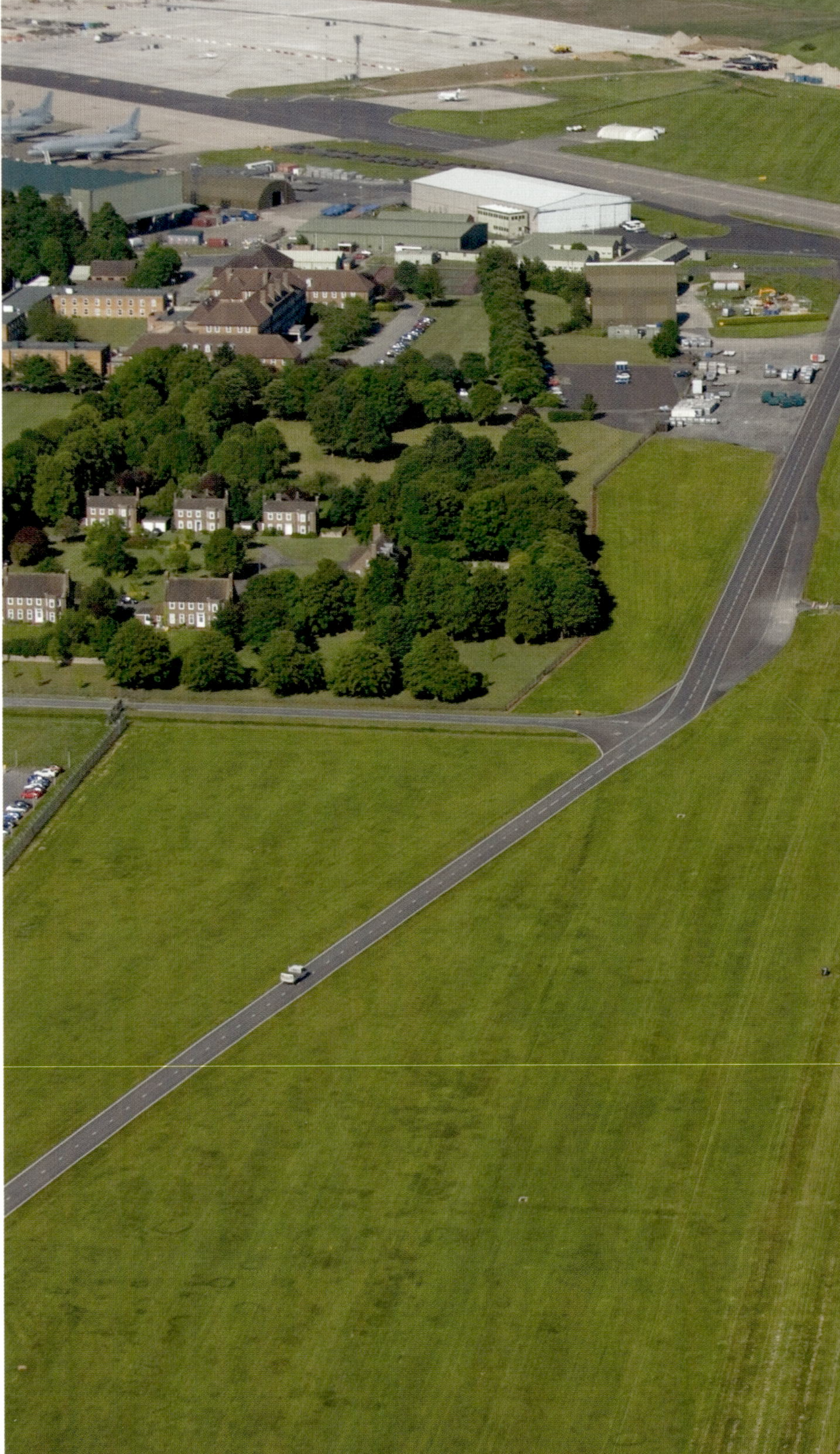

Looking along the runway RAF Brize Norton. This is the largest of all the RAF airbases in the UK.

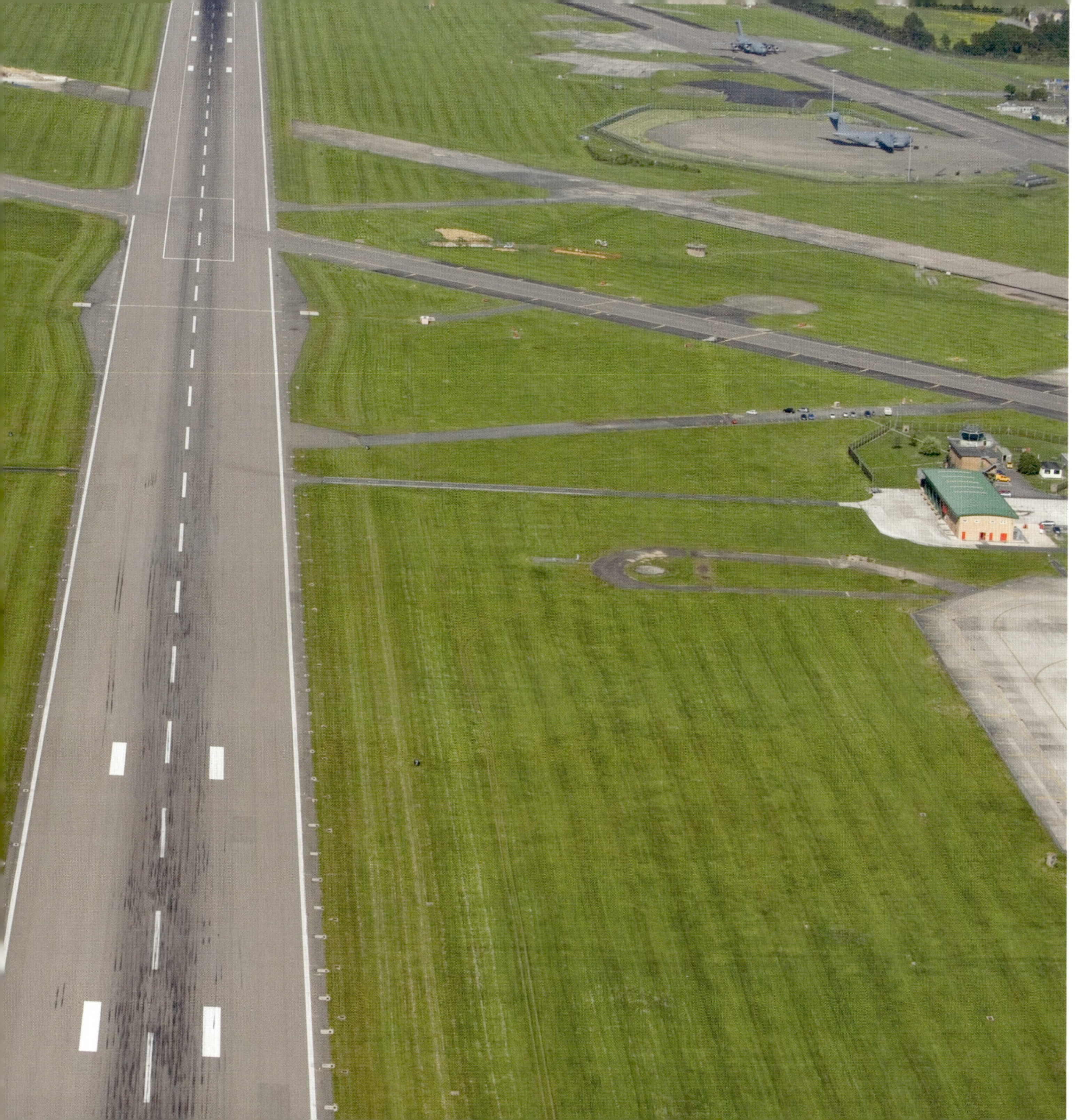

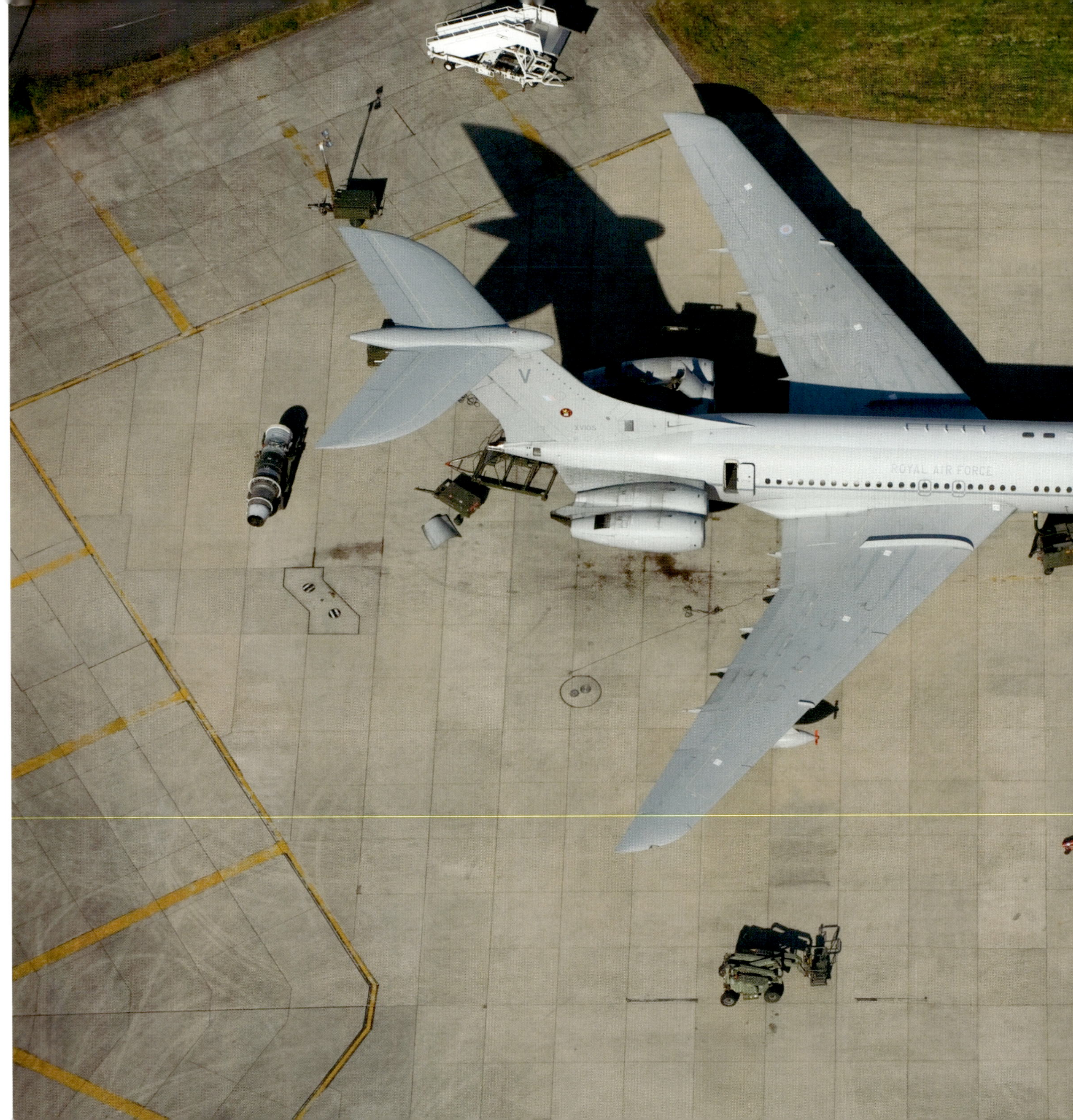

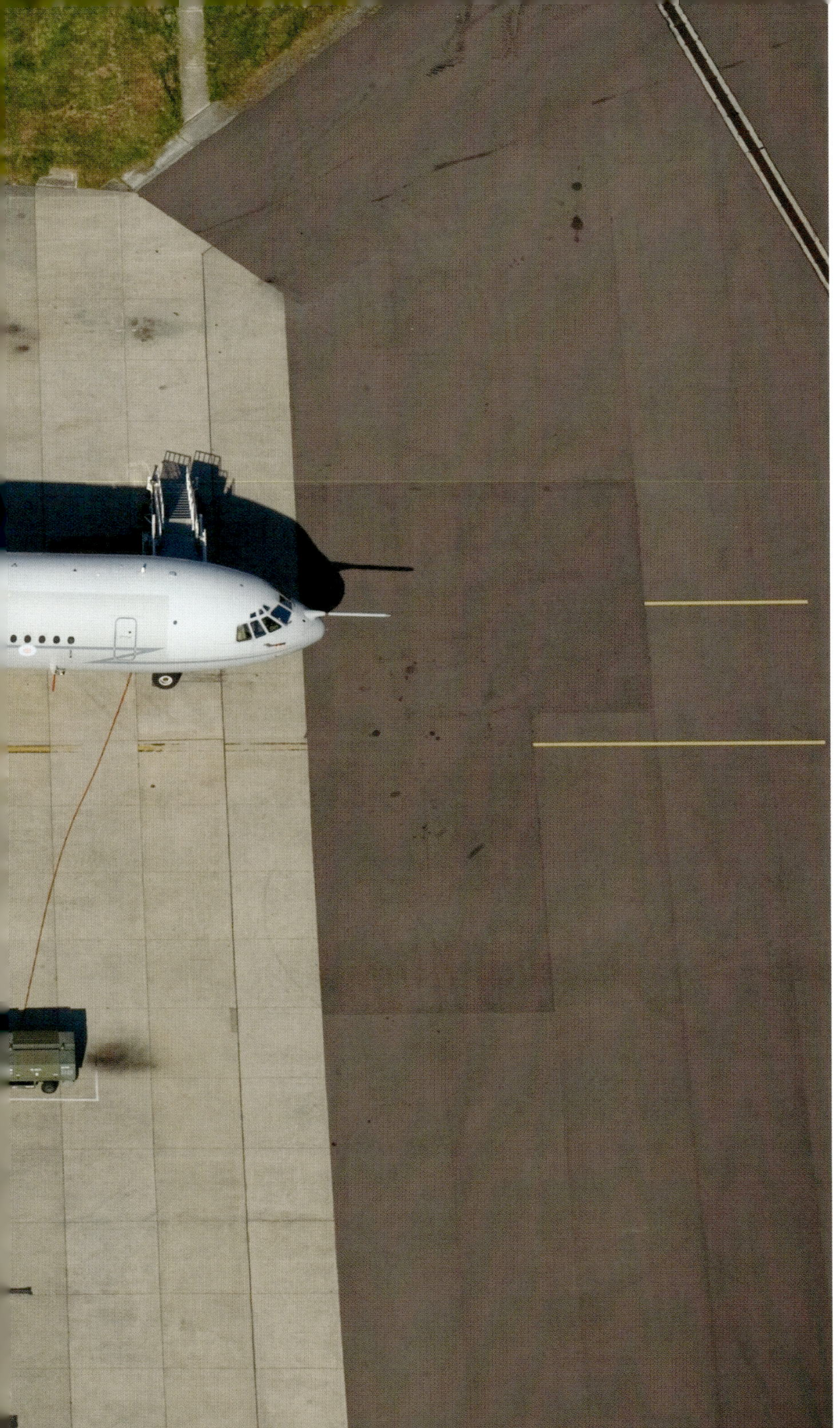

One of a handful of VC10 aircraft which remain in service as aerial refuelling and transport aircraft with the RAF. Here at RAF Brize Norton.

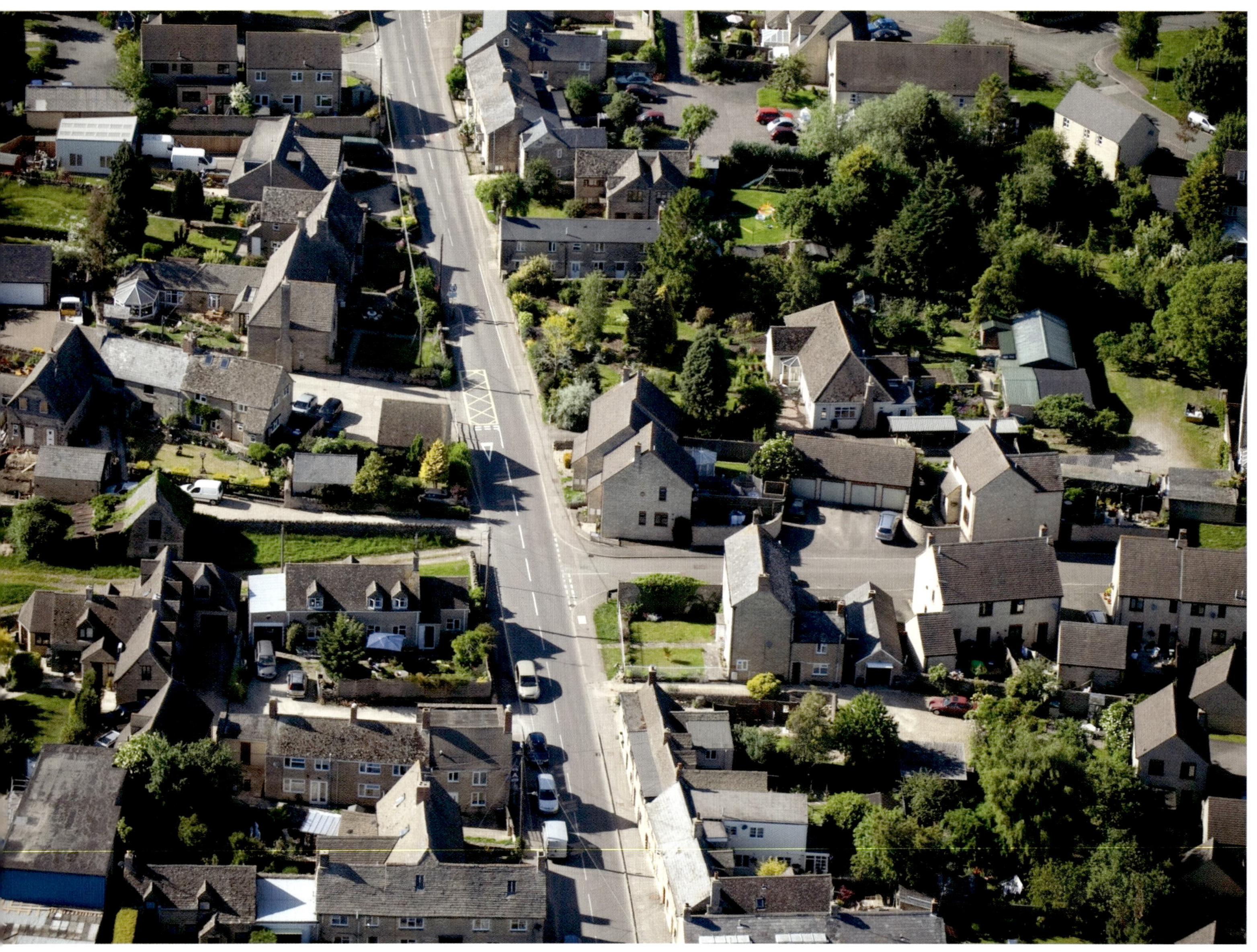

Above: Looking down on to Station Road in the village of Brize Norton, which gave its name to the RAF station.

Right: The immense size of the parish church of St Mary in Witney reflects the wealth that was created by the wool trade in the Middle Ages when it was enlarged from an earlier Norman building.

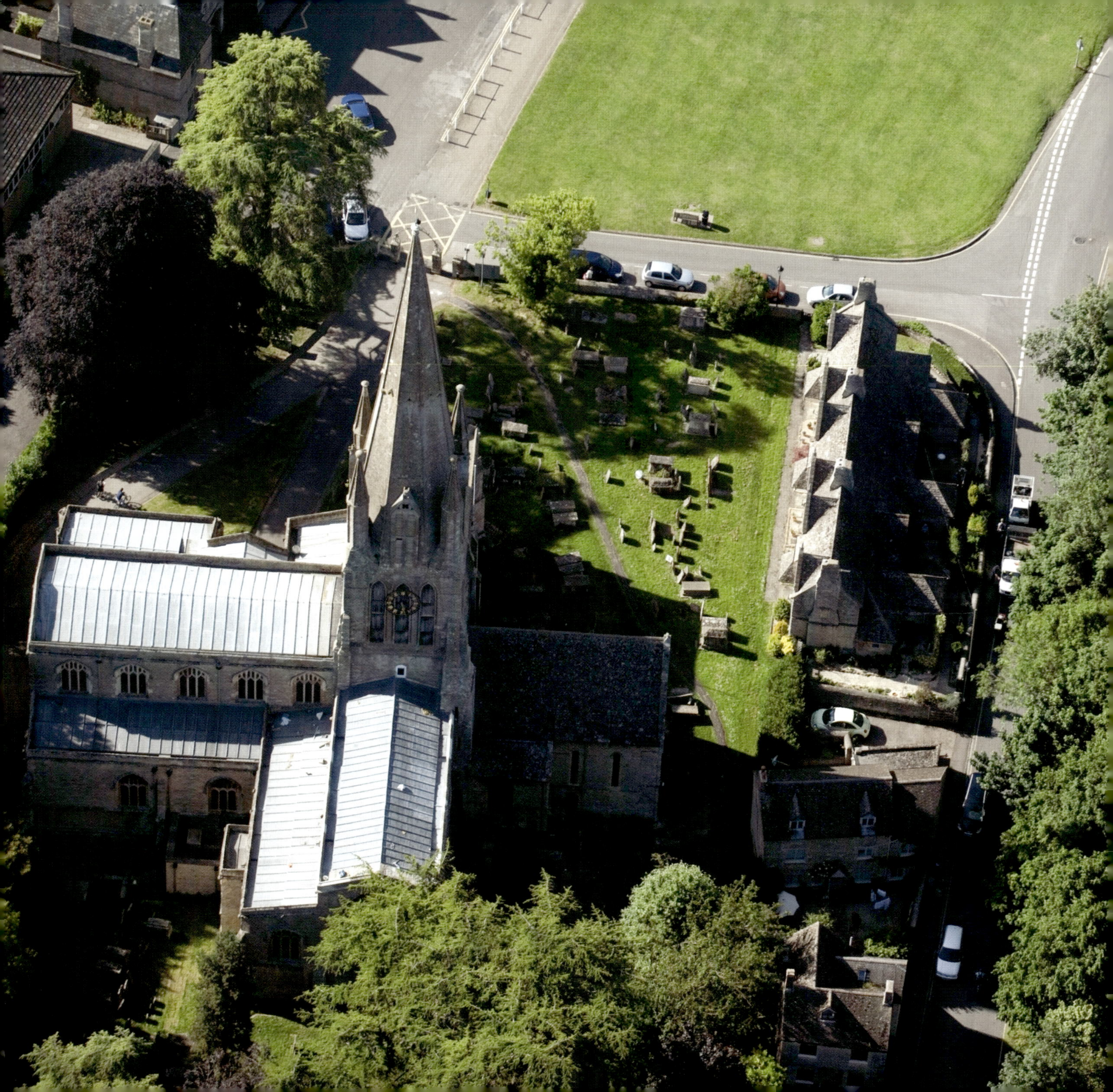

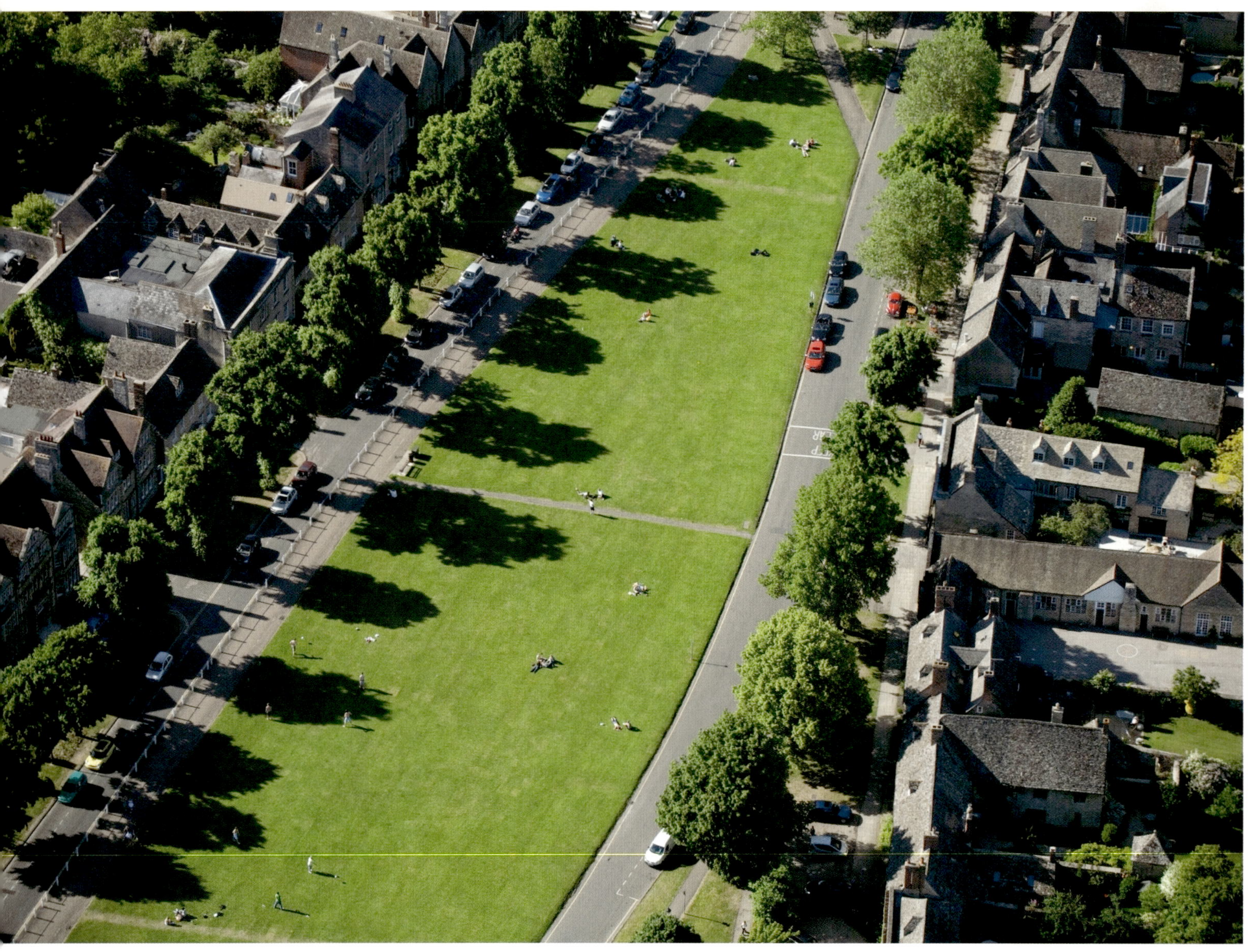

Above: Church Green, Witney. Famed for its woollen blankets, water for the production in the mills at Witney was drawn from the River Windrush.

Right: The market square Witney lies at the junction of the two main streets and contains the Buttercross, a medieval building where women from nearby villages gathered to sell butter and eggs.

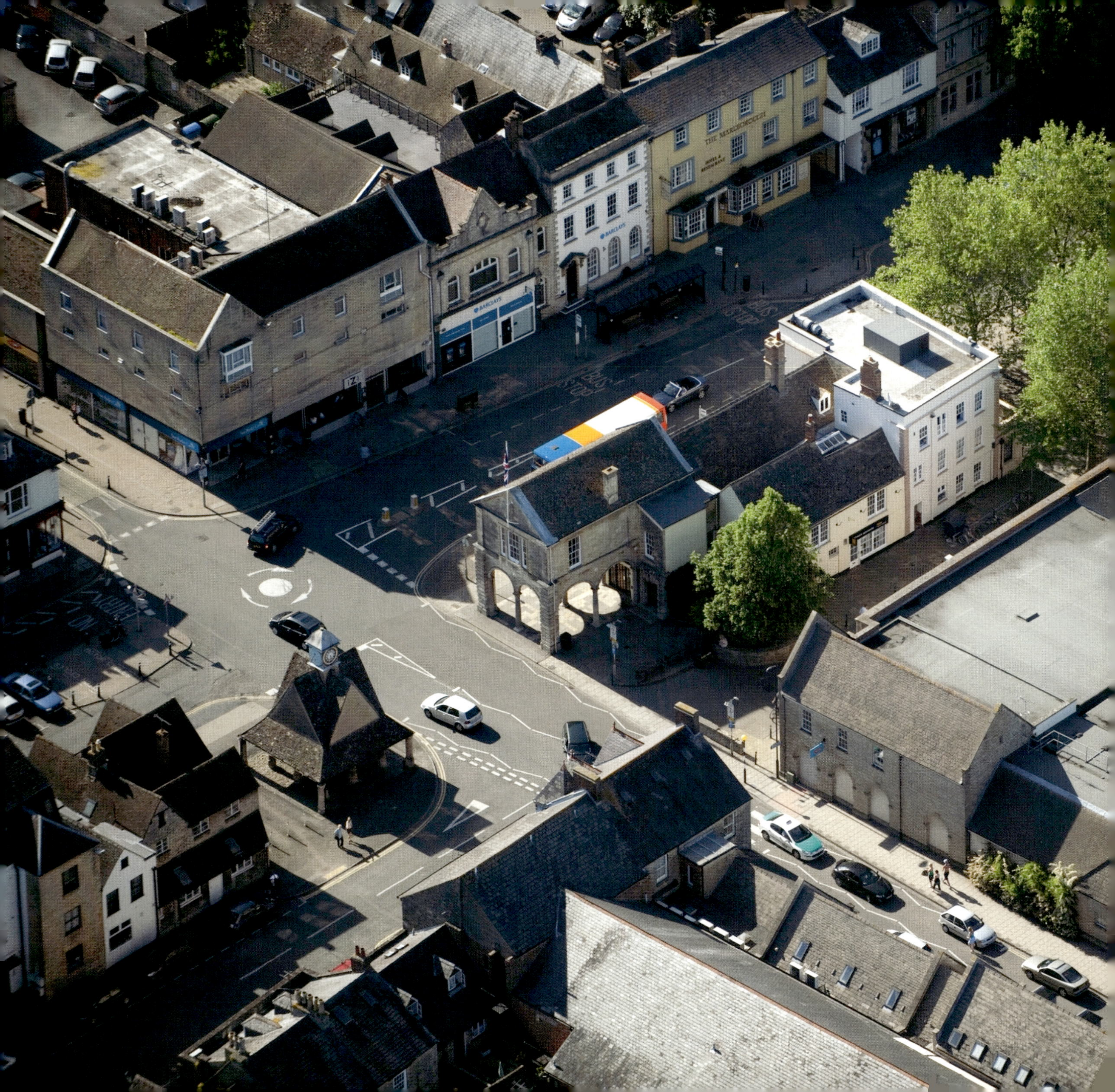

THE MARLBOROUGH
HOTEL & RESTAURANT
BARCLAYS
BARCLAYS
BUS STOP
BUS STOP
IZI

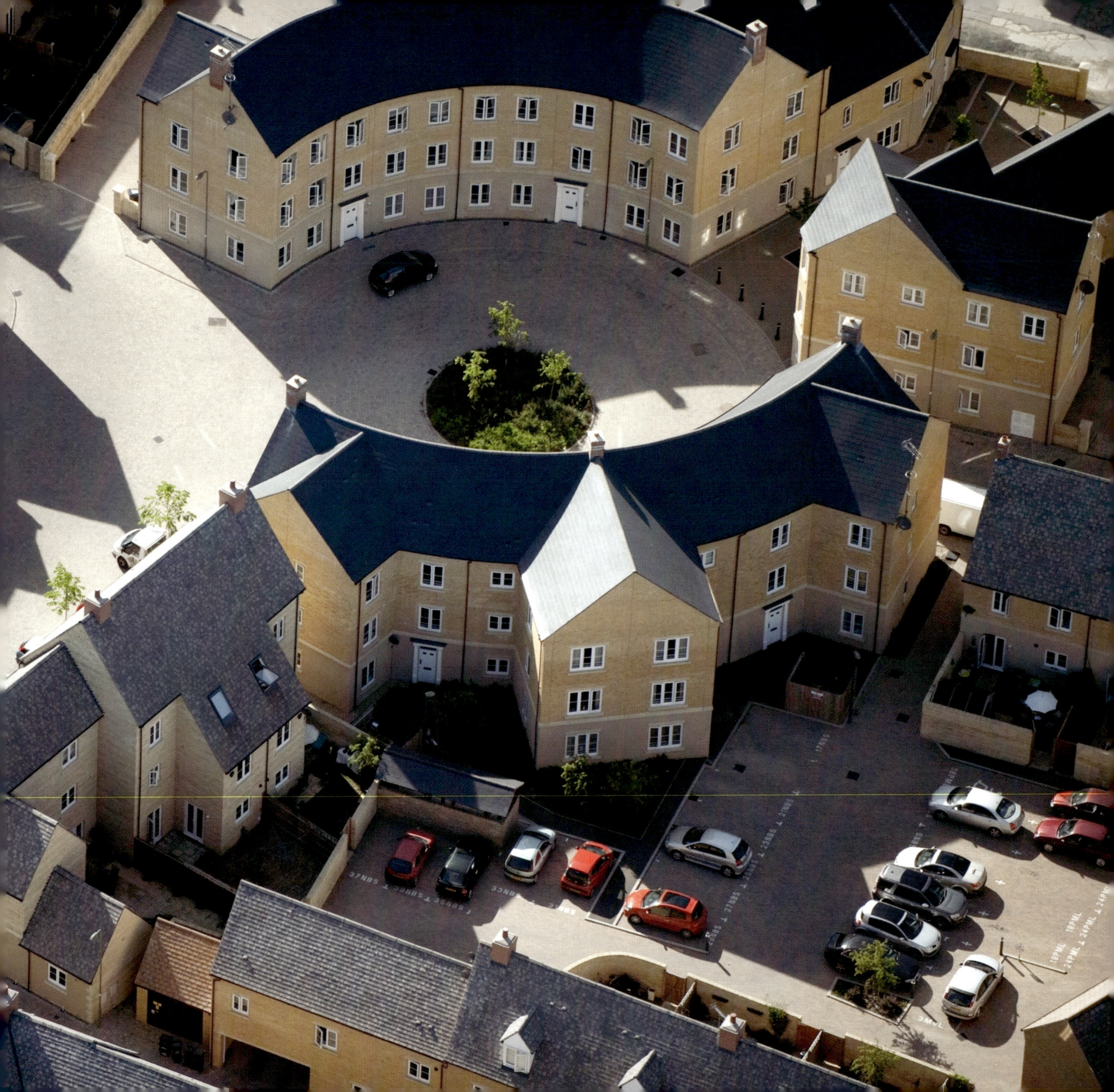

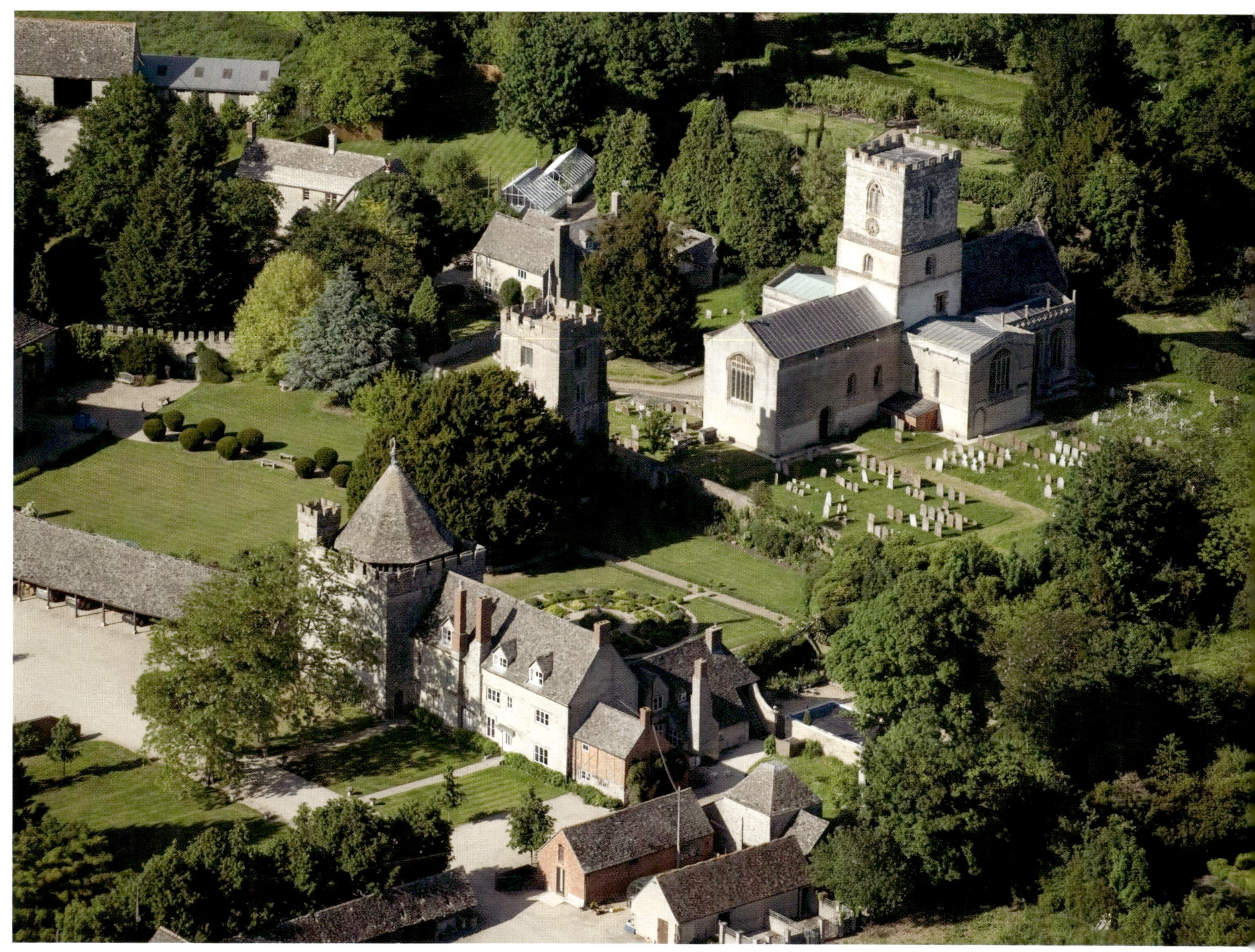

Left: Modern housing developments contrast with the older parts of Witney.

Above: The Manor House at Stanton Harcourt was built by the Harcourt family in the late fourteenth century. One of the surviving parts is the medieval kitchen with its octagonal roof seen here.

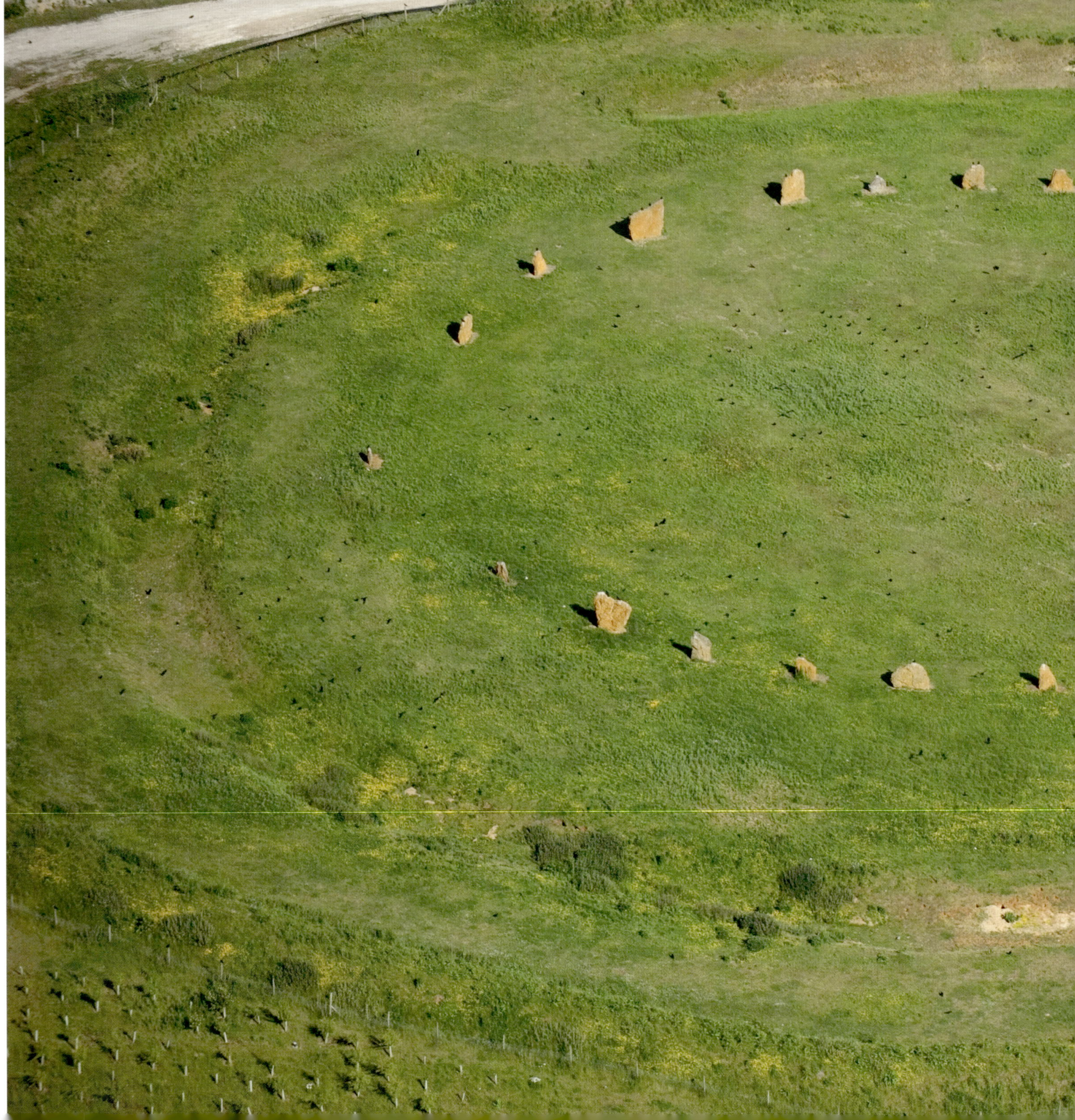

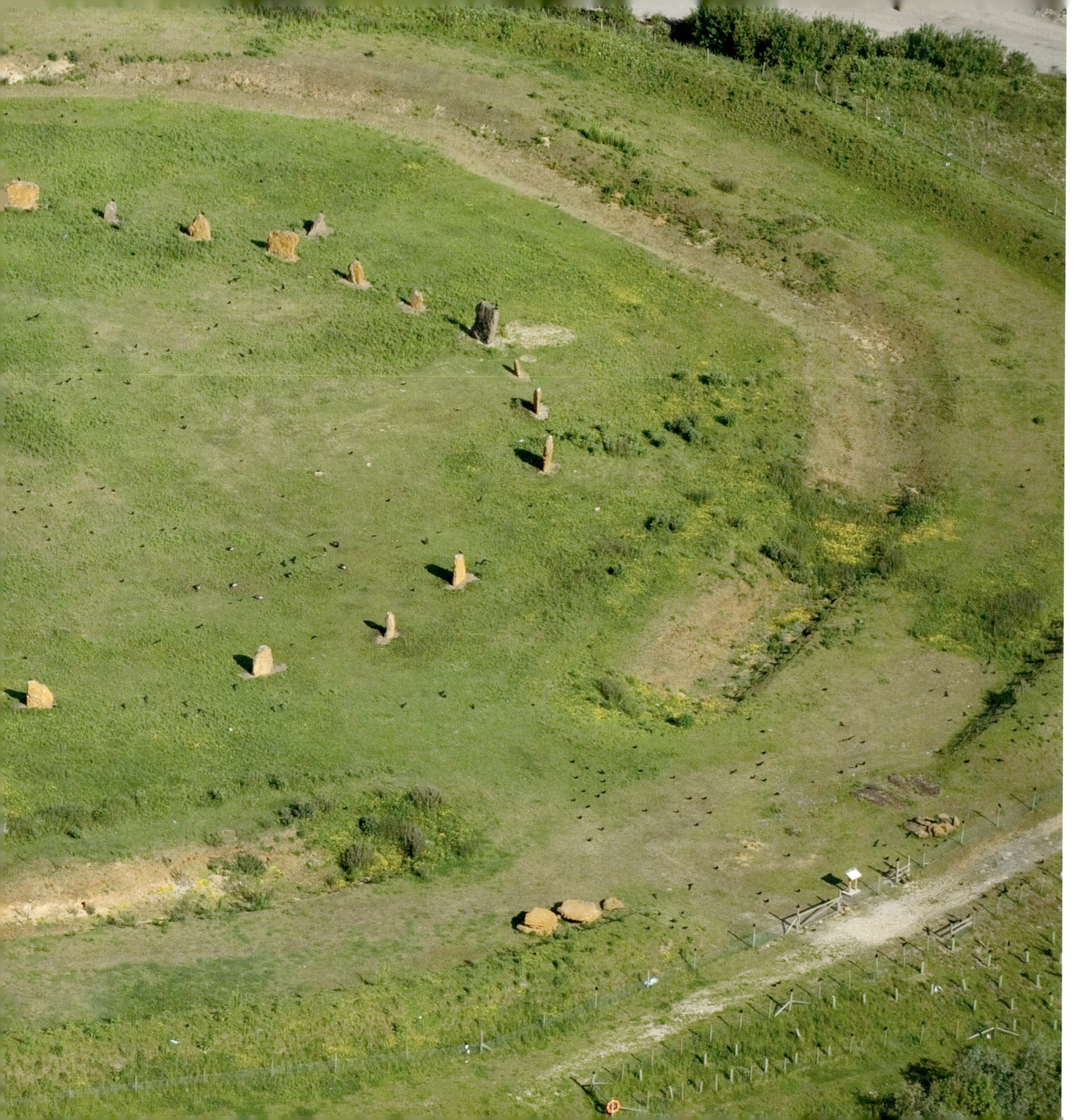

Previous page: The Devil's Quoits, Stanton Harcourt, would once have been one of the most important standing stone circle sites in Britain. The circle is now thought to be between 4000 and 5000 years old and is partly a Scheduled Ancient Monument. At one time much plundered so only a handful of stone remained, in 2008 a fully restored monument was reopened.

Boats moored at a secluded marina on the River Thames near to Eaton Hastings.

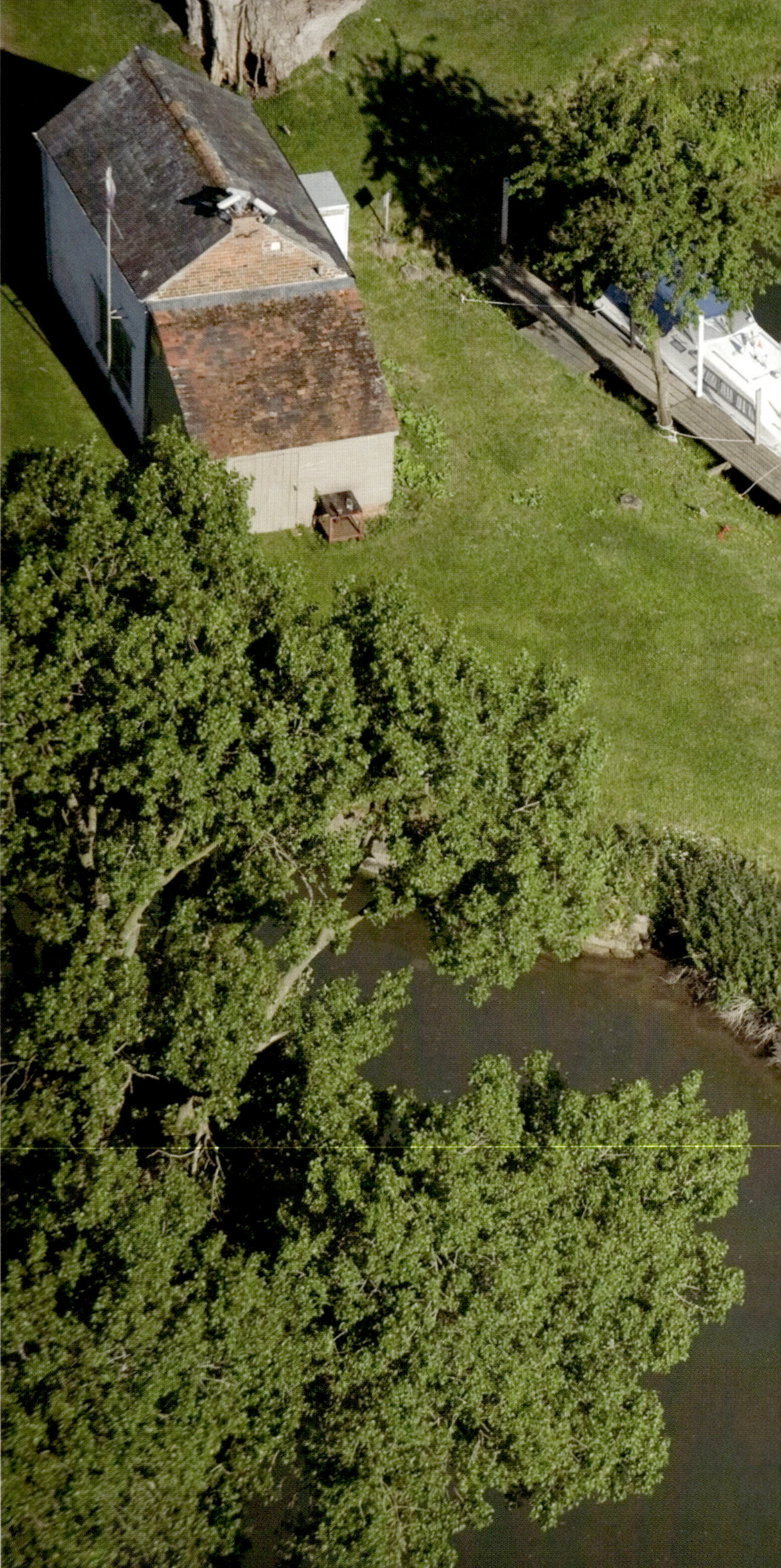

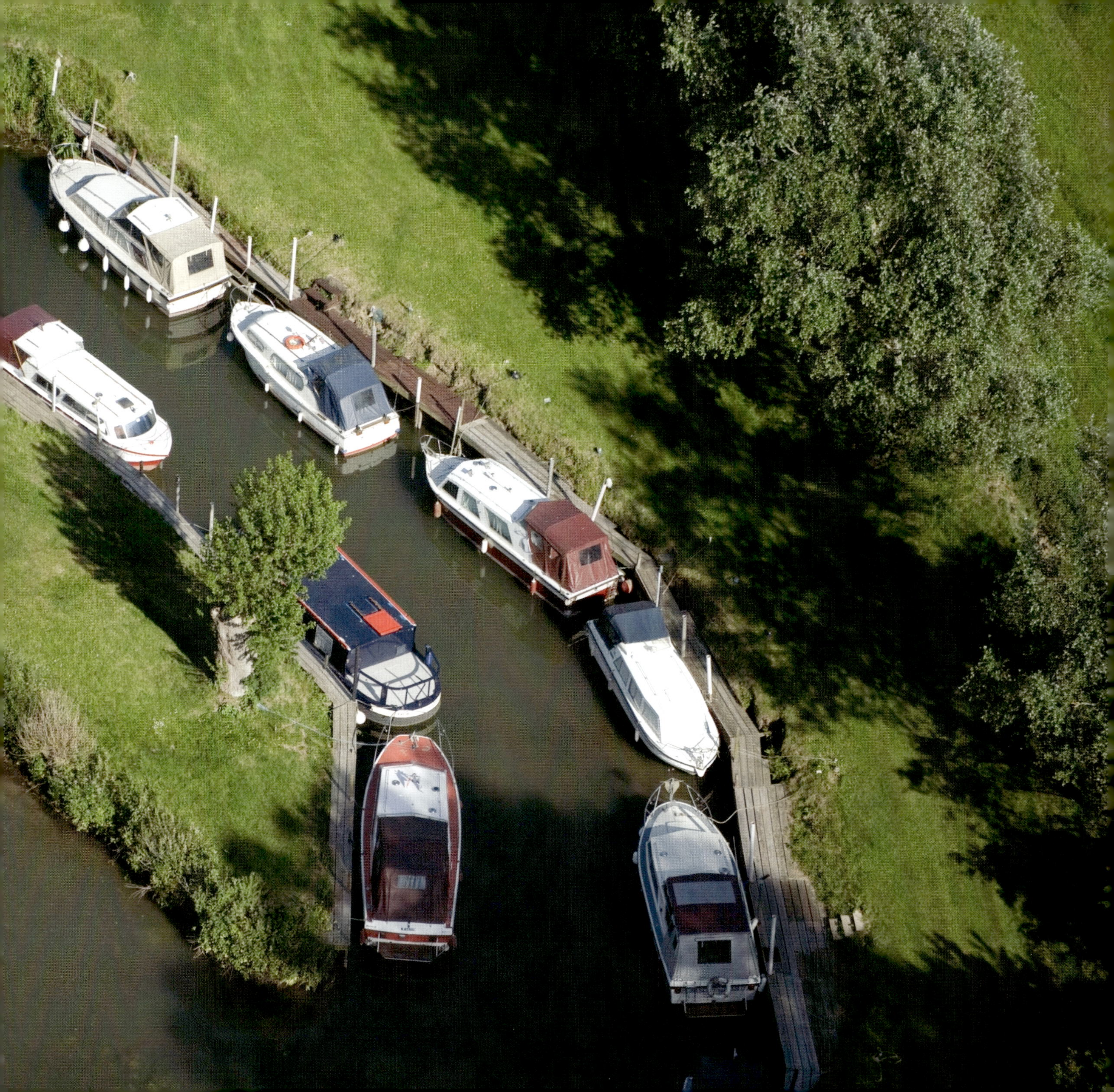

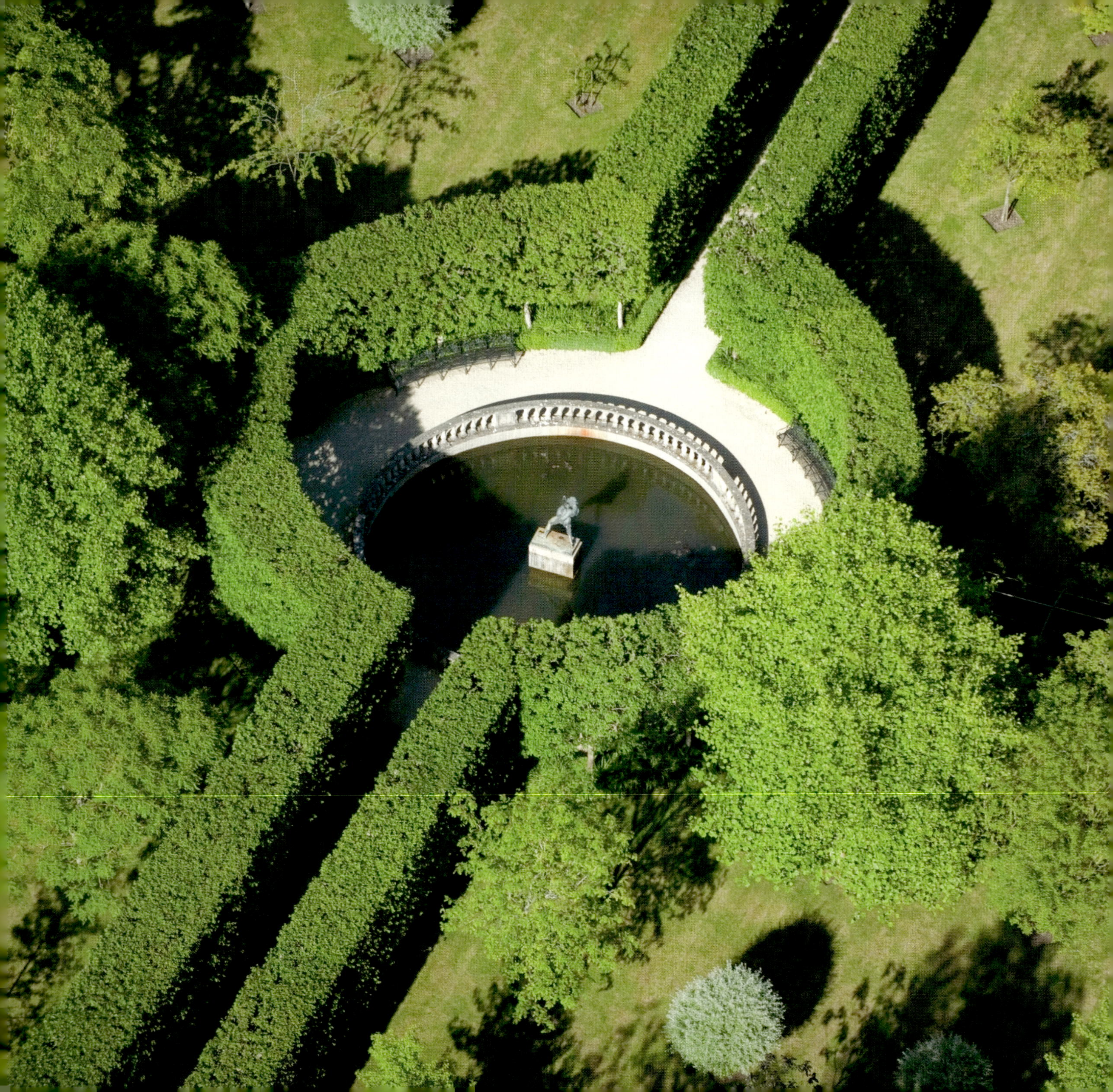

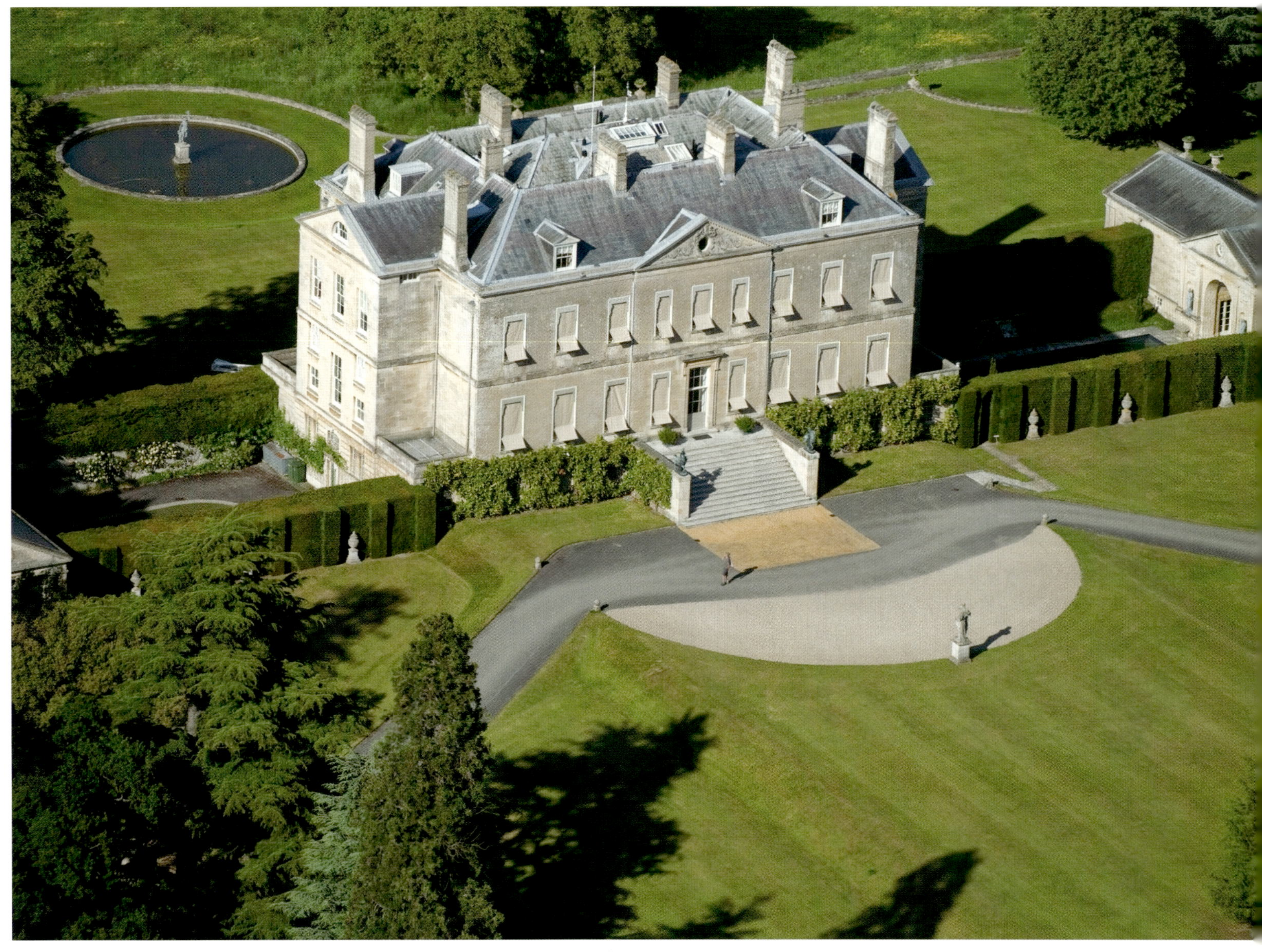

Left and above: Buscot Park is the home of Lord and Lady Faringdon. The house was built by Edward Loveden Townsend in the late eighteenth century at a cost of £20,000. The formal gardens include designs by the eminent twentieth century designer Sir Harold Peto. The garden is divided into four, called The Four Seasons Garden, and is joined in the centre by a lily pond complete with a fountain.

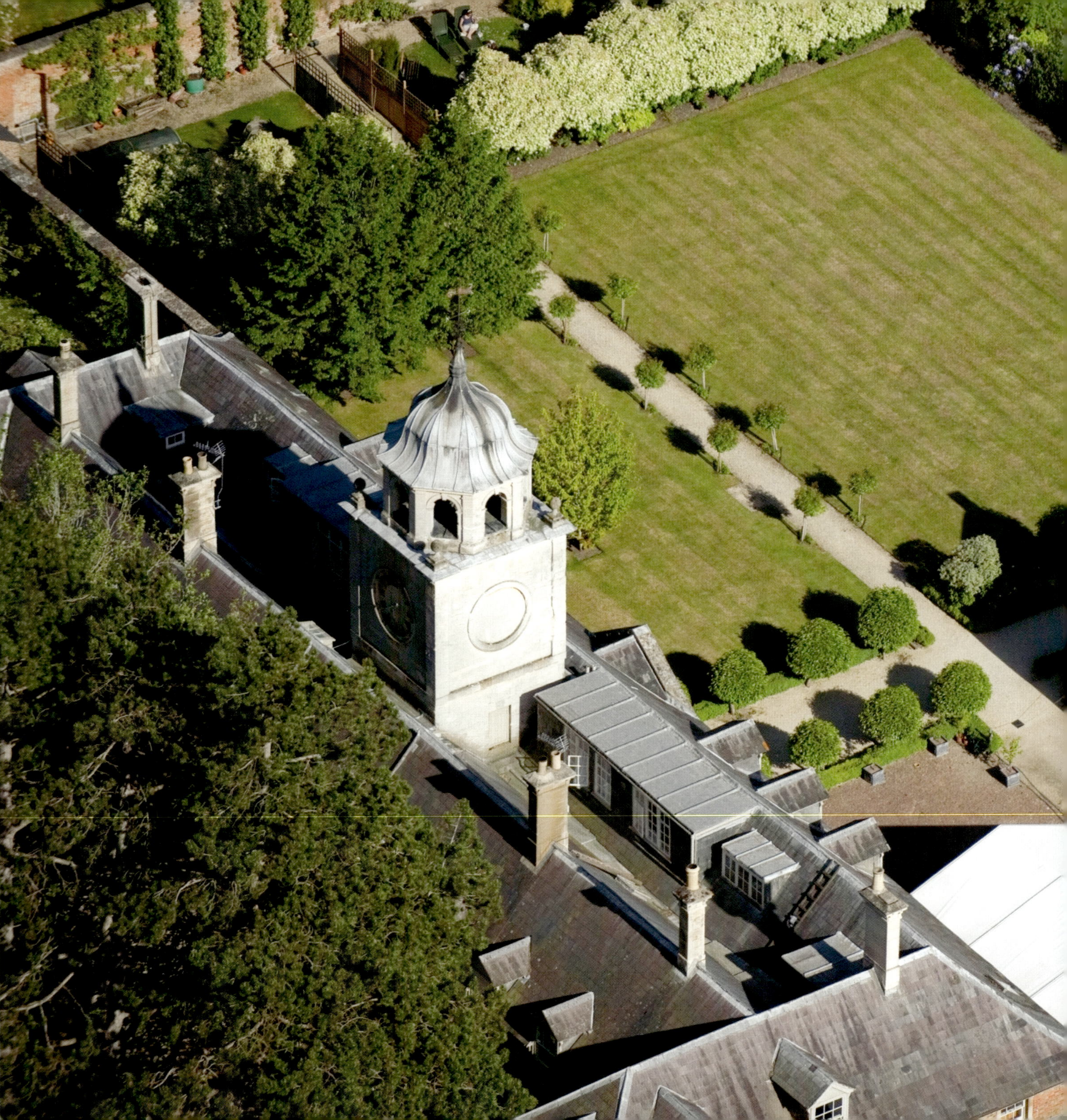

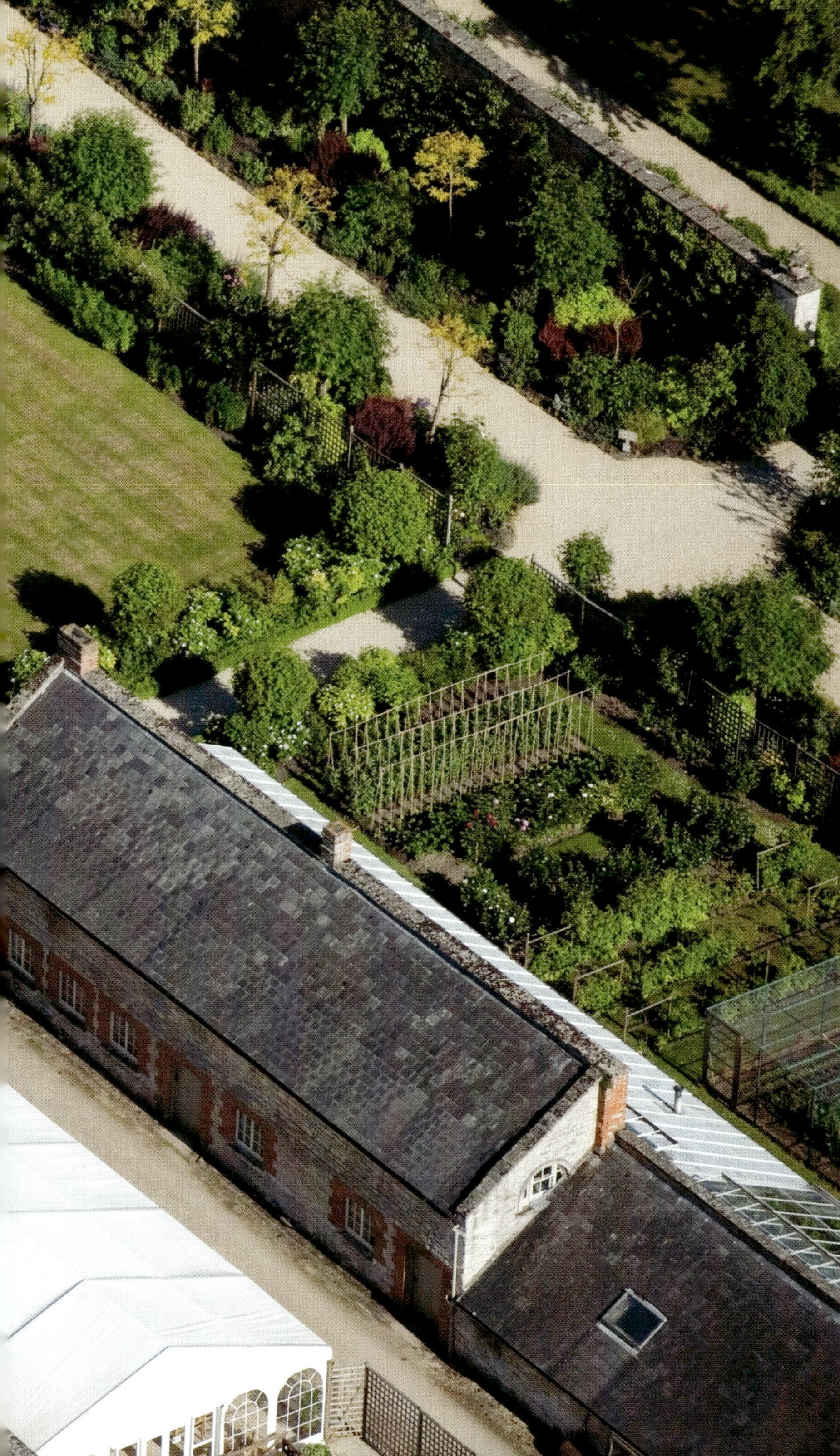 The walled garden at Buscot Park.

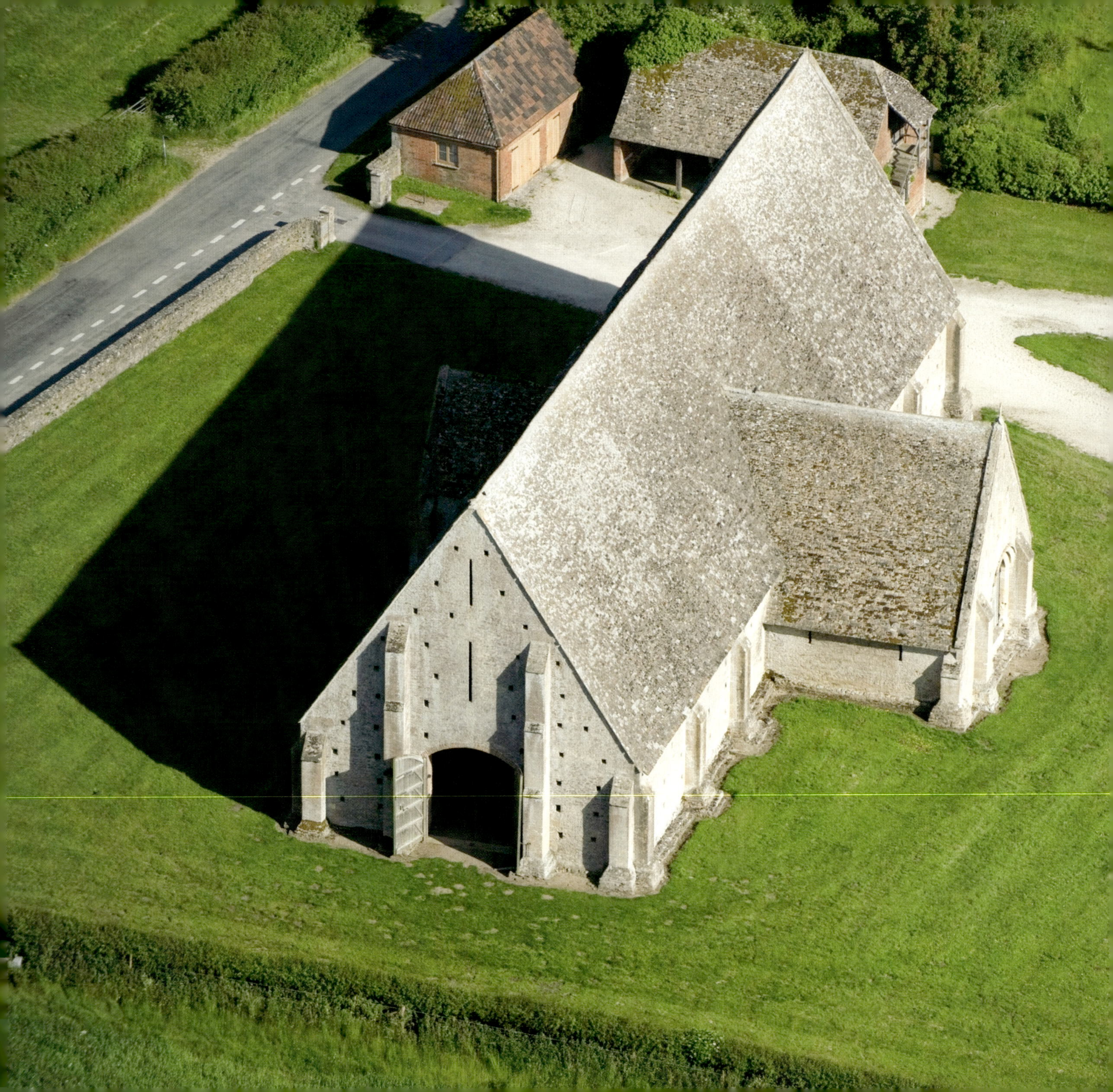

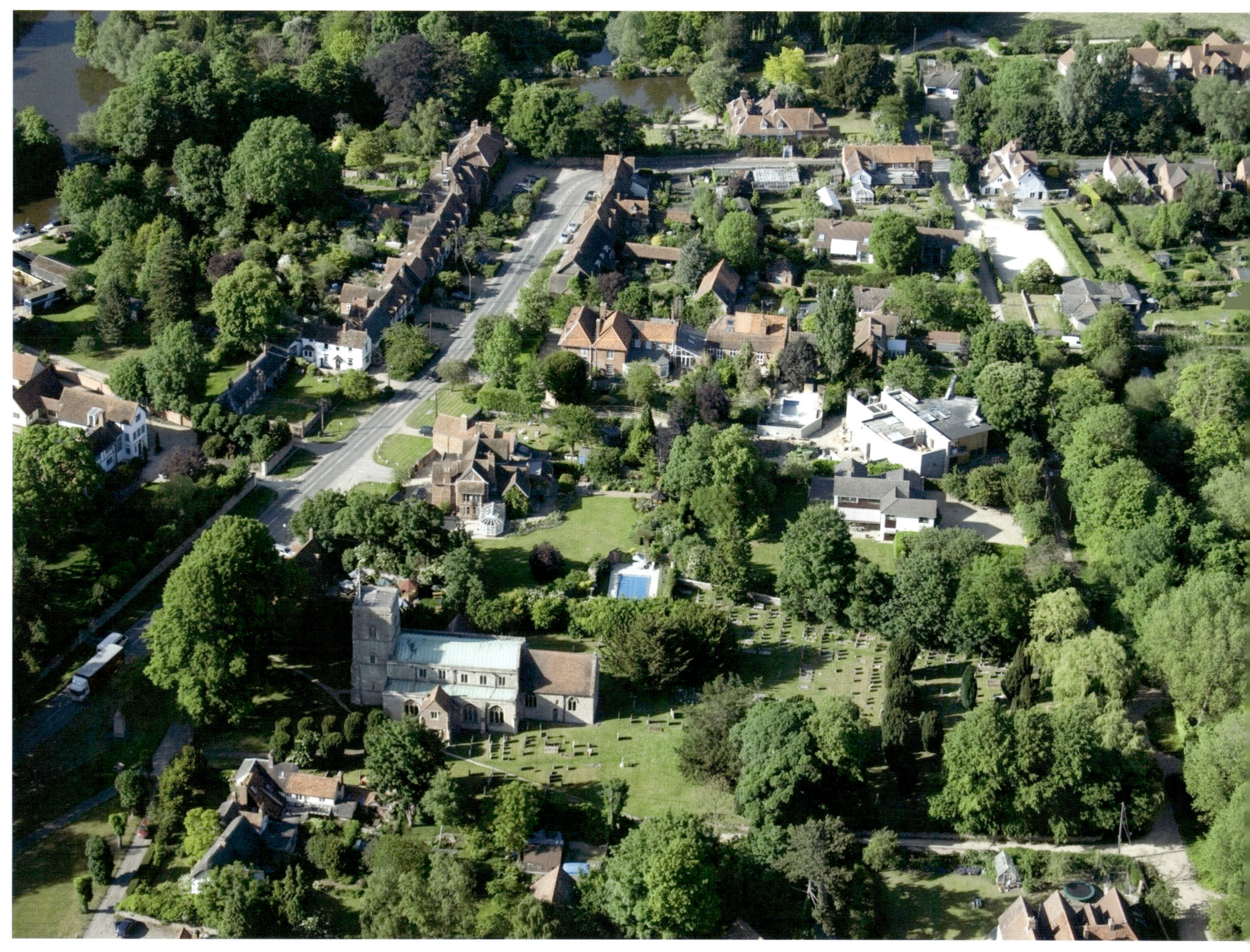

Left: The magnificent thirteenth century Tithe Barn at Great Coxwell is now in the care of the National Trust.

Above: The view above Sutton Courtenay and All Saints Church.

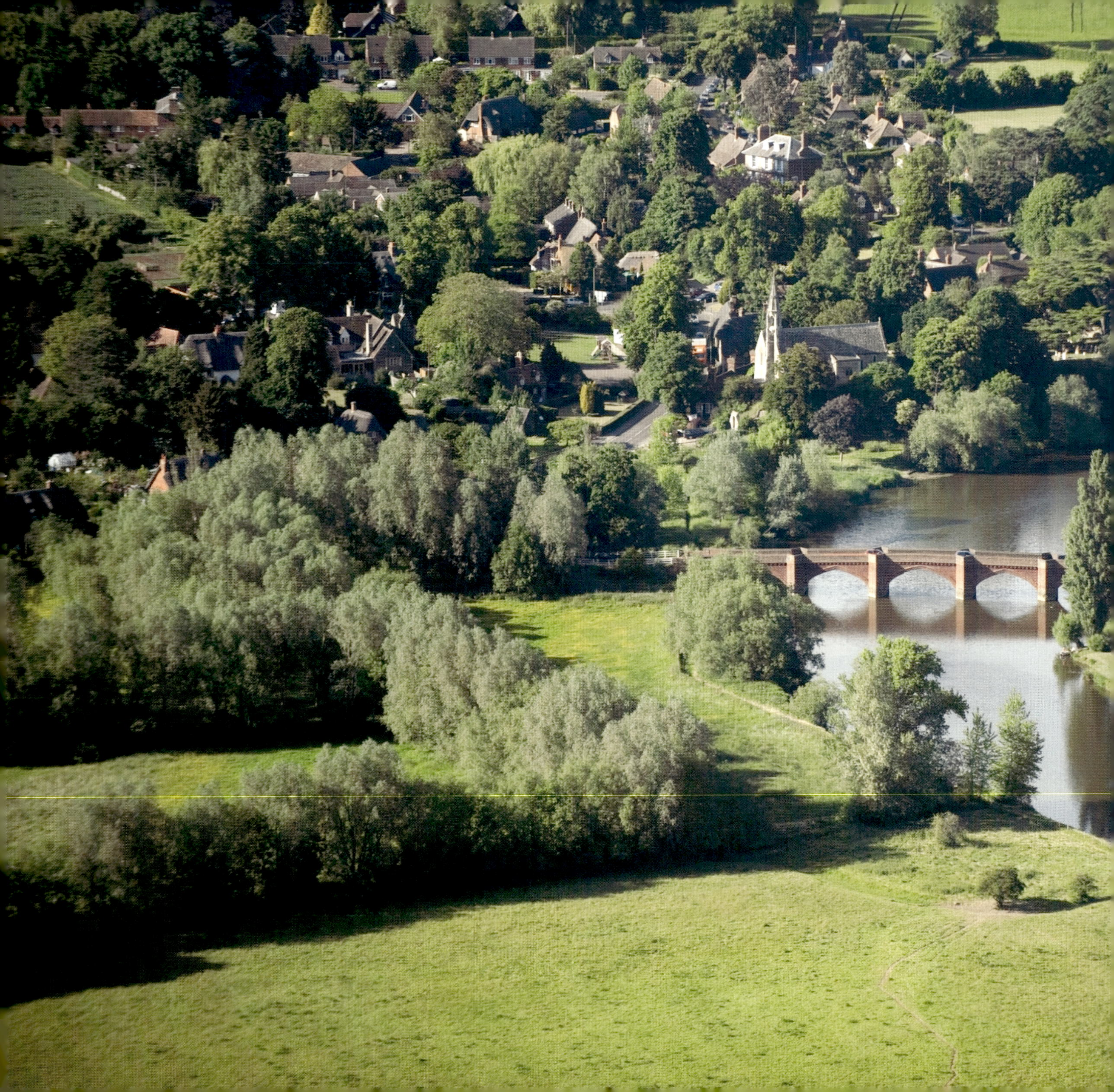

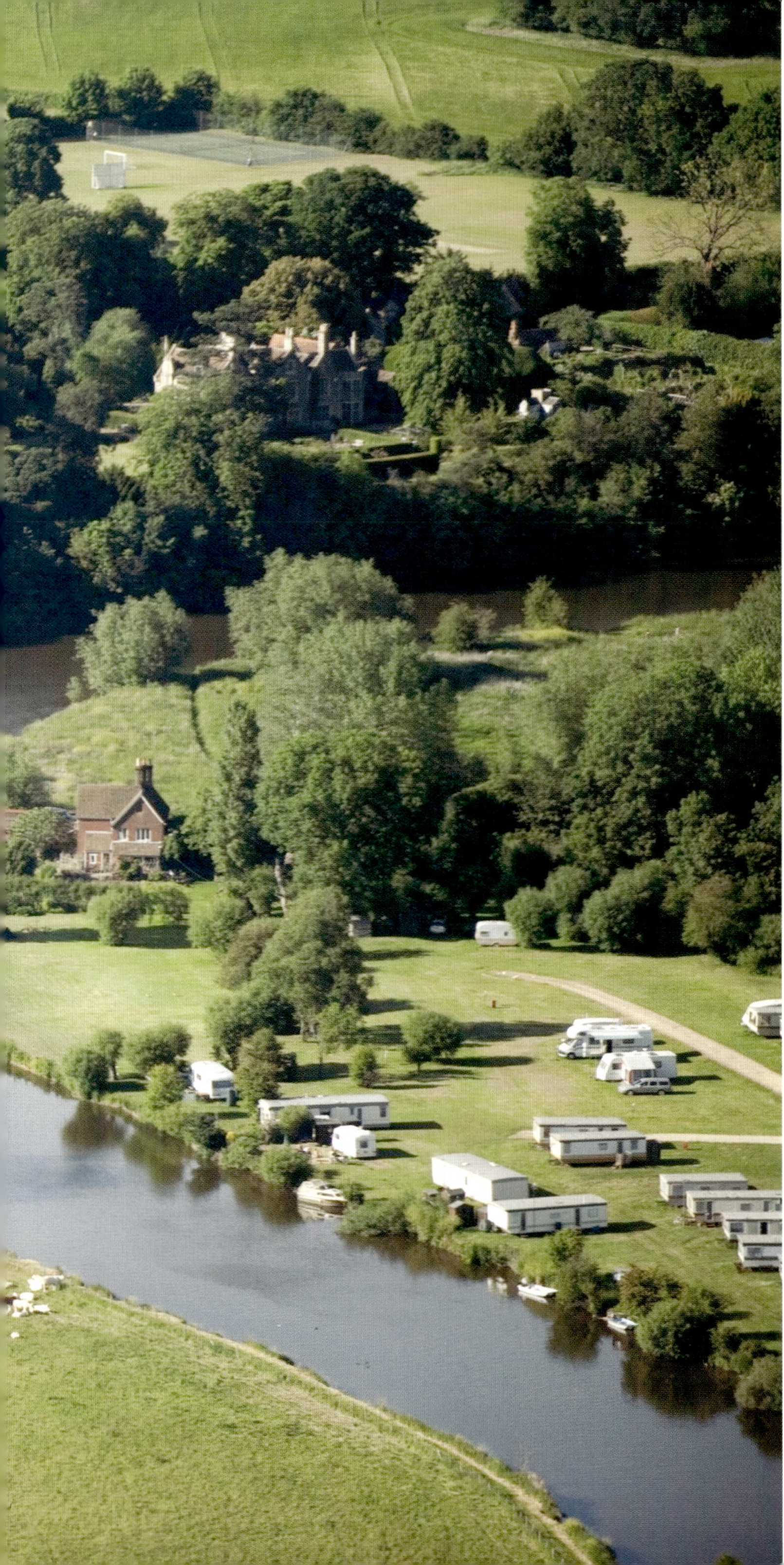

The elegant Clifton Hampden Bridge bestrides the River Thames at the village of Clifton Hampden. It was designed by Sir George Gilbert Scott and completed in 1867. The Barley Mow public house is close by, a hostelry that featured in the book *Three Men in a Boat*.

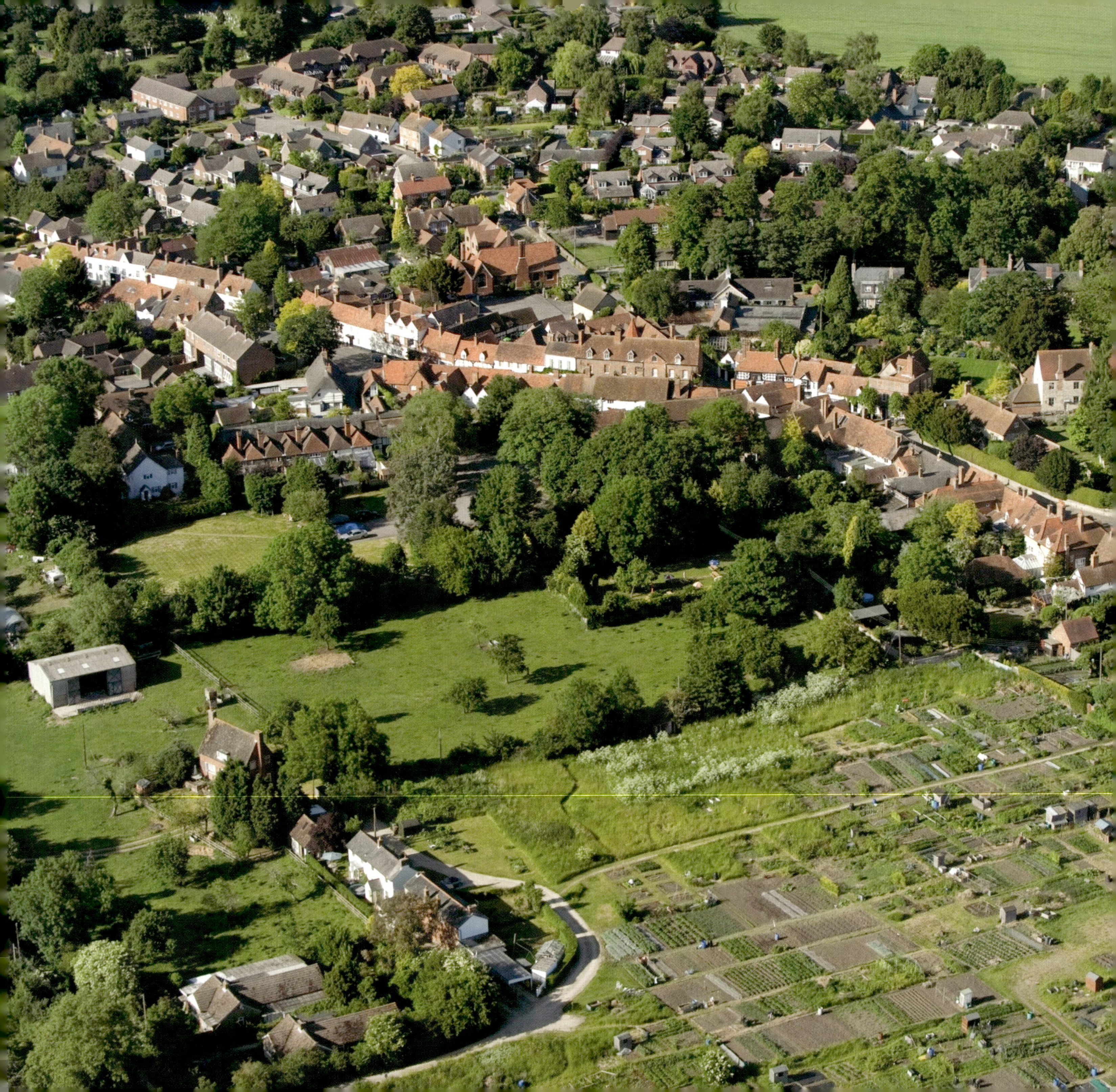

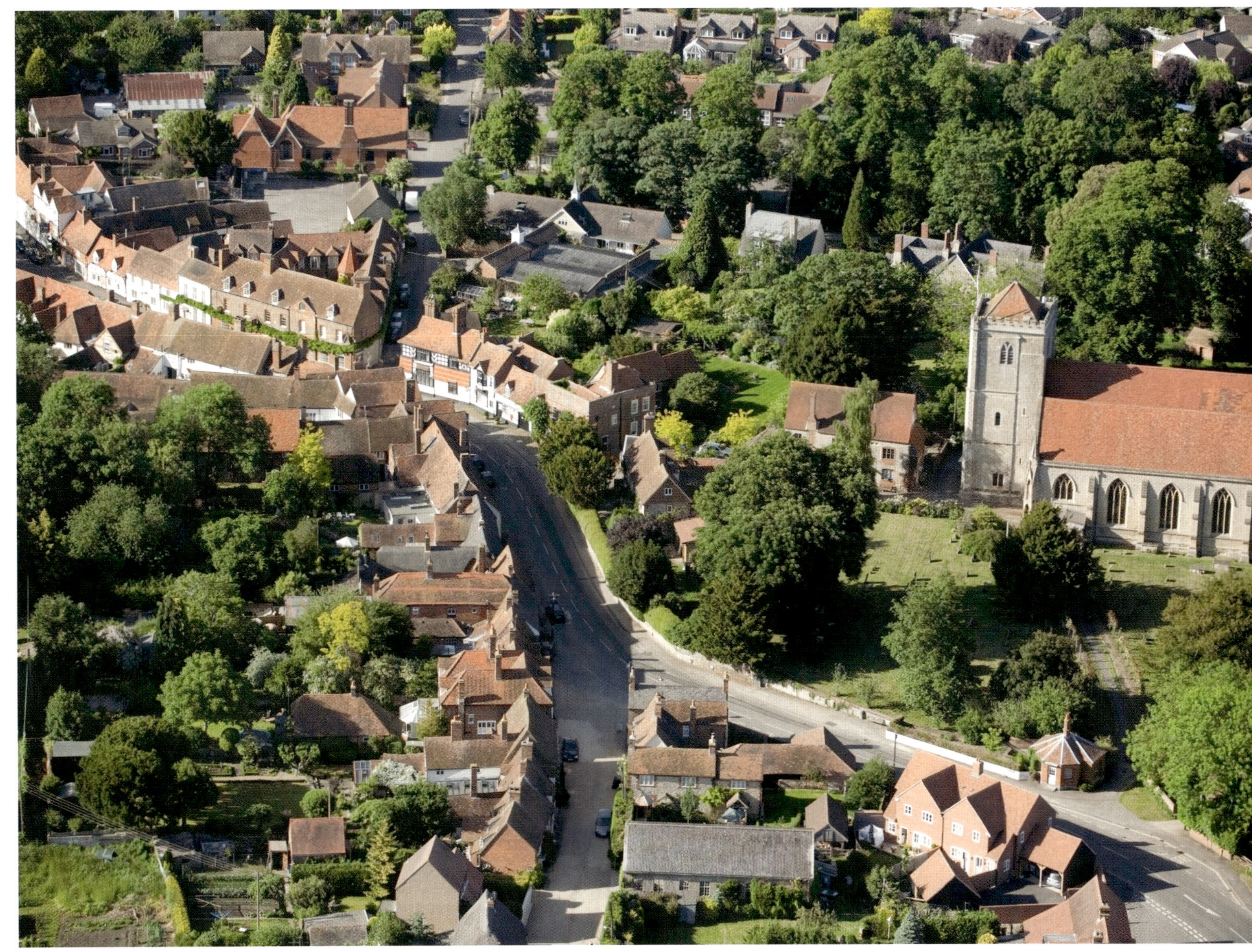

Left and above: Dorchester-on-Thames is an historic and charming village situated a few miles south of Oxford. The superb medieval Abbey church (seen right in the photograph above) is one of the most significant buildings of the Upper Thames Valley, dominating the delightful gathering of timbered houses, thatched cottages and ancient inns.

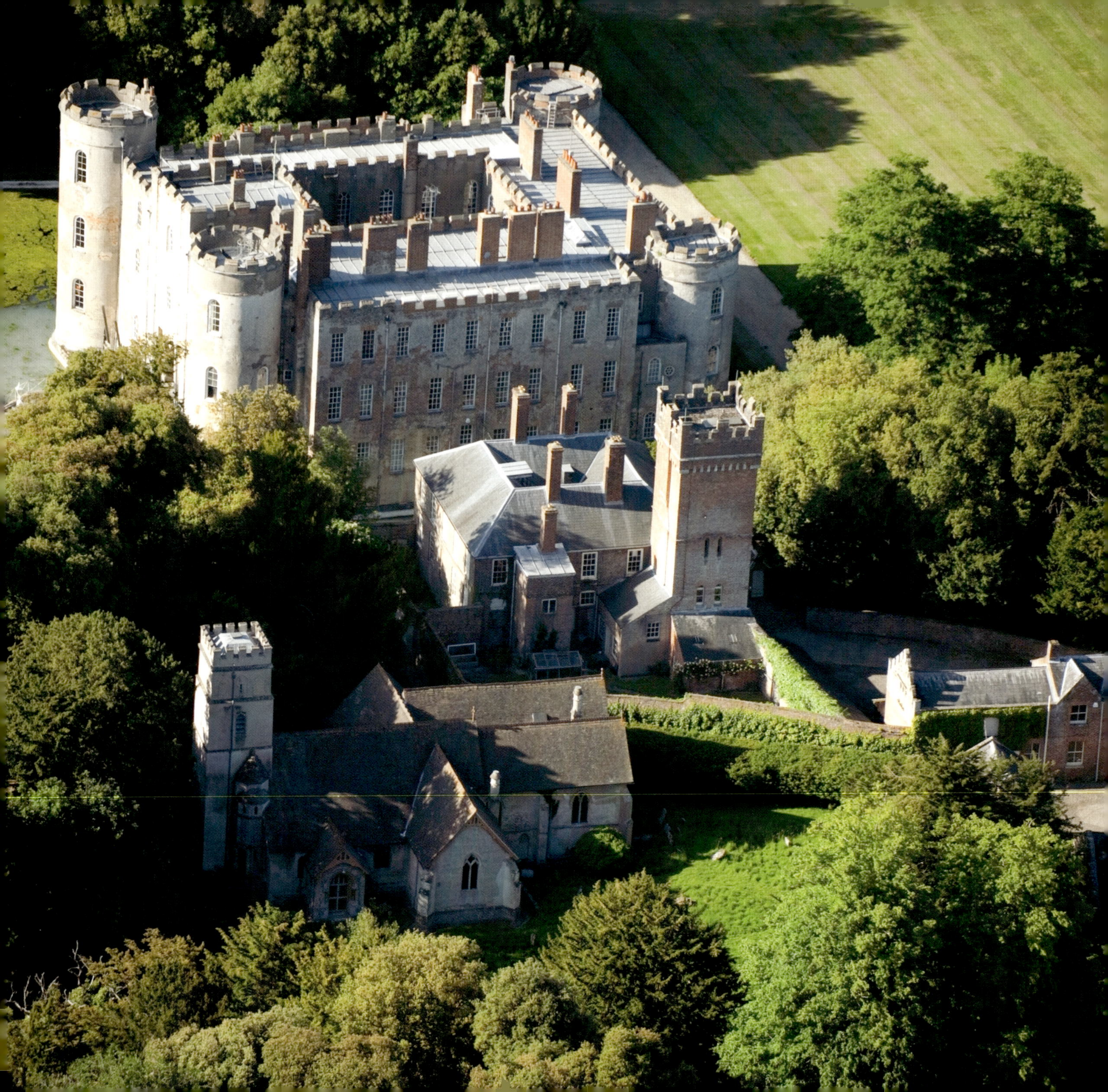

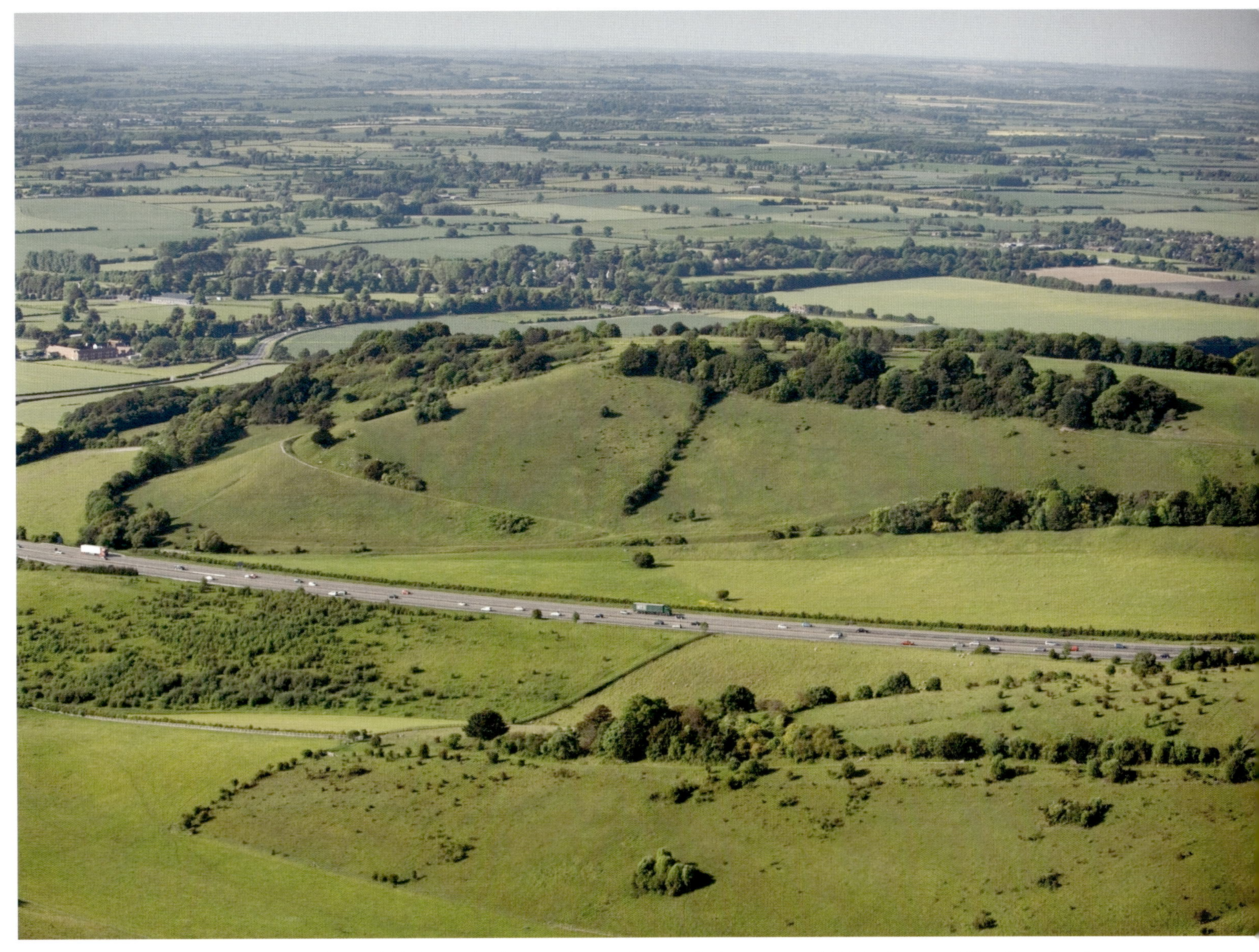

Left: Shirburn Castle is sited at the village of Shirburn, 6 miles south of Thame, it was formerly the home of the Earls of Macclesfield. It is privately owned.

Above: A view across M40 to Beacon Hill with Aston Rowant in distance.

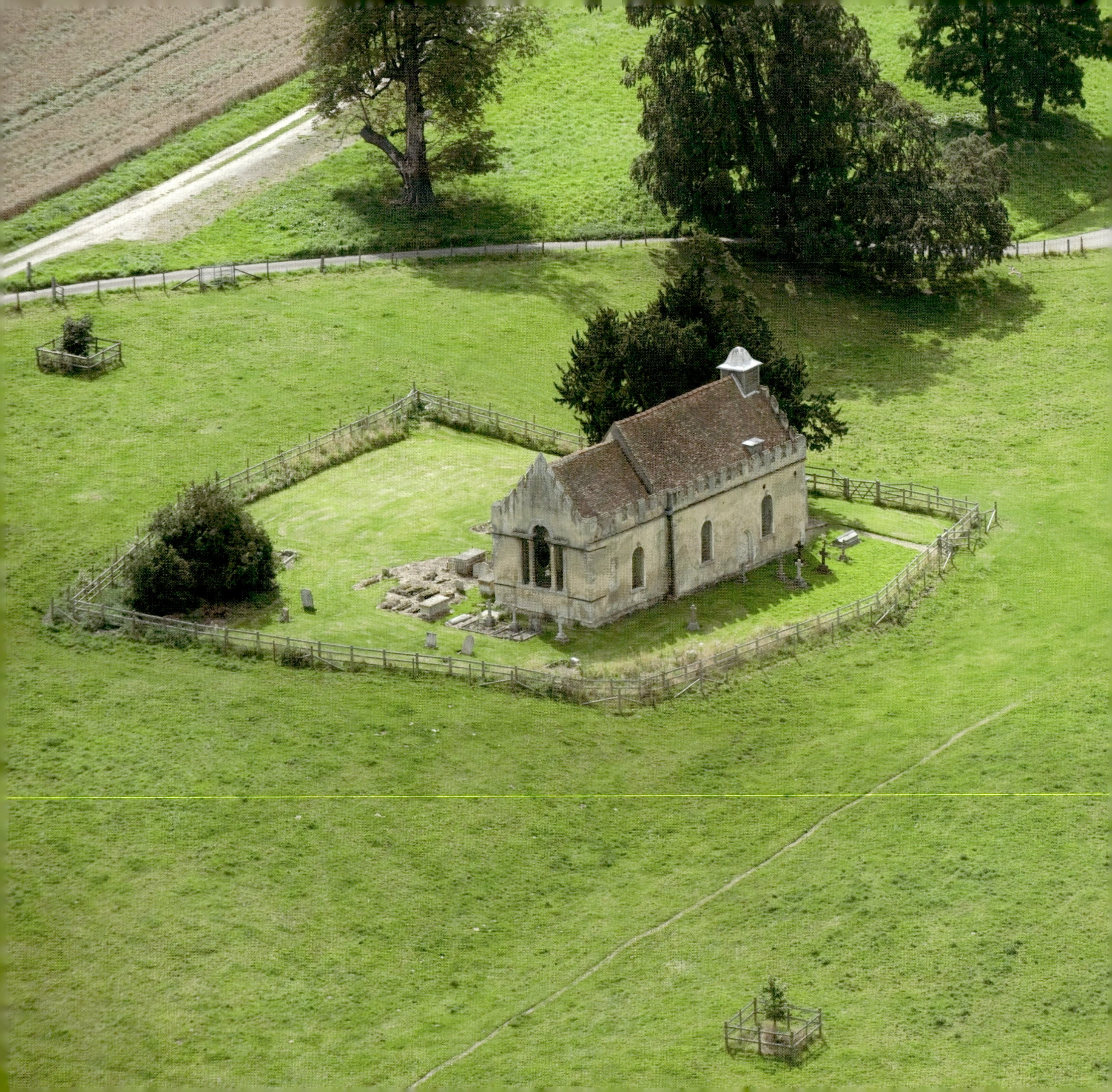

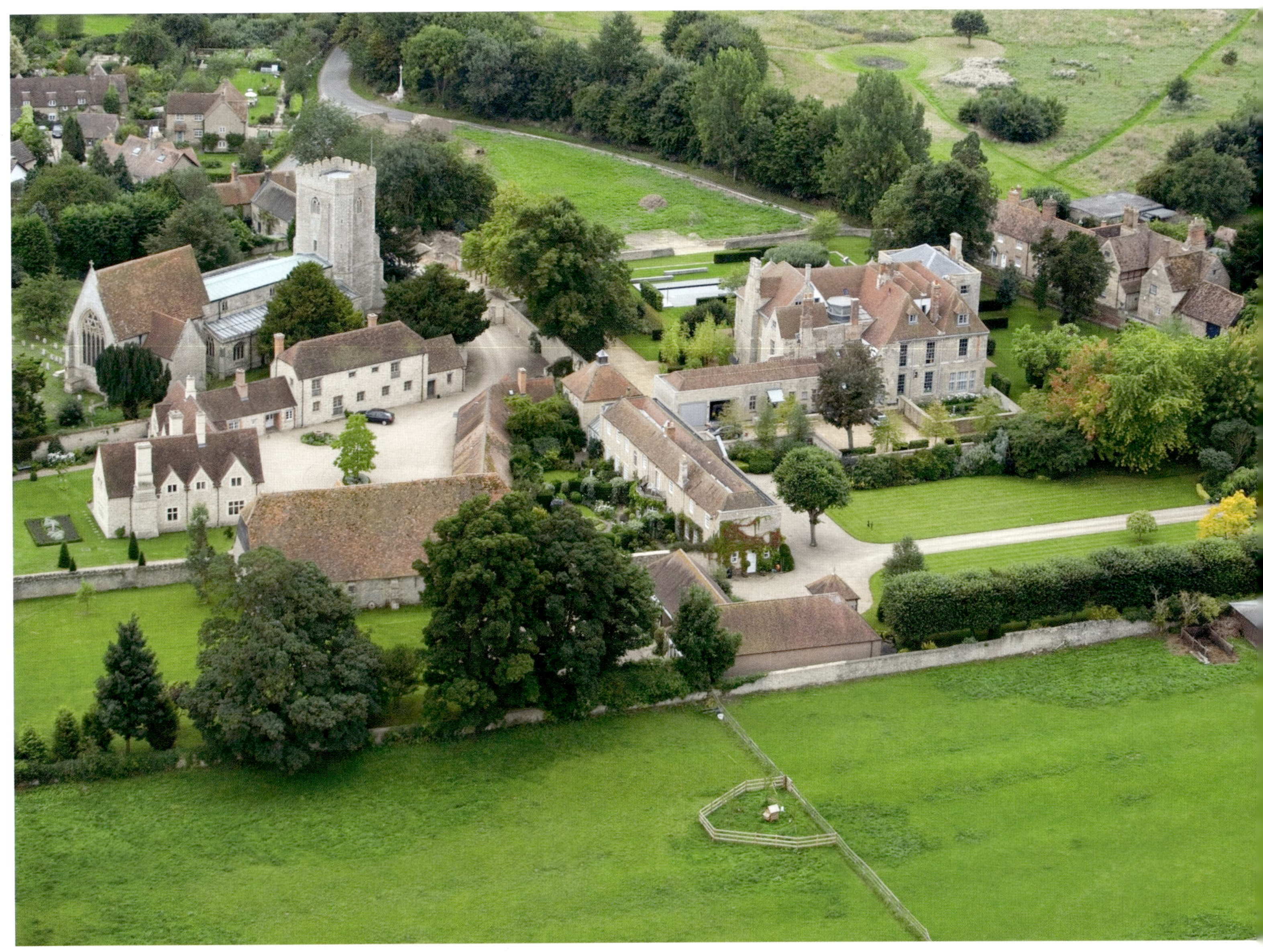

Left: The little church at Wheatfield, a settlement near Stoke Talmage (a few miles from Thame), has no electricity or water, although occasional services are still held here.

Above: Great Haseley is one of the village communities that make up the group known as The Haseleys and which also includes Little Haseley, Great Milton, Little Milton, Milton Common, Rycote, Standhill and North Weston.

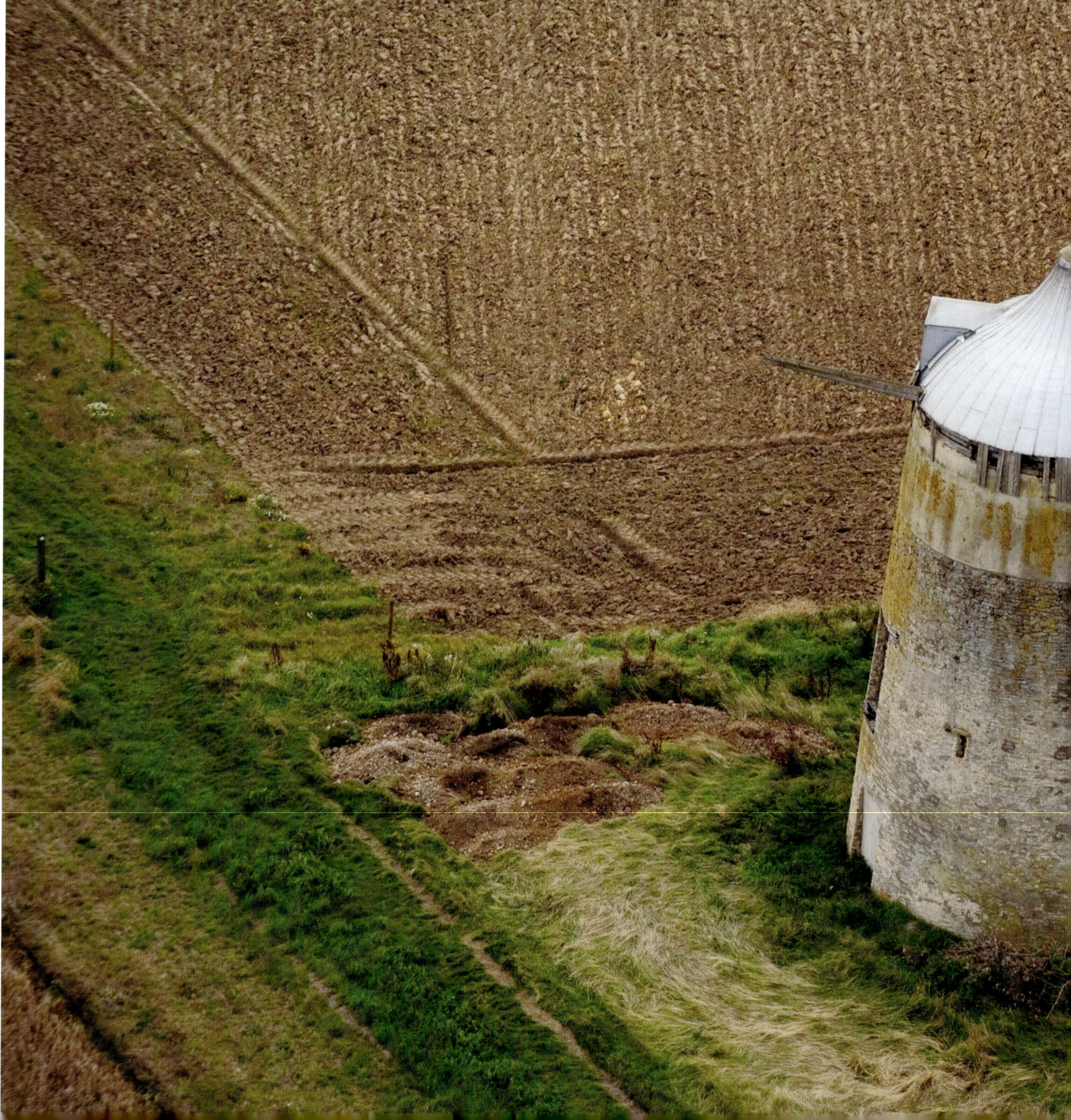

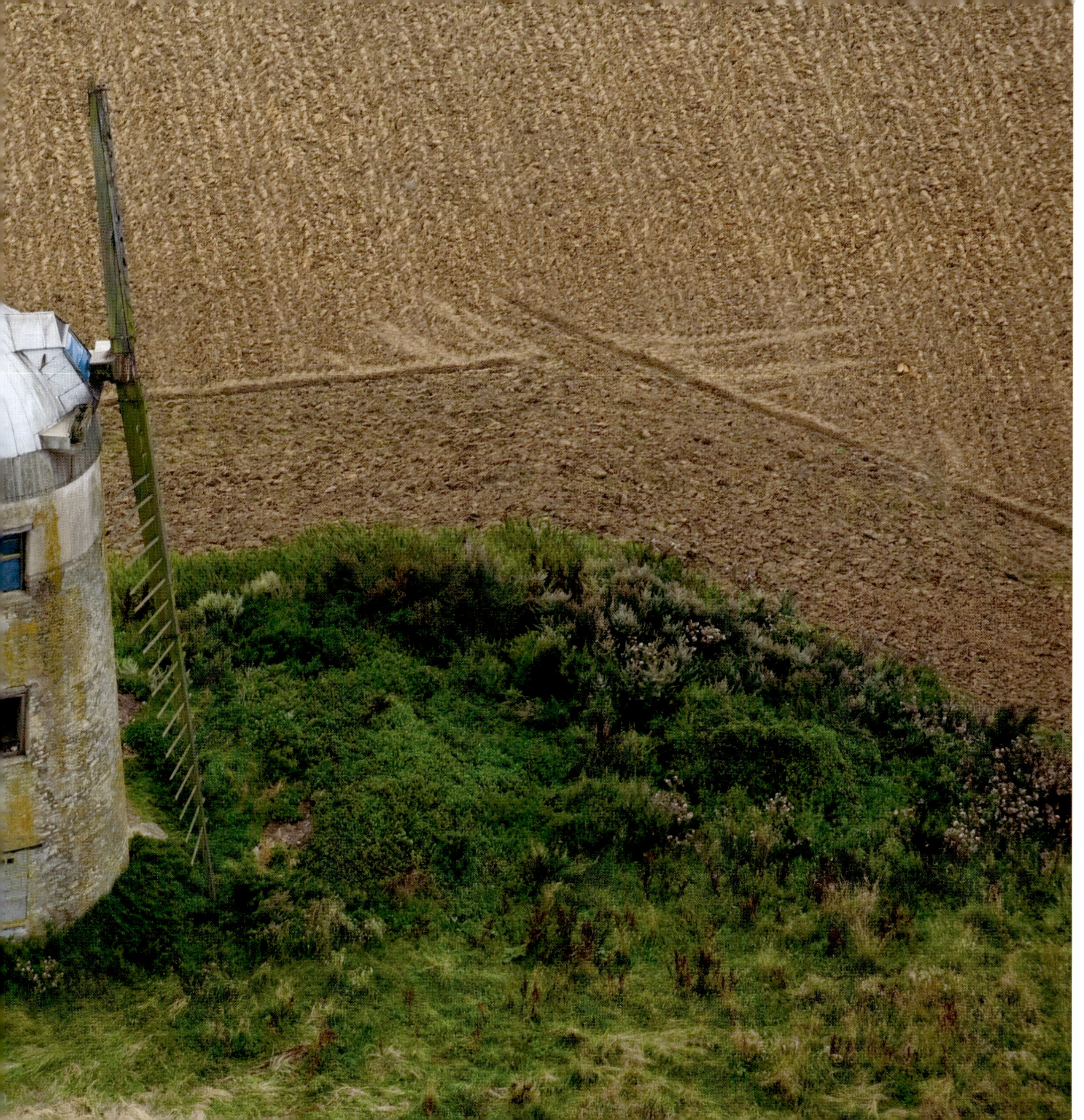

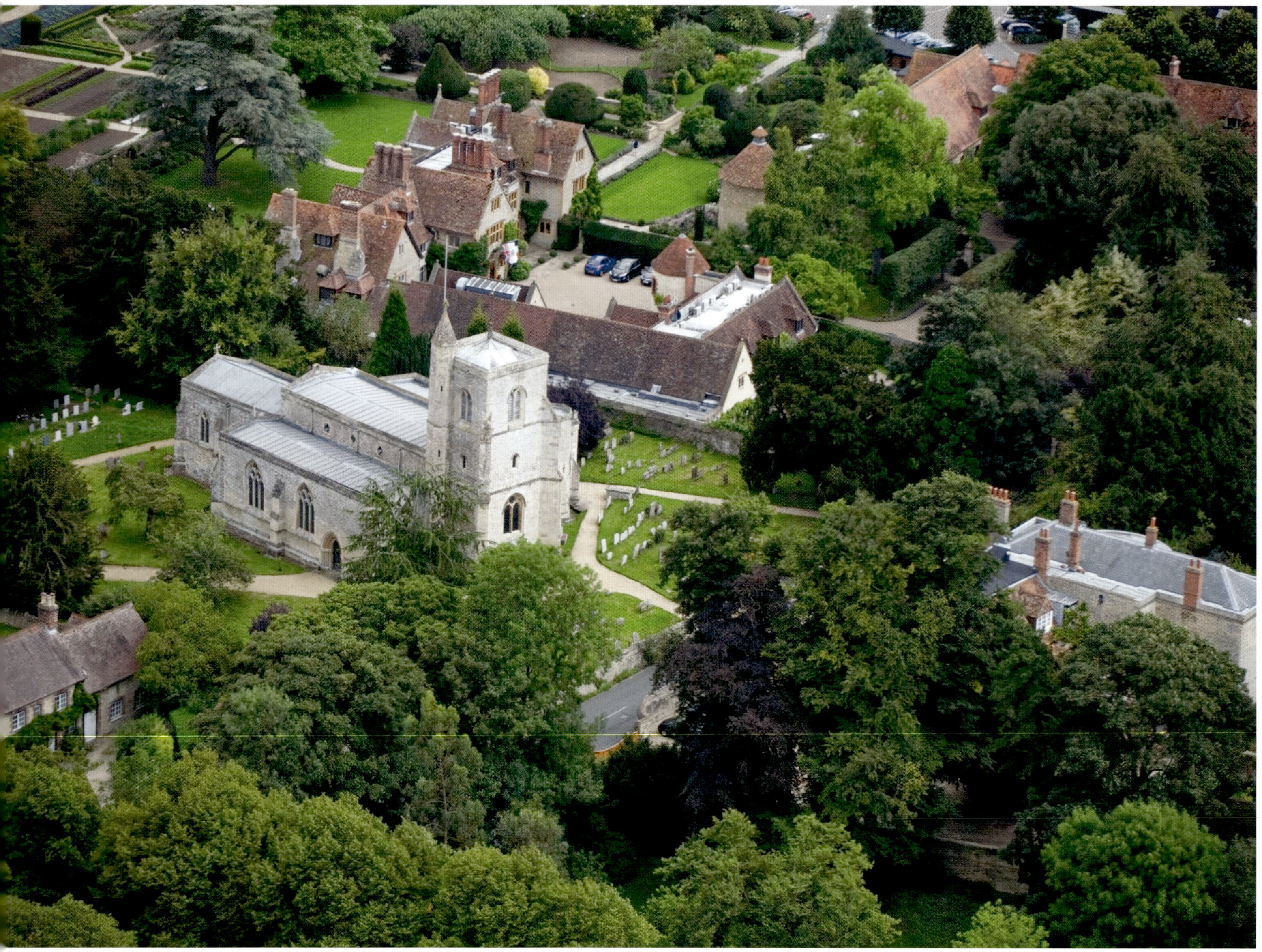

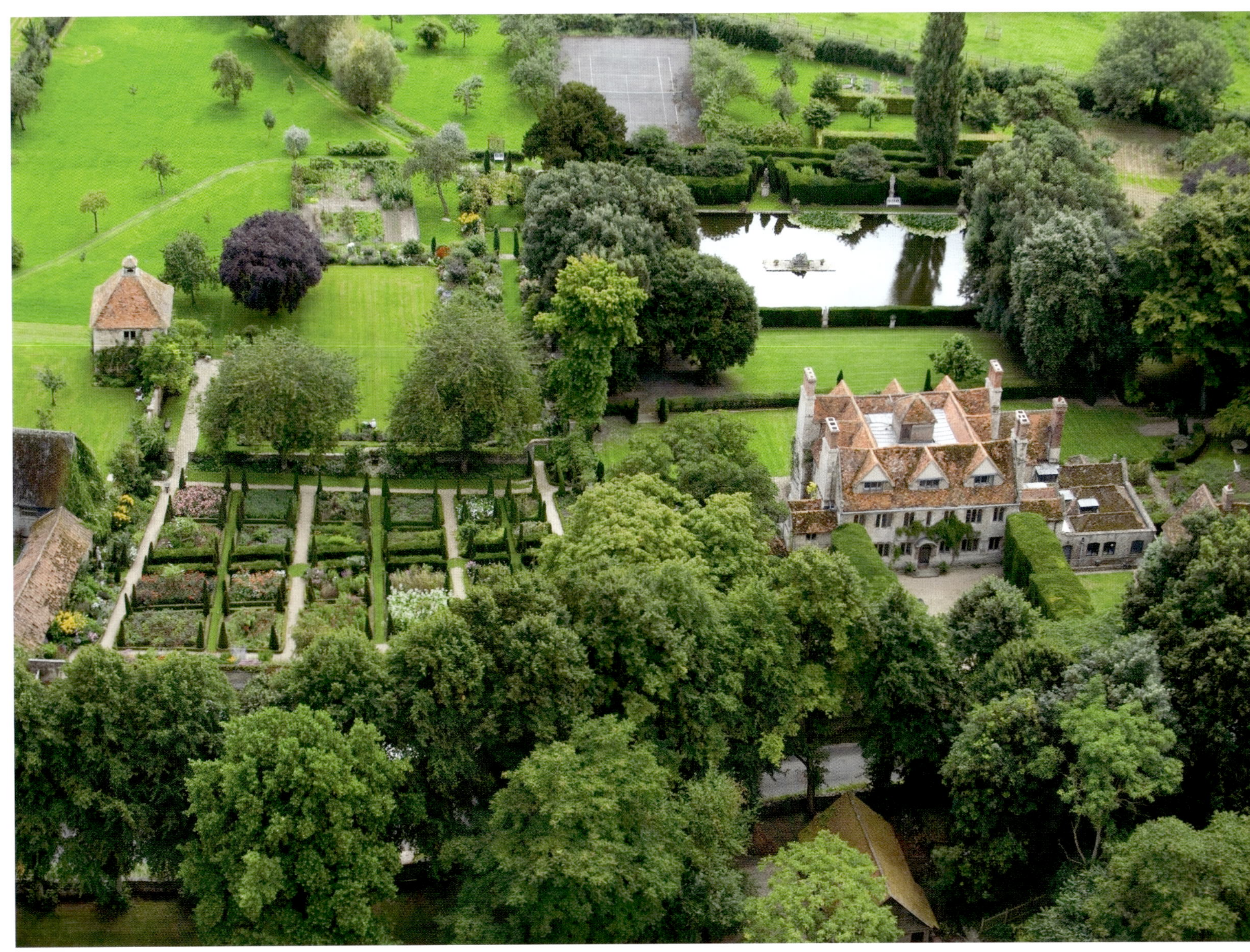

Left: In recent times the village of Great Milton is perhaps best known for its restaurant Le Manoir aux Quat' Saisons and the luxury hotel which is sited near the church of St Mary the Virgin.

Above: Garsington Manor, in the village from which it takes its name, hosts an annual open air festival of operatic performances.

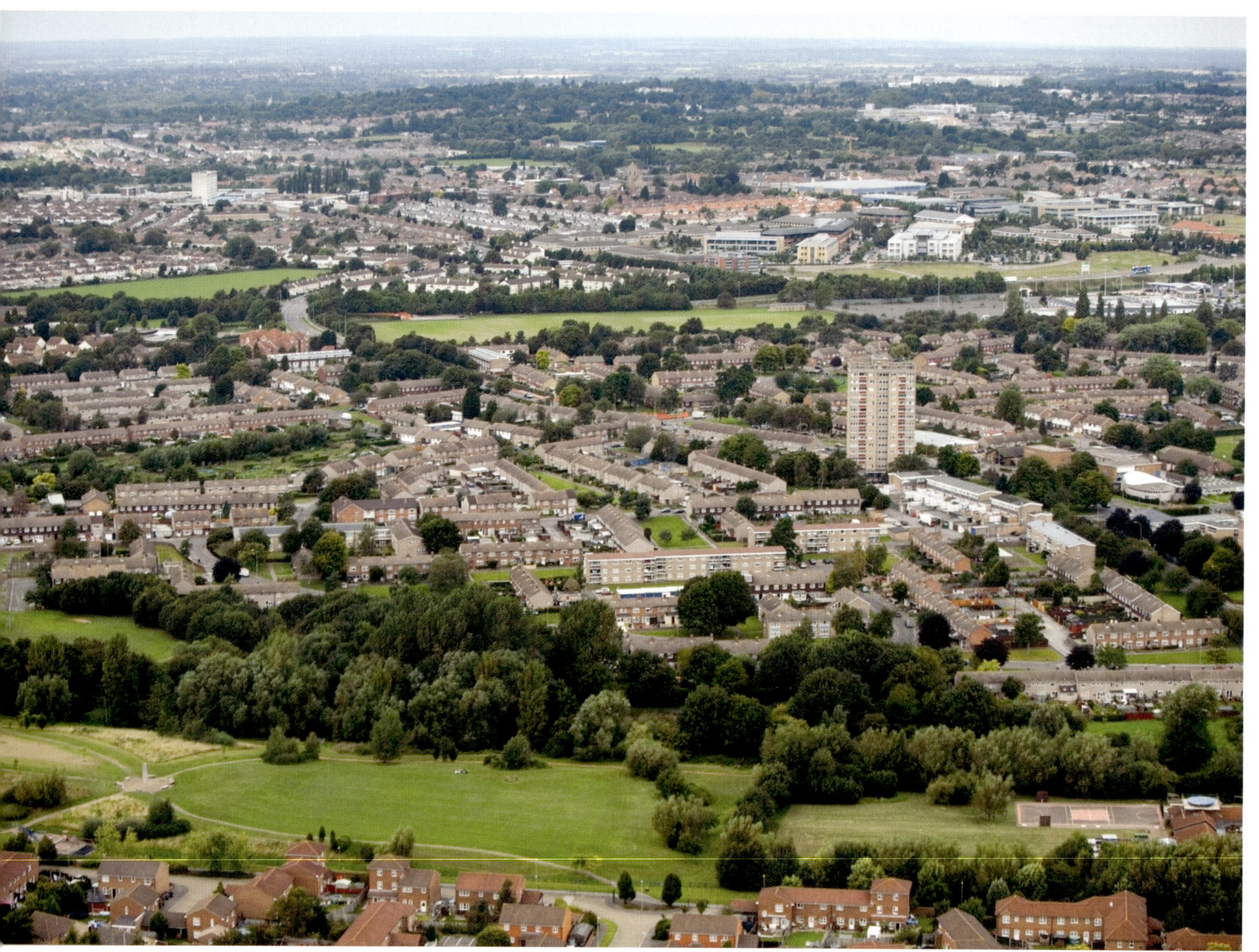

Above: A panoramic view over Cowley, one of the major suburbs of Oxford. Best known as a centre of car production; though much reduced in size, the industry is still vital to the area.

Right: South of the city, the River Thames leaves Oxford at Sandford Lock on its way to Abingdon.

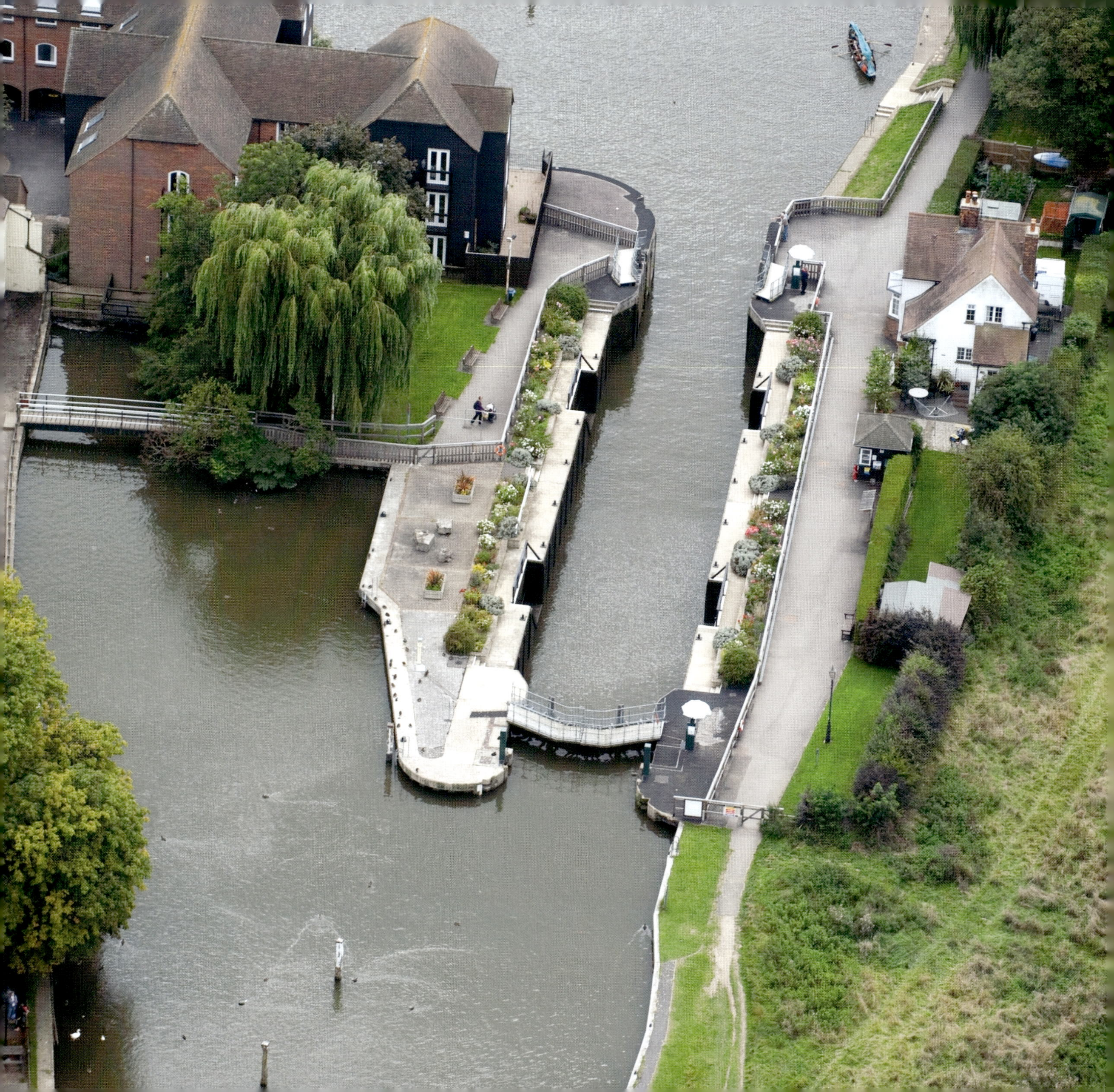

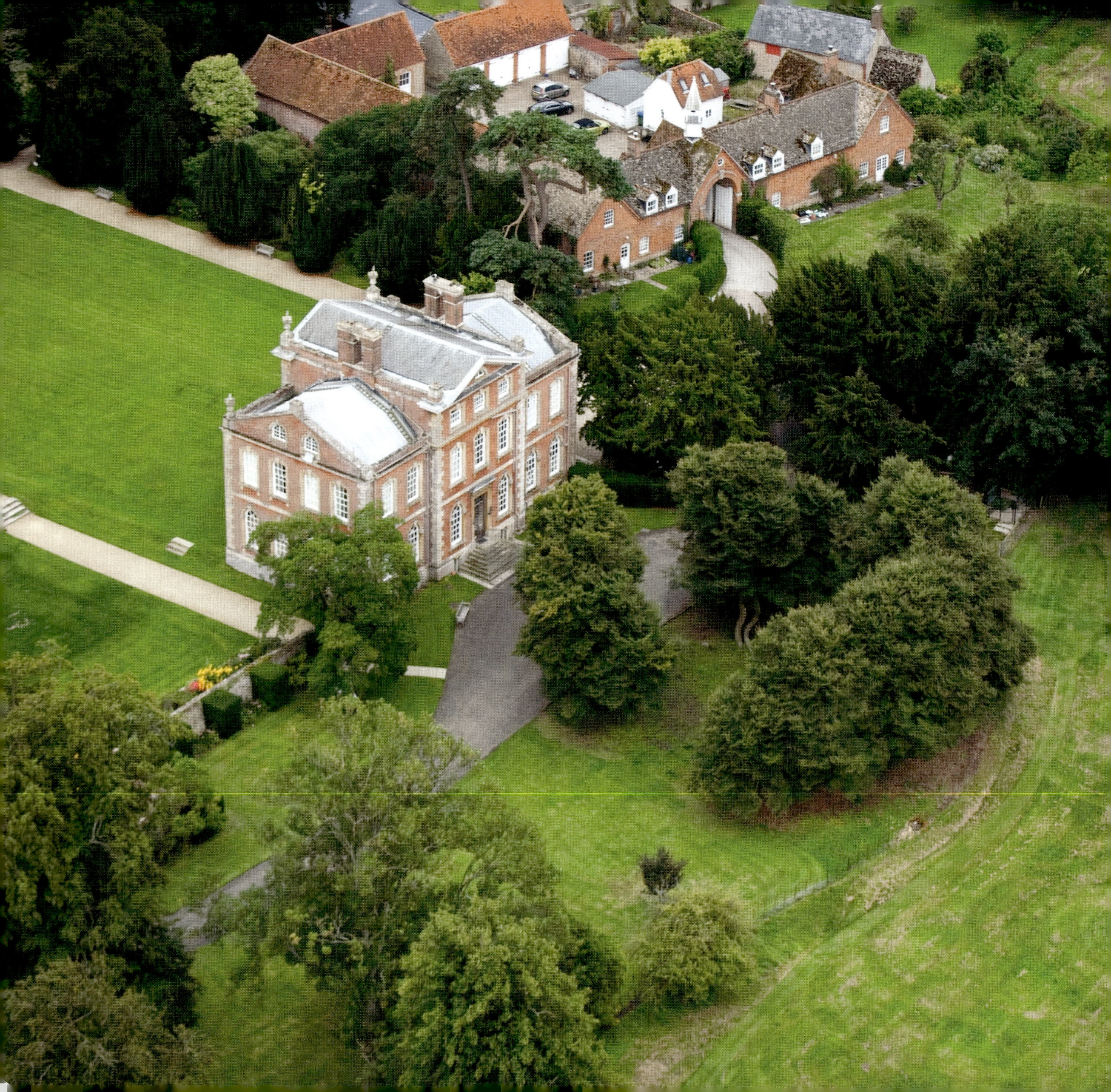

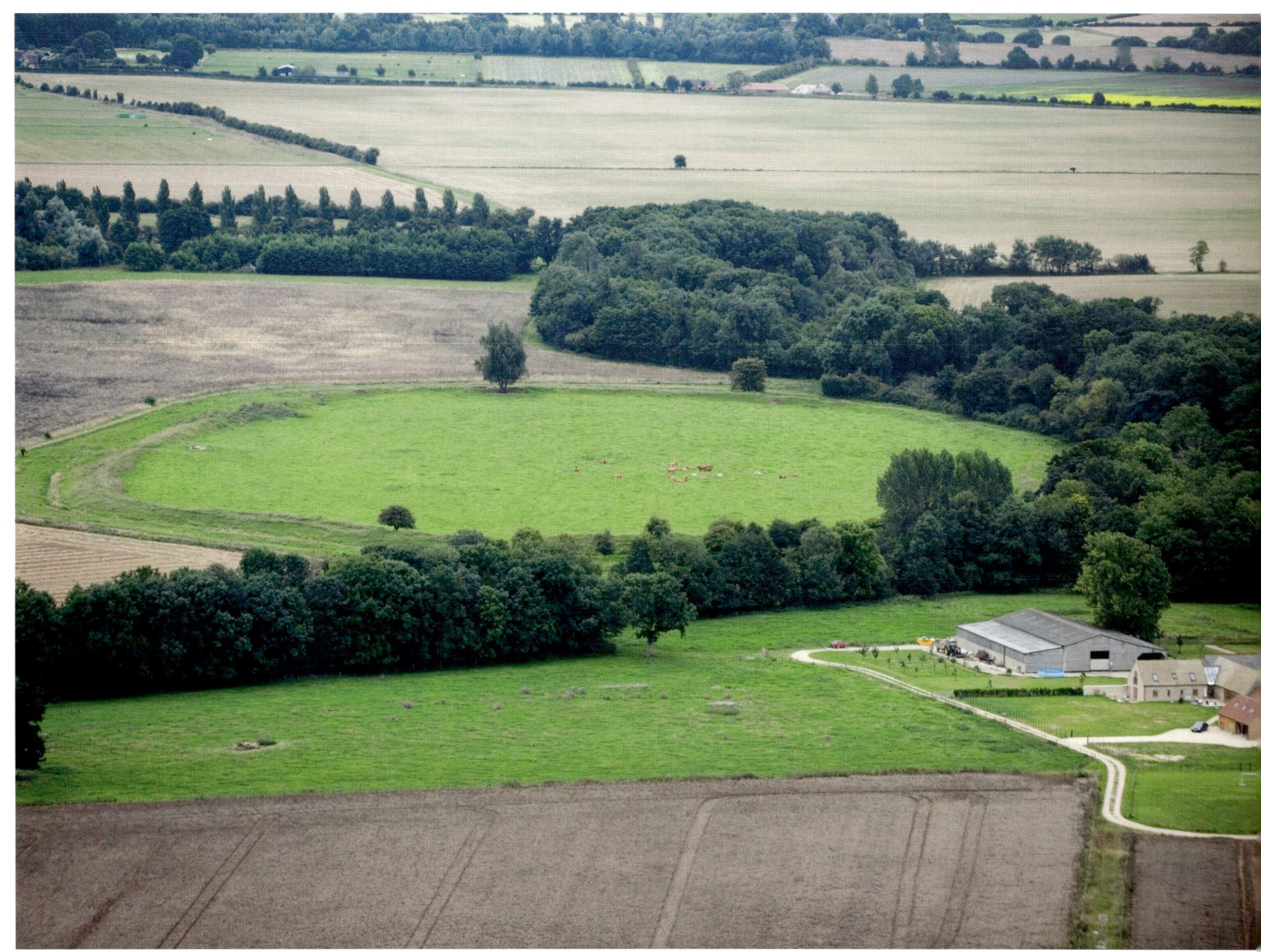

Left: Kingston Bagpuize House, west of Abingdon, was built in the mid seventeenth century and remodelled in the early 1700s. It is open to the public on selected days.

Above: The circular outline of Cherbury Camp, an Iron Age settlement in the Vale of the White Horse. It occupies an unusual position as counterpart hill forts are almost always sited on elevated strategic sites.

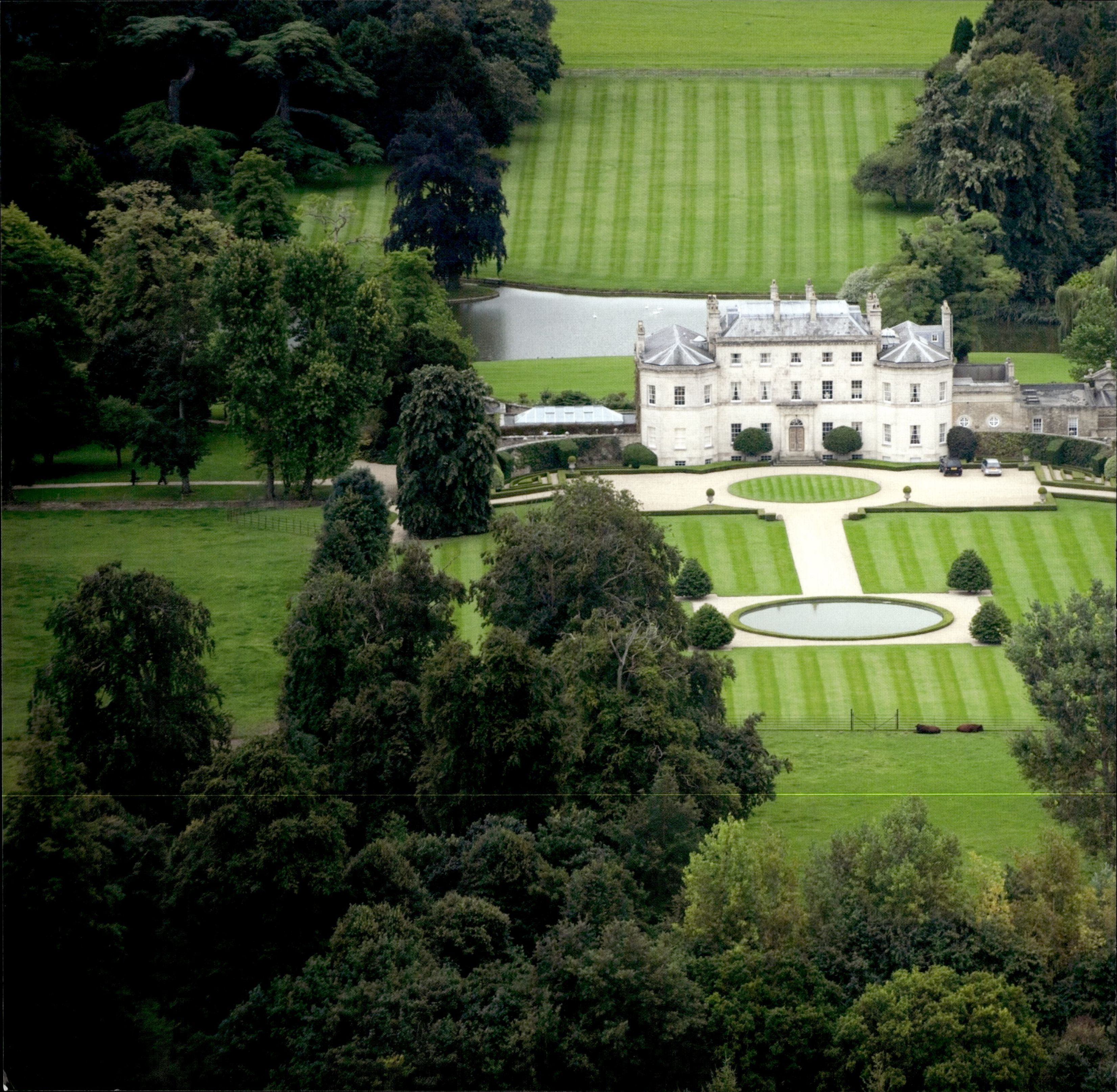

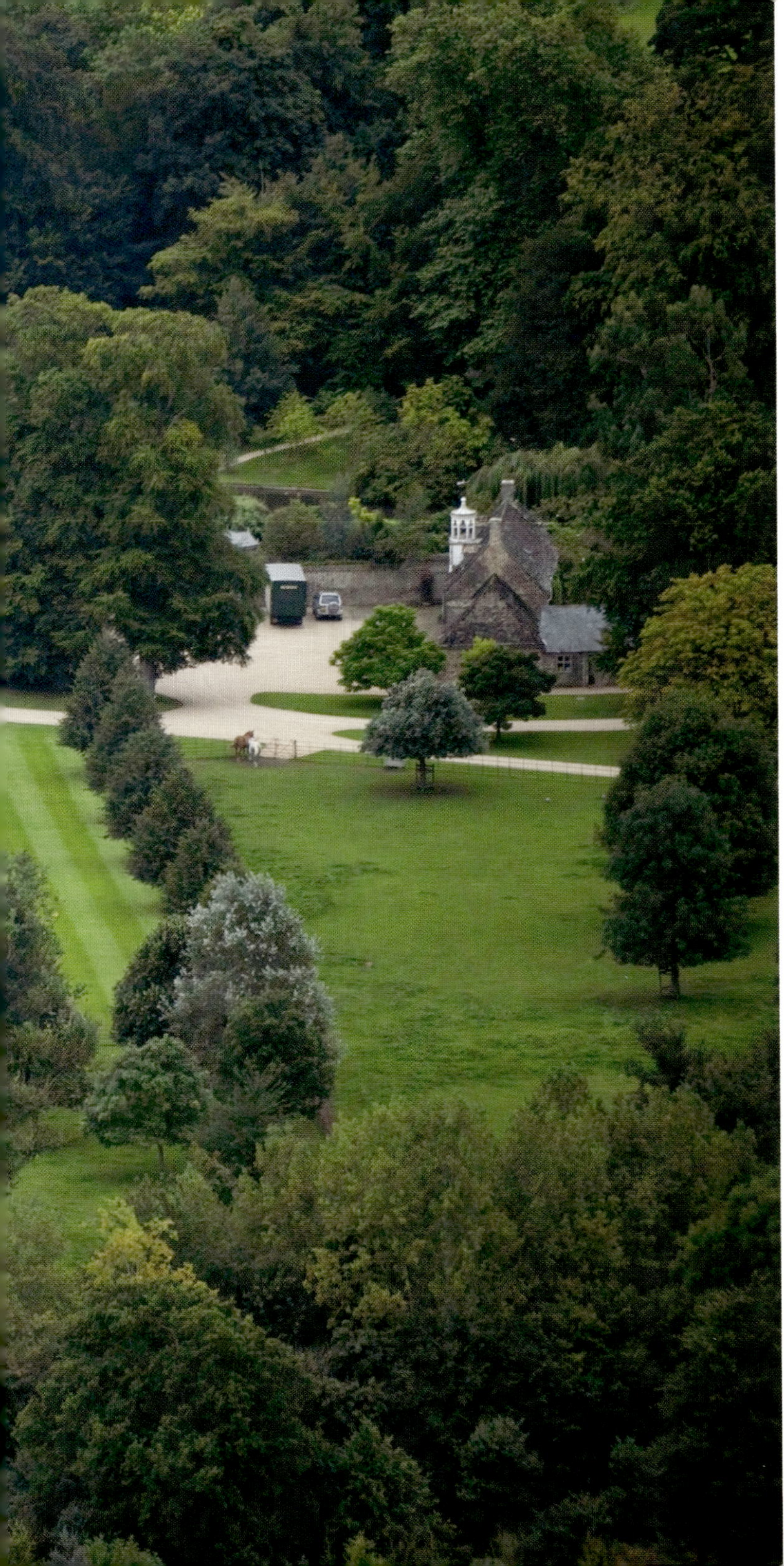

Pusey House, in the Vale of the White Horse, takes its name from the family who originally settled here, it is said in the tenth century. The present house, which remains in private ownership, dates from the mid eighteenth century.

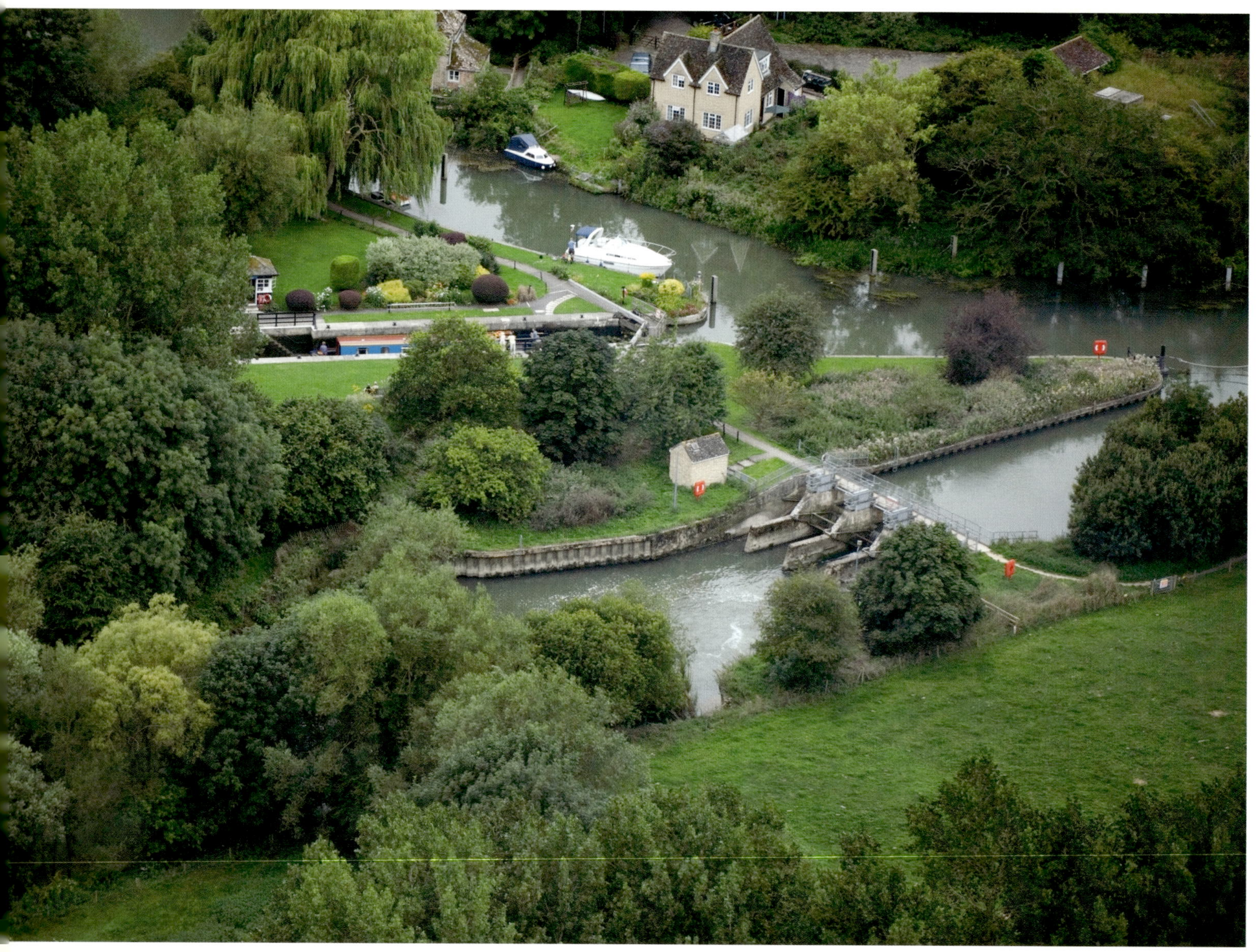

Above: Buscot Lock is on the River Thames near the village of Buscot. The lock, the smallest on the river, was built of stone by the Thames Navigation Commission in 1790.

Right: Stonor Park, north of Henley-on-Thames, is an impressive stately home, seat of the Stonor family for over 800 years. The house and gardens are open to the public.

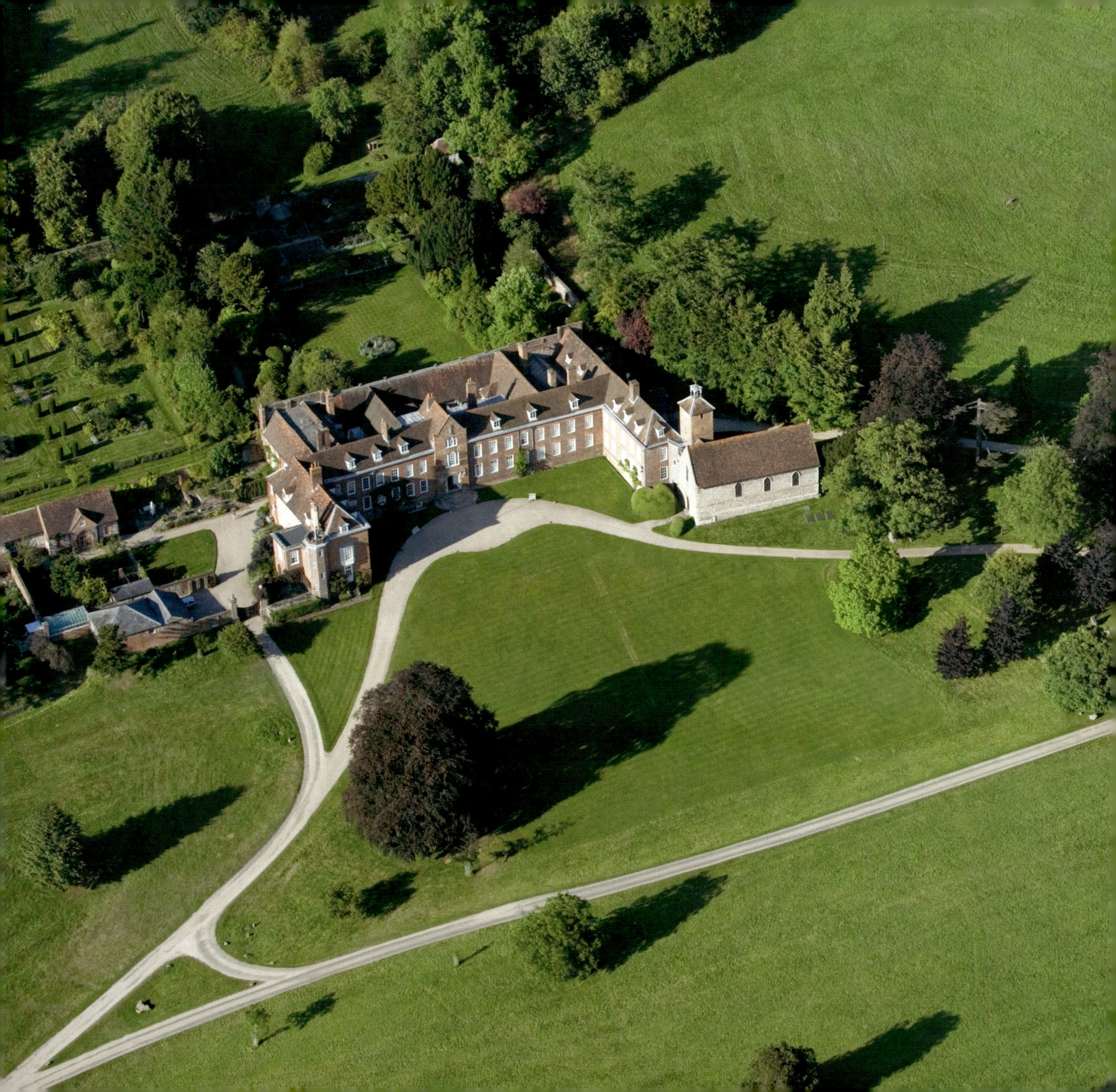

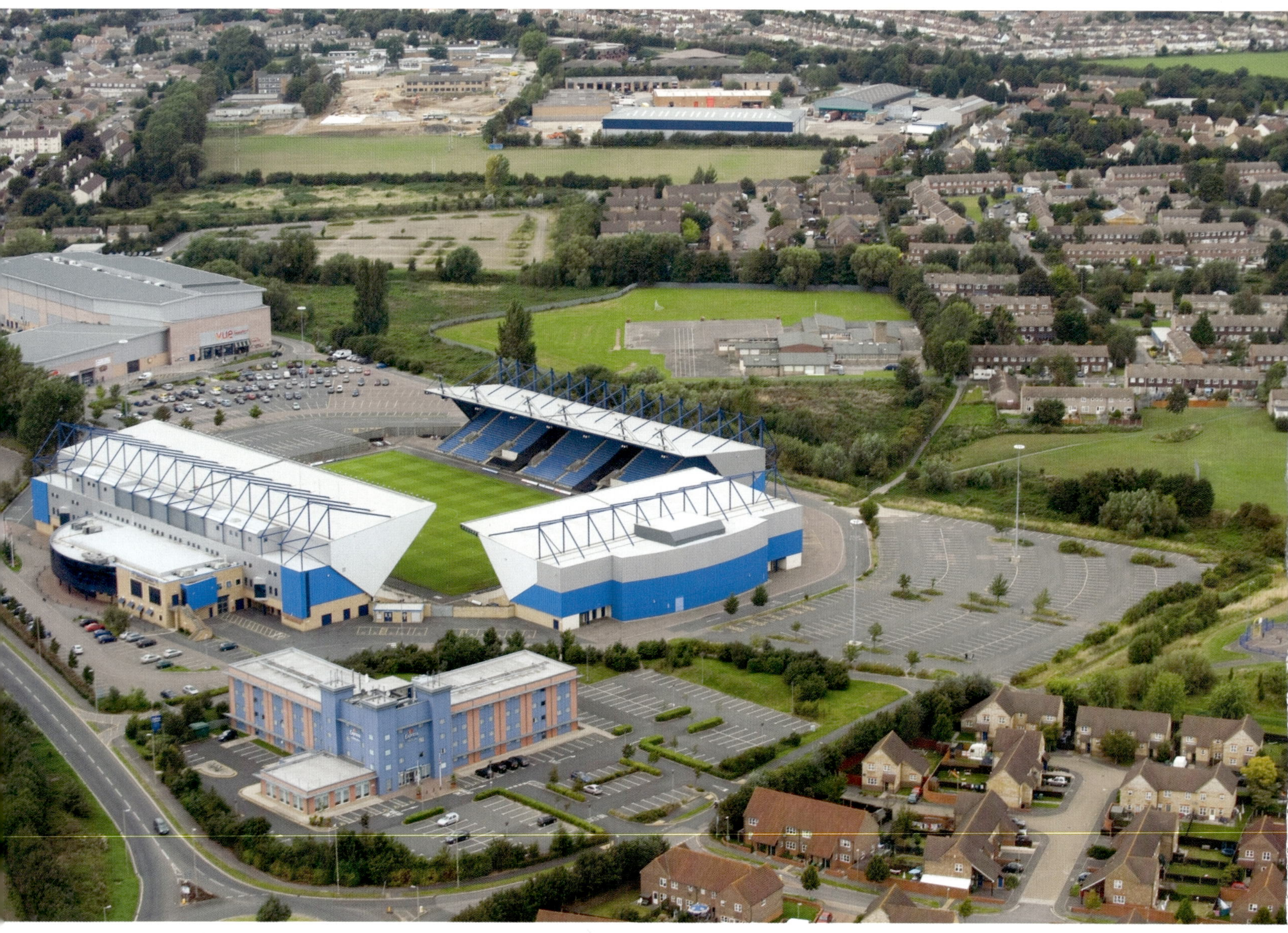

The Kassam Stadium is the home of Oxford United Football Club, named after the ground's owner, and former chairman of the club, Firoz Kassam. It lies to the south of city. Oxford United's former home, the Manor Ground, was sited in Headington.